TABLE OF CONTENTS

Preface

Every few years, the Pope calls bishops from around the world to come to Rome for a synod. The themes of these regular assemblies of the successors of the apostles reveal the key issues that the Church faces in these days as it follows the commission of Our Lord at the end of St Matthew's Gospel to evangelize the world (Matthew 28:16-20).

A few years ago (2005) there was a Synod on the Eucharist, and next year there will be a Synod on the New Evangelization (2012), as the bishops seek to find ways of proclaiming the good news of Jesus in our present age. Between the Synod on the Eucharist and the Synod on the New Evangelization was the Synod on the Word of God in October 2008.

Through the meditations on the Sunday Mass readings gathered in *Words Made Flesh: Biblical Reflections for Year B Volume II*, Father Thomas Rosica gives us all practical assistance in fulfilling the promise of these three synods. He helps us to prepare fruitfully for celebration of the Sunday Eucharist, which is the natural home of the Word of God, and the foundation for the mission of the new evangelization.

We need to prepare for the Sunday Eucharist, and one way of doing this is to spend some time before Mass prayerfully reflecting upon the readings that we will hear proclaimed, so that they are not words merely heard and forgotten, but rather saving words that bring new life to a heart and mind ready to receive them. We should have the attitude of the young Samuel in the Old Testament: "Speak, Lord. Your servant is listening." It is a principle of our faith that the Sunday eucharistic liturgy is the spiritual focal point of the Christian's week, and the reflections in this book will help all who participate in the Eucharist to make that principle effective in practice.

From the earliest times the proclamation of the Word of God has been a fundamental part of the Eucharist. Father Rosica's extensive knowledge of the scriptures will assist the reader of *Words Made Flesh* to gain a personal appreciation of the meaning of the sacred text.

The last words of the Mass exhort us to go in peace to serve the Lord in our daily lives. The encounter with Our Lord in Word and Sacrament in the Eucharist allows the disciple to engage day by day in the mission of the new evangelization.

May the regular use of Father Rosica's reflections on the Sunday Mass readings help each of us to grow in our love of the Eucharist, and of the Word of God, so that we can help to bring the Good News of Our Lord to this world of ours which is so much in need of it.

Most Reverend Thomas Collins,
Archbishop of Toronto
September 30, 2011
Feast of St. Jerome

Introduction

The idea for this collection of biblical reflections flows directly from the Synod of Bishops on the Word of God in the Life and Mission of the Church held at the Vatican during the month of October 2008. It was an extraordinary ecclesial experience, steeped in the Scriptures, Vatican documents, and the universality of the Church – an invitation to pastors, students, teachers, and to the entire Church, to examine carefully our relationship with the Word of God.

Having served as the English language Media Attaché at this universal gathering, I worked closely with Spanish language Media Attaché, Jesús Colina, a treasured friend and colleague, who is also founder and director of the Zenit International News Service. At the Synod's conclusion, Jesús Colina invited me to succeed the renowned Italian Capuchin scripture scholar and Preacher to the Papal Household, Fr. Raniero Cantalamessa, in offering weekly Scripture reflections for the Zenit audience beginning in Advent 2008. I accepted the invitation with no small amount of trepidation; aware of the great master and teacher I would be following.

This first of three published volumes of "Words Made Flesh" combines many of my biblical reflections that appeared weekly on the Zenit International News Service during the liturgical year "B" 2008-2009. The seeds of these reflections were first sown during my graduate studies in Sacred Scripture at the Pontifical Biblical Institute in Rome (1987-1990), and at the École Biblique et Archéologique Française de Jérusalem (1990-1994). During my years in Jerusalem, I also had the blessed opportunity of lecturing to many religious women, men, diocesan priests and laity in the Ecce Homo Centre for Biblical Formation. Upon return to Canada in 1994, I further developed those reflections for the vibrant parish community of the Newman Centre Catholic Mission at the University of Toronto that I was called to pastor from 1994-2000. In addition to the university chaplaincy, the biblical reflections matured among my students at the Faculty of Theology of the University of St. Michael's College from 1990-2008, as well as at St. Peter's Seminary in London, Ontario from 1997-2002.

Over the past twenty years, assemblies, conferences, and priests' and religious women's retreats in Canada, the United States, Colombia, French Polynesia, Australia, the United Kingdom, Italy, Egypt, Israel and Jordan afforded me many opportunities to share biblical reflections with pastoral ministers, young people, educators and catechists.

Year B: The Gospel of Mark

This first of three published volumes of weekly reflections will focus on the Gospel of Mark, briefest in length of the Gospels of the New Testament and most likely the first to have been written. Most scholars are in agreement that the gospel was written shortly before 70 A.D. in Rome, at a time of pending persecution and when the destruction of Jerusalem was imminent. The Gospel's detailed and vivid descriptions of the ministry of Jesus offer insights not provided by Matthew or Luke. For Mark, the Good News is the kingdom of God breaking and entering human history in a major way (1:14-15). Jesus is God's Good News in the flesh; God's son sent to save humanity through loving service and the total sacrifice of his life (10:45). Jesus is also the Son of Man. He appoints twelve disciples to help preach and drive out demons, just as he does (3:13-19). While Mark's depiction of the Twelve is often very negative, it is only after the Resurrection that the disciples would be given full sight and brought to single-minded faith and commitment to their Lord and Master.

Mark's Gospel account attempted to equip Christians under siege to stand faithful in the face of persecution (13:9-13), all the while continuing the joyful proclamation of the Gospel that Jesus began in Galilee. Mark insists that all who follow Jesus will be put to the test by great affliction. Whatever the form of these trials, Mark reminds us that we must remain vigilant and pray for single-minded devotion and fidelity.

Better Serving the Church's Mission

The reflections found in this volume are not ready-made homilies. They are attempts to bring together Catholic biblical exegesis, theological reflection, doctrinal topics and the rich culture and traditions of the Church. I would like to acknowledge one very positive influence on these weekly biblical reflections. In a major address to a conference under the theme "The Eloquence of Teaching" sponsored jointly by the United States Bishops' Committee on Doctrine and the Department of Theology of the University of Notre Dame in Indiana in 2008, Cardinal William Levada, Prefect of the Congregation for the Doctrine of the Faith and President of the Pontifical Biblical Commission called for "homilies that help people know better the rich content of the church's faith and how to live it in their lives."

Cardinal Levada said that homilies should "serve the Church's mission of preparing our laity to fulfill their baptismal vocation of evangelizing our culture and transforming our society to reflect Gospel values. When the homilist knows the clusters of texts that surround certain doctrines, then the appearance of these texts in a particular liturgy becomes an occasion for doctrinal teaching that is nonetheless thoroughly scriptural." (ORIGINS vol. 37 Issue 38, March 6, 2008 "The Homilist: Teacher of the Faith.")

Cardinal Levada's wise insight confirmed for me what I have always believed about good, Catholic preaching. While breaking open the Word of God is the main goal of our preaching, we are most effective when we help our hearers to make links between the Word of God, the treasure of Church teaching and tradition, and daily living. For this reason I have woven into my weekly reflections elements of Church teaching, the Catechism, conciliar and synodal documents, major ecclesial events, Catholic piety and devotion and the lives of the saints and blesseds. Each week in response to the publication of the Zenit article, many people from around the world sent messages of encouragement, questions or comments. These messages revealed a tremendous hunger for the Word of God, a quest to see links between the preached Word and the lived tradition and experience of the Church, and a desire to live the Catholic Christian life more deeply. It is hoped that these reflections might lead to an understanding of the mystery being celebrated, be a privileged moment of teaching for the Church, prepare the assembly for the Eucharistic liturgy, and serve as a summons to mission in the world. In this way, we can truly serve the Church's mission of preparing our laity to fulfill their baptismal vocation of evangelizing our culture and transforming our society to reflect Gospel values.

Gratitude

I am grateful to my religious family, the Congregation of Priests of St. Basil, whose charism of "Education in the Church's Mission of Evangelization" provided the opportunity to pursue scripture studies and put them into practice throughout my priestly ministry.

I express sincere gratitude to Matthew Harrison, Sébastien Lacroix, Sr. Marie-Noëlle Chaumette, X.M.C.J., and Ilona Huddart, of the Salt and Light Television Network who assisted me each week with these reflections over the past three years. Jesús Colina, Karna Swanson and Kathleen Naab of the Zenit International News Service manifested constant patience, professionalism and good cheer. I thank Zenit for allowing me to publish these weekly articles in book form.

My thanks to Dr. Glenn Byer, Director of Publications Services of the Canadian Conference of Catholic Bishops in Ottawa, his team and Albert Beaudry for their encouragement and generous assistance with the publication of these reflections in the English and French languages.

Finally I recall with profound gratitude those biblical figures in my own life who taught me to love the Word of God and allow the Words to become flesh in daily living. I am indebted to Fr. Ulysse Paré, C.S.B., scripture scholar and former Superior General of the Basilian Fathers for his biblical vision, and for assigning me to Scripture studies in the beginning; to Fr. James Swetnam, S.J., formerly of the Pontifical Biblical Institute in Rome, who taught me that we don't master the Word of God but must allow it to master us; to Fr. Justin Taylor, S.M., formerly of the École Biblique et Archéoloqique Française de Jéruslaem who modeled authentic, Catholic biblical scholarship at the service of the Church and to Cardinal Carlo Martini, S.J., Archbishop emeritus of Milan who nurtured my faith and love of the Lord through his brilliant use of the Word of God, and his mastery of *Lectio Divina* in his own pastoral ministry in the Ambrosian Church.

I would be remiss in not mentioning two towering giants, teachers, mentors and friends, who now enjoy the fullness of God's presence above, and who undoubtedly intercede for us here below: Fr. Raymond Brown, S.S., and Fr. Carroll Stuhlmueller, C.P. Both Frs. Brown and Stuhlmueller embodied the meaning of these words from *Verbum Domini*, Pope Benedict XVI's masterful Apostolic Exhortation that followed the Synod on the Word of God in the Life and Mission of the Church:

"In their work of interpretation, Catholic exegetes must never forget that what they are interpreting is the Word of

God. Their common task is not finished when they have simply determined sources, defined forms or explained literary procedures. They arrive at the true goal of their work only when they have explained the meaning of the biblical text as God's Word for today" (#33).

Fr. Thomas Rosica, C.S.B.

September 30, 2011

Feast of St. Jerome

Rehearsal of the Great History of Memories

Isaiah 63:16b-17; 64:1, 3-8;
1 Corinthians 1:3-9;
Mark 13:33-37

This weekend the Church enters into the liturgical season of Advent. Christians proclaim that the Messiah has indeed come and that God's reign is "at hand."

Advent does not change God. Advent deepens our longing and anticipation that God will do what prophets and the anointed have promised. We pray that God will yield to our need to see and feel the promise of salvation here and now.

During this time of longing and waiting for the Lord, we are invited to pray and to ponder the Word of God, but most of all, to become a reflection of the light of Christ, indeed of Christ himself. But we all know how difficult it is to mirror the light of Christ, especially when we have become disillusioned with life, accustomed to the shadowy existence of the world, or grown content with mediocrity and emptiness. Advent reminds us that we must be ready to meet the Lord at any and every moment of life. Just like a security alarm wakes up a homeowner, Advent wakes up Christians who are in danger of sleeping through their lives.

For what or for whom are we waiting in life? What virtues or gifts are we praying to receive this year? Do we long for healing and reconciliation in broken relationships? What meaning and understanding do we desire to have in the midst of our own darkness, sadness, and mystery? How are we living out our baptismal promises? What qualities of Jesus are we seeking in our own lives this Advent? Many times, the things, qualities, gifts, or people we await give us great insights into who we really are. Tell me whom you are waiting for and I will tell you who you are!

Advent is a time for opening eyes, focusing views, paying attention, keeping perspective on God's presence in the world and in our own lives.

In the first reading from the prophet Isaiah on the first Sunday of Advent, the Almighty One breathes hope back into the heart and soul of Israel and shapes Israel and events anew just as a potter shapes his pottery.

In the second Scripture reading, writing to his beloved community at Corinth, Paul looked forward to the "Day of our Lord" when the Lord Jesus will be revealed to rescue those whom he has called. And in the Gospel for the first Sunday of Advent this year, Mark's depiction of the doorkeeper watching out for the Lord whenever he "suddenly" appears is an image of what we are expected to be doing all year long but especially during the season of Advent.

Our own baptism is a share in the royal, messianic mission of Jesus. Anyone who shares this mission also shares royal responsibilities, in particular, care for the afflicted and the hurting. Advent is a wonderful opportunity to "activate" our baptismal promises and commitment.

Cardinal Joseph Ratzinger, now Pope Benedict XVI once wrote: "The purpose of the Church's year is continually to rehearse her great history of memories, to awaken the heart's memory so that it can discern the star of hope. It is the beautiful task of Advent to awaken in all of us, memories of goodness and thus to open doors of hope."[1]

This Advent, allow me to suggest that you mend a quarrel. Build peace. Seek out a forgotten friend. Dismiss suspicion and replace it with trust. Write a love letter. Share some treasure. Give a kind answer even though you would like to respond harshly. Encourage a young person to believe in him/herself. Manifest your loyalty in word and deed. Keep a promise. Find the time. Make time. Forego a grudge. Forgive an enemy. Celebrate the sacrament of reconciliation. Listen more. Apologize if you were wrong. Be kind even if you weren't wrong!

Try to understand. Flout envy. Examine the demands you make on others. Think first of someone else. Appreciate. Be kind, be gentle. Laugh a little. Laugh a little more. Deserve confidence. Take up arms against malice. Decry complacency. Express gratitude. Go to church. Stay in church a little while longer than usual. Gladden the heart of a child. Take pleasure in the beauty and wonder of the earth. Speak your love. Speak it once again. Speak it even more loudly. Speak it quietly. Rejoice, for the Lord is near!

---

1 Cardinal Ratzinger, *Seek That Which Is Above* (San Francisco: Ignatius Press, 1986).

John the Baptizer, the Advent Prophet

Isaiah 40:1-5, 9-11;
2 Peter 3:8-14;
Mark 1:1-8

One of the great stars of the Advent and Christmas stories, John the Baptizer, makes his appearance on the biblical stage today. Let us consider some of the details of John's life and see how he is such a good model for us.

John the Baptist didn't mince words. He got right to the point and said what needed to be said. He would speak with equally straightforward words to us – words that would zero in on the weak points of our lives. John the Baptist was a credible preacher of repentance because he had first come to love God's word that he heard in the midst of his own desert.

He heard, experienced and lived God's liberating word in the desert and was thus able to preach it to others so effectively because his life and message were one. One of the most discouraging things we must deal with in our lives is duplicity. How often are our words, thoughts and actions not coherent or one. The true prophets of Israel help us in our struggle against all forms of duplicity.

The desert wilderness

Throughout biblical history, leaders and visionaries have gone to the desert to see more clearly, to listen intently for God's voice, to discover new ways to live. The Hebrew word for wilderness, *midvar*, is derived from a Semitic root that means, "To lead flocks or herds to pasture." *Eremos*, the Greek word used to translate *midvar*, denotes a desolate and thinly populated area and, in a stricter sense, a wasteland or desert.

The term "wilderness" has two different but related meanings, referring to something judged to be wild and bewildering. It is probably the unknown (bewildering) and uncontrolled (wild) character of the place that earned it the name "wilderness." There is also another way of understanding the meaning of desert or wilderness.

A careful look at the root of the word *midvar* reveals the word *davar* meaning "word" or "message." The Hebraic notion of "desert" or "wilderness" is that holy place where God's word is unbound and completely free to be heard, experienced and lived. We go to the desert to hear God's Word, unbound and completely free.

The Spirit of God enabled the prophets to feel with God. They were able to share God's attitudes, God's values, God's feelings, God's emotions. This enabled them to see the events of their time as God saw them and to feel the same way about these events as God felt. They shared God's anger, God's compassion, God's sorrow, God's disappointment, God's revulsion, God's sensitivity for people, and God's seriousness. They did not share these things in the abstract; they shared God's feelings about the concrete events of their time.

John the Baptist is *the* Advent prophet. His image is often portrayed in the finger pointing to the one who was coming: Jesus Christ. If we are to take on John's role of preparing the way in today's world, our lives also will become the pointing fingers of living witnesses who demonstrate that Jesus can be found and that he is near. John gave the people of his time an experience of forgiveness and salvation, knowing full well that he himself was not the Messiah, the one who could save. Do we allow others to have experiences of God, of forgiveness and of salvation?

John the Baptist came to teach us that there is a way out of the darkness and sadness of the world and of the human condition, and that way is Jesus himself. The Messiah comes to save us from the powers of darkness and death, and to put us back on the path of peace and reconciliation so that we might find our way back to God.

The late Jesuit theologian, Father Karl Rahner, once wrote: "We have to listen to the voice of the one calling in the wilderness, even when it confesses: I am not he. You cannot choose not to listen to this voice, 'because it is only the voice of a man.' And, likewise, you cannot lay aside the message of the Church, because the Church is 'not worthy to untie the shoelaces of its Lord who goes on before it.' It is, indeed, still Advent."

We may not have the luxury of traveling to the wilderness of Judah, nor the privilege of a week's retreat in the Sinai desert this Advent. However, we can certainly carve out a little desert wilderness in the midst of our activity and noise this week. Let us go to that sacred place and allow the Word of God to speak to us, to heal us, to reorient us, and to lead us to the heart of Christ, whose coming we await this Advent.

Rejoicing and Waiting

Isaiah 61:1-2a, 10-11;
1 Thessalonians 5:16-24;
John 1:6-8, 19-28

Advent is the season of the prophets and the Scripture readings of these weeks before Christmas help us to focus our vision and deepen our longing for the Messiah.

In this year's Gospel for the Third Sunday of Advent, the figure of John the Baptist appears once again on the stage of salvation history. John's whole mission was a preparation for the Messiah's coming. When the time had come, John led his own disciples to Jesus and indicated to them the Messiah, the True Light, and the Lamb of God who takes away the sins of the world. John, himself, was not the light. He came to testify to the light. He didn't spend time thinking about his shadow. He just allowed the light to shine on him.

John considered himself to be less than a slave to Jesus, "Among you stands one whom you do not know, the one who is coming after me; I am not worthy to untie the thong of his sandal" (John 1:26-27). When John's own disciples came to him and were troubled about the meaning of Jesus' baptism in the Jordan, he answered them confidently: "No one can receive anything except what has been given from above." John says he is only the friend of the bridegroom, the one who must decrease while his master increases (John 3:27-30). The Baptizer defined his humanity in terms of its limitations.

In one of the most poignant scenes of Luke's Gospel, John the Baptist is imprisoned by Herod Antipas because of his public rebuke of the tetrarch for his adulterous and incestuous marriage with Herodias (Matthew 4:12; Mark 1:14; Luke 3:19). Alone, dejected and near the end of his life, John the Baptist, hailed as the "greatest of all prophets," had to ask the question, "Are you really the one who is to come?" (Luke 7:19) John probably expected a fiery social reformer to come and bring about the Kingdom, certainly not someone who would associate with the poor, the lame, the blind, outcasts and sinners. Yet Christ comes in the most unexpected ways and often in the most unlikely people.

Jesus invites John to look around and see the works that had already been accomplished in the midst of people. The blind recovered their sight and the lame were walking again. Diseases and illness were healed and all those who were deaf could hear. The Good News was now preached to the poor. That was the greatest wonder of all! This is a great consolation for us. We should never be surprised if we often find ourselves asking the same question – "Is Christian living really worth it?" "Is Jesus really the answer to all the evils and sadness of the world and of our own lives?"

The crowds came to John and asked him, "What should we do?" The Baptist advises no one to leave the world they are in, however ambiguous it may be. Rather he told those with two coats to share one with those who had none. Likewise, those with an abundance of food were to share with the hungry. Tax collectors were told to collect no more than was appointed to them. Soldiers were to rob no one by violence or by false accusation. They were to be content with their wages. What were people to do to prepare for the imminent coming of the Messiah? To be generous, just, honest, grateful and compassionate (cf. Luke 3:10-14).

John the Baptist's life and mission reminds us how badly we need a Saviour to save us, in order that we might be all that we are called to be and do all that we have to do to live in the Light. How are we courageous and prophetic in our Christian witness to the Light, who has already come into our world? So often we fail to recognize the one among us who is our True Light.

May John the Baptist give us strength and courage to bear the light to others, and the generosity and ability to rejoice as we wait. "Rejoice always, pray without ceasing," Paul writes in his first letter to the Thessalonians. We can also reverse the order of these two sentences: "Pray without ceasing, so that we will be able to rejoice always."

In prayer we experience God's gathering up all of our concerns and hopes into his own infinite love and wisdom, his setting us back on our feet, and his giving us fullness of life and light.

How Do We Solve a Problem Like Maria?

FOURTH SUNDAY OF ADVENT

2 Samuel 7:1-5, 8b-12, 14a, 16;
Romans 16:25-27;
Luke 1:26-38

The Sound of Music stage play and I are the same age – both from that vintage year of 1959 – and the film version was the first motion picture I saw as child in the mid 1960s with my family. God alone knows how many times I have seen it since on stage, at the theatre and on television!

A few years ago, the Rodgers and Hammerstein famed musical *The Sound of Music* delighted audiences in Toronto's Princess of Wales Theatre in the downtown theatre district. The city was "alive" with the sound of music. This magnificent production first opened in England under the direction of Andrew Lloyd Weber. The Toronto version of the show did justice to the musical that contains some of the best-loved songs of all time.

Solving the problem of Maria von Trapp

One of the memorable songs of the play is "Maria," sometimes known as "How Do You Solve a Problem Like Maria?" It is sung brilliantly by Sister Berthe, Sister Sophia, Sister Margaretta and the Mother Abbess as portrayed at the Benedictine Nonnberg Abbey in Salzburg, Austria. The nuns are exasperated with Maria for being too frivolous, flighty and frolicsome for the decorous and austere life at the abbey. It is said that when Oscar Hammerstein II wrote the lyrics for this song, he was taken by the detail of her wearing curlers in her hair under her wimple!

When older Austrians in Salzburg speak of Maria, it is the *Gottesmutter*, the Mother of the Lord! When the foreigners, especially North Americans, arrive in Salzburg and speak about Maria, it is usually the other one: Maria Augusta Kutschera, later Maria Augusta von Trapp, who was a teacher in the abbey school after World War I and whose life was the basis for the film *The Sound of Music.*

Because of this Maria, the abbey acquired international fame, to the consternation of some of the sisters! Having visited Nonnberg Abbey on several occasions while I was studying German in nearby Bavaria, I spoke with a few of the elderly sisters about the impact of *The Sound of Music* on their life. The prioress told me that they have no plaques up about Maria von Trapp and her escapades neither at the abbey nor in Salzburg! One elderly sister said to me, with a smile, "Das ist nur Hollywood!" (That is only Hollywood!)

Solving the problem of Maria von Nazareth

The Gospel story of the Annunciation presents another Maria, the great heroine of the Christmas stories – Mary of Nazareth – the willing link between humanity and God. She is the disciple par excellence who introduces us to the goodness and humanity of God. She received and welcomed God's word in the fullest sense, not knowing how the story would finally end. She did not always understand that word throughout Jesus' life but she trusted and constantly recaptured the initial response she had given the angel and literally "kept it alive," "tossed it around," "pondered it" in her heart (Luke 2:19). At Calvary she experienced the full responsibility of her "yes." We have discovered in the few Scripture passages relating to her that she was a woman of deep faith, compassion, and she was very attentive to the needs of others.

Maria von Trapp followed the captain and his little musical family through the Alpine mountain passes of Austria, fleeing a neo-pagan, evil regime that tried to deny the existence of God and God's chosen people. Some would say that they lived happily ever after in Vermont in the United States, and that their musical reputation lives on through the stage production that enchanted Toronto audiences. The hills are still alive with their music!

The "problem" of Maria of Nazareth began when she entertained a strange, heavenly visitor named Gabriel. The young woman of Nazareth was greatly troubled as she discovered that she would bear a son who would be Saviour and Son of the Most High.

"How can this be," Mary asked the angel, "since I am a virgin?" (Luke 1:34)

The angel answered, "The Holy Spirit will come upon you, and the power of the Most High will overshadow you; therefore the child to be born will be holy; he will be called Son of God."

"Here am I, the servant of the Lord," Mary answered. "let it be with me according to your word." The angel left her and then the music began: *Magnificat anima mea Dominum.* It would become a refrain filling the world with the sound of its powerful music down through the ages.

The message Mary received catapulted her on a trajectory far beyond tiny, sleepy Nazareth and that little strip of land called Israel and Palestine in the Middle East. Mary's "yes" would impact the entire world, and change human history.

Problem solved.

Mary of Nazareth accepted her "problem" and resolved it through her obedience, fidelity, trust, hope and quiet joy. At that first moment in Nazareth, she could not foresee the brutal ending of the story of this child within her. Only on a hillside in Calvary, years later, would she experience the full responsibility of her "yes" that forever changed the history of humanity.

Although there are no plaques commemorating Maria von Trapp's encounter with destiny at Nonnberg Abbey, there is one small plaque commemorating Mary of Nazareth's life-changing meeting in her hometown. Standing in the middle of the present day city of Nazareth in Galilee is the mammoth basilica of the Annunciation, built around what is believed to be the cave and dwelling of Mary. A small inscription is found on the altar in this grotto-like room that commemorates the place where Mary received the message from the angel Gabriel that she would "conceive in your womb and bear a son, and you will name him Jesus" (Luke 1:31). The Latin inscription reads *Verbum caro hic factum est* (Here the word became flesh).

I can still remember the sensation I had when I knelt before that altar for the first time in 1988. That inscription in the grotto of the Annunciation is profound, otherworldly, earth shaking, life changing, dizzying and awesome. The words *Verbum caro hic factum est* are not found on an ex-voto plaque in the cave of the Nativity in Bethlehem, nor engraved on the outer walls of the Temple ruins or on governmental tourist offices in Jerusalem. They are affixed to an altar deep within the imposing structure of Nazareth's centrepiece of the Annunciation. "This is where the word became flesh." This is where history was changed because Mary said "yes."

Could such words be applied to our own lives, to our families, communities, and churches – "Here the word becomes flesh"? Do we know how to listen to God's Word, meditate upon it and live it each day? Do we put that word into action in our daily lives? Are we faithful, hopeful, loving, and inviting in our discourse and living? What powerful words to be said about Christians – that their words become flesh!

However beautiful and catchy are the tunes of Maria of Salzburg, the music of the other Maria, the one from Nazareth, surpasses anything I have ever heard.

For Unto Us a Child Is Born ...

HANUKKAH AND THE NATIVITY OF THE LORD

Midnight: Isaiah 9:2-4, 6-7; Titus 2:11-14; Luke 2:1-16
Dawn: Isaiah 62:11-12; Titus 3:4-7; Luke 2:15-20
Day: Isaiah 52:7-10; Hebrews 1:1-6; John 1:1-18

One of my personal Advent and Christmas traditions each year has been to attend (or at least listen to) Handel's Messiah. My "Messiah night" took place this past week, not in a concert hall or church, but in my residence.

The choral section from the Nativity cycle of Handel's work never ceases to move me each time I listen to Isaiah's prophecy set to glorious music: "For unto us a Child is born, unto us a Son is given, and the government shall be upon his shoulder; and his name shall be called Wonderful, Counselor, the Mighty God, the everlasting Father, the Prince of Peace" (cf. Isaiah 9:6). Those marvelous words are taken from the prophet Isaiah and the first reading that we hear proclaimed each year at Midnight Mass on Christmas Eve.

Immediately preceding Chapter 9, Isaiah's testimony has built up a frightening picture of the darkness and distress about to descend upon both Judah and the northern kingdom of Israel. But that darkness and distress were not the prophet's final words. Precisely upon this land has shined a great light. The opening line of Chapter 9 forms a transition from the darkness of the previous chapter. "But there will be no gloom for those who were in anguish. In the former time he brought into contempt the land of Zebulun and the land of Naphtali, but in the latter time he will make glorious the way of the sea, the land beyond the Jordan, Galilee of the nations. The people who walked in darkness have seen a great light; those who lived in a land of deep darkness – on them light has shone" (9:1-2).

The great light that comes decisively into this profound darkness tears people away from their confusion and emptiness, from the violence and tyranny of the oppressor. On the inhabitants of a country in the shadow dark as death, light has blazed forth! The symbols of the Assyrian oppression: the yoke of their burden, the bar across their shoulders, the rod of their oppressor, shall be broken. The garments of war shall feed the flames. The destruction of warlike equipment heralds an age of peace.

The royal child whose birth is so poetically announced will possess the wisdom of Solomon, the valour and piety of David, the great virtue of Moses and the patriarchs. Presumably the child spoken of would be King Hezekiah. Contemporary kings of Judah had been disastrously advised and were powerless in warfare.

By the title "Wonderful Counselor," the new king will have no need for advisers such as those who led King Ahaz astray. "Everlasting Father" describes the quality of his rule. The virtues of judgment, justice and righteousness that sustain the Davidic throne are summed up in the word "Shalom," whose Hebrew root means wholeness, harmony, fulfillment and completion.

As a result of this new king's reign, people will live in harmony with God, each other and nature. It is no wonder, then, that the Church has appropriated Isaiah's exultation of this brilliant light and royal birth for our celebration of the birth of Jesus.

During the past years, who has not felt deeply the darkness and gloom of our world? Consider the tragic and violent situations of the lands we call "holy." Lands that were once touched by God, the patriarchs and prophets, and the Messiah himself, are killing fields. Think of the uncertainty and despair that has set in because of the collapse of economic structures. Such strong feelings of darkness and gloom usually stem from our attempts to act as isolated beings or islands, instead of communities of people genuinely concerned about one another and about the suffering of so many people in our world.

During this festival season, Jews continue to long for the Messiah's coming and Christians celebrate his birth in human history. But Jews and Christians are also invited to go beyond the outward symbols and ask the deeper questions: How do we continue to long for and actualize the salvation that the Messiah will bring? The prophetic texts read during the Hanukkah, Advent and Christmas feasts are a new summons to the synagogue and to the church to reach out to one another, to recommit ourselves to bearing God's light to the nations, and to recognize each other as partners in building up the Kingdom of God.

Both Christianity and Judaism seal their worship with a common hope: "Thy Kingdom come!" And we must utter this prayer more loudly and clearly in these days of shadows and darkness for so many in the world, especially for the people of Afghanistan, Iraq, the Holy Land that is torn apart by warfare, hatred, oppression and sadness, as well as for those living in other regions suffering through war, poverty, injustice.

Our common longing for the fruits of the Messianic Kingdom invites us – Christians and Jews – into a knowledge of our communion with one another and a recognition of the terrible brokenness of the world. As Blessed John Paul II and now Pope Benedict XVI have taught us through word, gesture and deed, nothing and no one can ever wrench us away any longer from that deep communion that unites us together. The *tikkun ha'olam*, Hebrew for the healing of the world, its repair, restoration and redemption – including the redemption of Israel, incarnate in the person of Jesus, is the work of God's Son, our redeemer and Lord, working through each one of us.

Zooming in on Joseph

FEAST OF THE HOLY FAMILY

Sirach 3:2-6, 12-14;
Colossians 3:12-21
or
Genesis 15:1-6, 17:3b-5, 15-16, 21:1-7;
Hebrews 11:8, 11-12, 17-19;

Luke 2:22-40

In the afterglow of Christmas, the Church celebrates the feast of the Holy Family. This weekend we are invited to reflect on the gift and mystery of life and the blessing of family life in particular.

In the longer form of Luke's Gospel scene of the Presentation of the Child Jesus in the Temple in Jerusalem, we encounter four individuals who embrace the new life of Jesus held in their arms: the elderly and faithful Simeon, the old, wise prophetess Anna, and the young couple, Mary and Joseph, who in faithful obedience offer their child to the Lord. Simeon's beautiful prayer is nothing more than an anthology of the prayer of ancient Israel:

"Master, now you are dismissing your servant in peace, according to your word; for my eyes have seen your salvation, which you have prepared in the presence of all peoples, a light for revelation to the Gentiles and for glory to your people Israel" (Luke 2:29-32).

The whole scene of the Presentation, and the carefully chosen words of Simeon's prayer, raise several questions for us: How do I see God's glory in my life? Do I thirst for justice and peace? What are the new situations and who are the new people who have entered my life in the last little while? How am I light and salvation for other people?

Today I would like to borrow from my new profession of television production and zoom in on Joseph, one of the characters found in this most touching Gospel scene of the Presentation. To "zoom" in on the foster father of the Lord gives us some profound insights into the family background of our Saviour.

Joseph is often overshadowed by the glory of Christ and the purity of Mary. But he, too, waited for God to speak to him and then responded with obedience. Luke and Matthew both mark Joseph's descent from David, the greatest king of Israel (Matthew 1:1-16 and Luke 3:23-38). Scripture has left us with the most important knowledge about him: he was "a righteous man" (Matthew 1:19).

Joseph was a compassionate, caring man. When he discovered Mary was pregnant after they had been engaged, he knew the child was not his but was as yet unaware that she was carrying the Son of God. He planned to divorce Mary according to the law but he was concerned for her suffering and safety. Joseph was also a man of faith, obedient to whatever God asked of him without knowing the outcome. When the angel came to Joseph in a dream and told him the truth about the child Mary was carrying, Joseph immediately and without question or concern for gossip, took Mary as his wife. When the angel came again to tell him that his family was in danger, he immediately left everything he owned, all his family and friends, and fled to a strange country with his young wife and the baby. He waited in Egypt until the angel told him it was safe to go back (Matthew 2:13-23).

We are told that Joseph was a carpenter, (more likely a builder), a man who worked to provide for his family. Joseph wasn't a wealthy man, for when he took Jesus to the Temple to be circumcised and Mary to be purified he offered the sacrifice of two turtledoves or a pair of pigeons, allowed only for those who could not afford a lamb.

Joseph revealed in his humanity the unique role of fathers to proclaim God's truth by word and deed. His paradoxical situation of "foster father to Jesus" draws attention to the truth about fatherhood, which is more than a mere fact of biological generation. A man is a father most when he invests himself in the spiritual and moral formation of his children. He was keenly aware, as every father should be, that he served as the representative of God the Father.

Joseph protected and provided for Jesus and Mary. He named Jesus, taught him how to pray, how to work, how to be a man. While no words or texts are attributed to him, we can be sure that Joseph pronounced two of the most important words that could ever be spoken when he named his son "Jesus" and called him "Emmanuel." When the child stayed behind in the Temple we are told Joseph (along with Mary) searched with great anxiety for three days for him (Luke 2:45).

Joseph's life reminds us that a home or community is not built on power and possessions but goodness; not on riches and wealth, but on faith, fidelity, purity and mutual love.

The present challenges to fatherhood and masculinity cannot be understood in isolation from the culture in which we live. The effect of fatherlessness on children is deeply alarming. How many young people today have been affected by the crisis of fatherhood and paternity! How many have been deprived of a father or grandfather in their life?

It is not for naught that St. Joseph is patron of the Universal Church and principal patron of Canada. If there was ever a time when we needed a strong, saintly male role model who is a father, it is our time. And the feast of the Holy Family is a very significant day to go to Joseph and beg him to send us good fathers who will head families.

Joseph and Mary, more than anyone else, were the first to behold the glory of their One and Only who came from the Father, full of grace and truth (John 1:14). May St. Joseph make of us good priests, religious and laymen who will imitate the humble worker from Nazareth, who listened to the Lord, treasured a gift that was not his, all the while modeling to Jesus how the Word becomes flesh and lives among us.

Nations Will Come to Your Light

SOLEMNITY OF THE EPIPHANY

Isaiah 60:1-6;
Ephesians 3:2-3a, 5-6;
Matthew 2:1-12

What "stirring" readings we hear in the Epiphany liturgy! Consider the scene from Isaiah's prophecy (60:1-6). Gentiles come from distant places, attracted by the splendour of Jerusalem, bringing gifts and tenderly carrying the sons and daughters of the Holy City! Though darkness may have surrounded the people, the glory of the Lord allows the light to burst forth and shine like a bright new dawn. What a fitting way to describe what we have just celebrated at Christmas!

Matthew's Gospel story of the Magi (2:1-12) reveals to us the inevitable struggle that God's manifestation in Christ implies for the world. If we read the story carefully, we realize that far from being a children's tale, it is a tragic adult story. The battle lines are drawn and the forces are being marshaled. A child is born at the same time as a death-dealing power rules. Jesus was a threat to Herod and to them: to the throne of one, to the religious empire of the others.

At home in their distant, foreign lands, the Magi had all the comfort of princely living, but something was missing – they were restless and unsatisfied. They were willing to risk everything to find the reality their vision promised. Unlike the poor shepherds, the Magi had to travel a long road; they had to face adversity to reach their goal. The shepherds also knew adversity, and it had prepared them to accept the angels' message. But once they overcame their fright, they simply "crossed over to Bethlehem" to meet the Christ Child.

The Magi, on the other hand, had a much more difficult journey to Bethlehem. It was anything but a romantic, sentimental pilgrimage that we often see in our manger scenes! The Magi were not just holy visionaries or whimsical religious figures; they were willing to wager their money, their time and their energy, and perhaps even their lives to seek out someone who would bring true peace.

The Magi were not completely lost upon their arrival in Jerusalem – the city did not stop their pilgrimage. In fact, in Jerusalem, they were redirected to Bethlehem. These men of the East, foreigners in every sense of the word, were guided not only by their own wisdom and knowledge of the stars, but were aided by the Hebrew Scriptures that now form the Old Testament. The meaning of this is important – Christ calls all peoples of all nations, Gentiles as well as Jews, to follow him. We could say that Jerusalem and the Old Testament serve as a new starting point for these Gentile pilgrims on their road to faith in Jesus. The people of the big city, indeed even Herod himself, were instrumental in leading the Magi to Christ.

What could this mean for our own pilgrimages to the truth today? More than the obvious fact that the Old Testament must be a central part of our path to Christ, might it not also mean that our own cities, with all of their confusion and ambiguity, might also serve as a starting point for our journey of faith?

At the centre of this whole Gospel story of striking contrasts lies a Baby, Jesus of Bethlehem, who is joy. Herod is afraid of this "great joy for all the people" (see Luke 2:10). From Matthew's Gospel, we do not know what happened to the Magi when they returned to their native lands, but we can be sure that they were changed men. They discovered in Jerusalem and in Bethlehem that there is no longer a God of this or that country, nor an oracle uttered in some distant place, but a God and Saviour who has become flesh and blood for of all humanity. And the Saviour is joy.

In the end, the Magi went their own way, and because they refused to be seduced by cynicism, because they allowed themselves to be surprised by this great joy, the star to which they had committed themselves appeared again. This is not only the description of the times into which Jesus was born, but also our times. When we have found our lasting joy in the midst of the encircling gloom, cynicism, despair, indifference and meaninglessness, the only thing to do is to kneel and adore.

Gaspar, Melchior and Balthasar, bless our hearts and our homes with your peace and humility! When we hear the voices of old kings of death and fear and cynicism, may we have the courage to go our own way … rejoicing, because we, too, have seen and experienced the glory of the coming of the Lord.

I conclude with the words of St. Teresa Benedicta of the Cross (Edith Stein), that great Carmelite mystic and lover of the cross, who wrote so beautifully about the Christmas mysteries:

"Those kneeling around the crib are figures of light: the tender innocent children, the trustful shepherds, the humble kings, Stephen, the enthusiastic disciple, and John the apostle of love, all those who have followed the call of the Lord. They are opposed by the night of incomprehensible obstinacy and blindness: the scribes, who know indeed when and where the Saviour of the world is to be born, but who will not draw the conclusion: 'Let us go to Bethlehem,' King Herod, who would kill the Lord of Life. Ways part before the Child in the manger ..."

Some will choose the path of life; others will choose the path of death. Today as we move away from the manger of our newborn King and Lord, let us recommit ourselves to the cause of life that is the heart and the joy of Christmas.

The Baptismal Difference

BAPTISM OF THE LORD

Isaiah 42:1-4, 6-7
Acts 10:34-38
or
Isaiah 55:1-11
1 John 5:1-9

Mark 1:7-11

Christmas has come and gone, and the Magi are now off on the distant horizon, having returned to their native lands by another road. The feast of the Baptism of the Lord seemingly brings an end to the Christmas season, although, in reality, it is the feast of the Presentation of the Lord on February 2 that marks the great conclusion of the Christmas season.

Nonetheless, it is useful to ask ourselves some hard questions today of what we have just experienced in the Nativity celebrations.

A great tragedy of Christmas is that for many, it is a religion of one night, however lovely and shining it may be. The Incarnation of Jesus is reduced to mere sentimentality, tradition or a cultural feast. But Jesus is not a meteor. It is not enough to come to the manger and get stuck there; we must turn from it. And then, accepting what the occupant of the manger means, we must begin to live out that meaning, choosing what may be new directions, challenging previous ways and assumptions, continuing the journey of our life with the knowledge that something has changed. One person has

42Words Made Flesh: Biblical Reflections for Year B

made a huge difference in our life and has literally changed history.

The theme of Christ's epiphany – of Jesus inaugurating his divine mission on earth – reaches its fulfillment in today's feast of the Baptism of the Lord. The beautiful text from Evening Prayer on the feast of the Epiphany reads: "Three mysteries mark this holy day: today the star leads the Magi to the infant Christ; today water is changed into wine for the wedding feast; today Christ wills to be baptized by John in the river Jordan to bring us salvation." Each event is accompanied by a theophany, by startling evidence of divine intervention: the star, the water into wine, the voice from heaven and the dove. Today we witness the baptism of the Lord, the one into whom we ourselves are baptized.

In today's Gospel, the appearance of John the Baptist seems to send us back to Advent...to look carefully at the evidence of the Baptizer and of Jesus, and to make some decisions about our lives and our future. Mark's account of the baptism of Jesus is the earliest account we have in the Scriptures. The Baptizer's preaching is both abrasive and attractive. His very opening statement detracts the attention from himself and places it on the one who is coming, the "one who is more powerful than I" (v 7). John's whole mission was a preparation for the Messiah's coming. When the time had come, John led his own disciples to Jesus and indicated to them the Messiah, the True Light, and the Lamb of God who takes away the sins of the world.

Jesus was attracted to John and he accepted to be baptized because he identified totally with the human condition. He felt our struggle and our need to be washed from the guilt of our sins. Through his own baptism by John in the waters of the Jordan, Jesus opens the possibility to us of accepting our human condition and of connecting with God the way we were intended to. We are baptized into Christ's death and resurrection. Heaven opens above us in the sacrament. The more we live in contact with Jesus in the reality of our baptism, the more heaven will open above us.

While I was studying in Rome, I came across a story from the early Church that is very fitting for us on the feast of the Baptism of the Lord. During the third century, Cyprian of Carthage wrote to his friend Donatus: "It's a bad world, Donatus, in which we live. But right in the middle of it I have discovered a quiet and holy group of people. They are people who have found a happiness that is a thousand times more joyful than all the pleasures of our sinful lives. These people are despised and persecuted, but it doesn't matter to them. They are Christians, Donatus, and I am one of them."

As we remember Jesus' baptism in the Jordan, let us echo Cyprian's words without fear: "We too are one of them." Our own baptism invites us to recall the past with gratitude, to accept the future with hope and the present moment with wonder and awe. Each time we celebrate the Eucharist, we are invited to the banquet of the Lord, so lavishly spread out before us. Our sharing in the Eucharist bonds us together with our brothers and sisters who have been immersed into the life of Christ through the waters of baptism. Let us pray that the grace of our own baptism will help us to be light to others and to the world, and give us the strength and courage to make a difference.

The Cost of Our Discipleship

1 Samuel 3:3b-10, 19;
1 Corinthians 6:13c-15a, 17-20;
John 1:35-42

Reflecting on today's readings, especially the call of Samuel and of Andrew and his brother, I remembered something that the German Lutheran Pastor Dietrich Bonhoeffer wrote from his prison in Nazi Germany, that "only by living unreservedly in this life's duties, problems, successes and failures, experiences and perplexities ... does one become a man and a Christian." Bonhoeffer experienced what he called so poignantly "the cost of discipleship."

The Prophet Samuel and Andrew and Simon Peter experienced this cost in their own lives. First let us consider the story of Samuel's call – a dramatic story exemplifying the dynamics of God's call, and offering to us a model to follow in our own lives. Eli was old and nearly blind. His sons, who were the priests of the temple, had been unfaithful to God. Their time was nearing an end, so God called Samuel to begin a new era.

Samuel needed help in discerning his call, and Eli's wisdom and friendship with the young man were necessary so that Samuel could really hear the Lord's voice. Once Samuel recognized that it was truly the Lord who was calling him, he became the great prophet who would discern God's will regarding religious, social and political matters for the people.

When we come before the Lord to listen to his Word, our deepest prayer and cry of the heart should be: "Speak Lord, your servant is listening." But is it not true that that cry often turns out to be: "Listen Lord, your servant is speaking!"

At the 2008 world Synod of Bishops on "The Word of God in the Life and Mission of the Church," Bishop Luis Antonio Tagle of the Diocese of Imus in the Philippines, made one of the most significant interventions. Bishop Tagle spoke about the disposition of listening to God's Word that leads people to true life. He said: "Listening is a serious matter. The Church must form hearers of the Word. But listening is not transmitted only by teaching but more by a milieu of listening."

Bishop Tagle proposed three points to develop a disposition of listening:

1. Listening in faith means opening one's heart to God's Word, allowing it to penetrate and transform us, and practicing it. It is equivalent to obedience in faith. Formation in listening is integral to faith formation.

2. Events in our world show the tragic effects of the lack of listening: conflicts in families, gaps between generations and nations, and violence. People are trapped in a milieu of monologues, inattentiveness, noise, intolerance and self-absorption. The Church can provide a milieu of dialogue, respect, mutuality and self-transcendence.

3. God speaks and the Church, as servant, lends its voice to the Word. But God does not only speak. God also listens, especially to the just, widows, orphans, persecuted, and the

poor who have no voice. The Church must learn to listen the way God listens and must lend its voice to the voiceless.

In the Gospel story for the Second Sunday in Ordinary Time, it is Jesus who takes the initiative or the first step. His question to the disciples is intriguing: "What are you looking for?" (1:38). Far from any simple interrogation, these words are deeply religious and theological questions. "Why" Jesus asks, "are you turning to me for answers?" They ask him, "Rabbi, where are you staying?" (v 38). The verb "live," "stay," "remain," "abide," "dwell," "lodge," occurs 40 times in the Fourth Gospel. It is a verb that expresses concisely John's theology of the indwelling presence.

The disciples are not only concerned about where Jesus might sleep that night, but they are really asking where he has his life. Jesus responds to them: "Come and see" (v 39). Two loaded words throughout John's Gospel: to "come" to Jesus is used to describe faith in him (cf. John 5:40; 6:35, 37, 45; 7:37); for John, to "see" Jesus with real perception is to believe in him.

The disciples began their discipleship when they went to see where he was staying and "they remained with him that day" (John 1:39). They responded to his invitation to believe, discovered what his life was like, and they "stayed on"; they began to live in him, and he in them. After Andrew had grown in his knowledge of who Jesus was, he "found his brother" Simon (Peter) and "brought him to Jesus (v 41, 42). This whole experience will be fulfilled when the disciples see his glory on the cross.

What can we learn from the call stories in today's readings? We are never called for our own sake, but for the sake of others. Israel was called by God for the benefit of the godless around it. God calls all Christians for the sake of the world in which we live.

To be called does not require perfection on our behalf, only fidelity and holy listening. Samuel and the prophets of Israel, the fishermen of Galilee and even the tax collectors that Jesus called were certainly not called because of their qualifications or achievements. Paul says that Jesus calls "the foolish," so that the wise will be shamed. It is a dynamic call that involves a total response on our part. We will never be the same because he has called us, loved us, changed us and made us into his image. Because he has called us, we have no choice but to call others to follow him.

How have you been called away from the routine of your life, away from the frustrations of daily life and work? What new purpose do you find emerging in your life because of the ways that God has called you? Through whom have you encountered the call of the Lord in your life? Have you called anyone to follow the Lord recently?

The Big Fish, the Great Catch, the Ultimate Commission

Jonah 3:1-5, 10;
1 Corinthians 7:29-31;
Mark 1:14-20

Those with literal minds will question many things about the Jonah story (Jonah 3:1-5, 10): the great fish, the size and population of this immense city, and the conversion of the Assyrians.

On the other hand, those who really listen to and view this story with ears and eyes of faith will take all of these other factors in stride. What is essential is not the size of God's sea monsters, nor the distances to be covered within cities, nor the large numbers of those converted.

For people of faith, the rather amazing Jonah story contains a far greater message: Because the people of Nineveh repented at the preaching of Jonah and turned from their evil ways, God repented of the evil that he had threatened to do to them. No person, place or situation is beyond God's mercy and healing reach!

It is no wonder, then, that Christianity saw Jonah as a positive figure prefiguring Christ and his universal Gospel message. Through Christ, God approaches his world in a new, decisive way in order to fulfill all the expectations and hopes of the Old Testament.

Jesus to the city

When the disciples in today's Gospel (Mark 1:14-20) leave their nets and present occupations in order to submit to God's Kingdom, they model what this turning from and turning toward means. How can we bring the Good News of God and of Jesus to our cities that are often so vast, so impersonal, and so busy and filled with noise?

At times do we not often run the other way to the lake and wait for some speedboat or cruise ship to pick us up and take us to a quiet, peaceful place that is much less complicated and less hostile to our message? How can we Christians be the souls of our cities?

We begin by celebrating the Eucharist with devotion and love. We must pray incessantly. We continue to do many hidden, quiet sacrifices each day of our lives with love, peace and joy. We take our baptism seriously and activate the Beatitudes in daily living. We must never give up in living God's Word and preaching it to others in words and deeds.

Remaining faithful

Whenever I read the story of Jonah, I am reminded of a story I heard in Jerusalem during the four years of my graduate studies in the Holy Land. One day my Muslim neighbours had invited me to meet their Imam. As we sat and sipped tea in the Old City of Jerusalem, the religious leader of the small mosque near my house spoke about the mercy of Allah.

He recounted a story about a certain Muslim – Youssef ben-al-Husayn – who died in the year 917. Youssef had received from his master the order to preach incessantly. He had however been very misunderstood and ostracized, and the time came when he had no more people who would listen to his words and messages.

One day Youssef entered the mosque to preach and not a soul was present. He was leaving the mosque when an old woman cried out to him: "Youssef, if the people are absent, the Almighty, he is surely present. Even though no one is here, teach the Word of Allah!"

Thus Youssef preached the word for 50 years, whether or not anyone was present to hear it. He didn't give up because of people's indifference, cynicism, absence or wickedness. He simply remained faithful to his vocation of preaching the word of Allah.

Youssef ben-al-Husayn and Jonah probably experienced a bit of prophetic fatigue in their day. They continued to preach the Word of God in season and out of season. We know what happened because of Jonah's persistence and fidelity to that word.

I am sure that Jesus must have felt the same way on many occasions. Was anyone really listening to his message? And with January 25 marking the feast of the Conversion of St. Paul, how could we not think of the great Apostle to the Gentiles, and his trials and tribulations endured as he preached the Gospel?

In the Acts of the Apostles (18:8-10), Paul arrives in Corinth, and we are told that "many of the Corinthians who heard Paul became believers and were baptized." One night the Lord said to Paul in a vision, "Do not be afraid, but speak and do not be silent; for I am with you, and no one will lay a hand on you to harm you, for there are many in this city who are my people."

The Year of St. Paul

One of the great hopes and goals of Benedict XVI in proclaiming the Year of St. Paul in June 2008, was to have every Catholic hold up a mirror to his or her life and to ask, "Am I as determined and as energetic about spreading the Catholic faith as St. Paul was?"

Our Catholic faith only grows when we consciously and conscientiously share it with others. Christ will look at each one of us with his merciful eyes at our individual judgment and ask what efforts we made during the course of our lifetime to invite people into communion with Jesus Christ and his Church. In the end, the Lord will ask us: "Did you love me? To whom did you preach the Good News? How many people did you bring with you?"

The Ultimate Commission

What does Jesus Christ demand of us today? Repentance, conversion, a turning away from our own ideas about how God's Kingdom should operate and a turning toward belief in Christ's teaching and example about God's Kingdom that is among us here and now. Our ultimate commission is to preach the word of God in season and out of season.

May the fire that the Holy Spirit poured into the heart of St. Paul of Tarsus, inflame our hearts to be vibrant and effective missionaries throughout our lives. May it strengthen us never to give up, especially when it seems like no one is listening any more. For it is precisely at such moments that the Lord will say again to us: "Do not be afraid, but speak and do not be silent; for I am with you, and no one will lay a hand on you to harm you, for there are many in this city who are my people" (Acts 18:9-11).

Speaking the Word of God with Authority

Deuteronomy 18:15-20;
1 Corinthians 7:32-35;
Mark 1:21-28

At the beginning of Mark's story of the Son of God, we read of the calling of the first disciples (1:16-20) and the confrontation with evil (1:21-28). The calling, influenced by the compelling calls of the prophets (e.g., Isaiah 6:1-13; Jeremiah 1:14-19), is a model of discipleship. Jesus is not a solitary prophet but one who calls companions "to be with him" (Mark 3:14); he enters the lives of four people engaged in their ordinary occupations, simply says, "Follow me" (Mark 1:17), and they immediately leave everything to follow him.

The story of Jesus in the Capernaum synagogue inaugurates the first day of his ministry that consists of exorcisms and healings. The story reflects contemporary Jewish thought that the coming of God's kingdom would mark the defeat of evil, which is personified in an array of demons and unclean spirits. Jesus' word is so powerful that people abandon their occupations and follow him, and even demonic powers are powerless before it. Jesus summons people to a change of heart, to take a new look at their lives and put their trust in the good news. This is not simply a story from the past, but one that continues to speak powerfully and prophetically to people today.

On this Fourth Sunday of Ordinary time, both the first reading (Deuteronomy 18:15-20) and the Gospel (Mark 1:21-28) raise the issue of the authority of those who speak the Word of God. Authentic prophets taught with authority because God put his own words into their mouths. In the first reading, Moses tells the people that God will send a prophet from the line of the Israelites. God commands everyone to listen to this prophet, whom we come to recognize as Jesus.

Jesus astonishes the people in the Capernaum synagogue with his teaching and authority. He taught with authority because he is the living Word of God. We are all witnesses to this living Word who is Jesus. We have no authority of our own; we simply proclaim his Word. Each member of the Church, by virtue of baptism and confirmation, has a prophetic role, and echoes the Word of God himself, both by words and example. We must walk our talk!

Authentic prophets were strident opponents of the status quo. They recognized and felt the injustice that kings and priests and false prophets wanted to whitewash. They shared the groans of the oppressed poor, of widows, orphans and the dispossessed, and articulated those groans in cries of woe. They denounced the system, but denounced a system in which they were often enmeshed. They experienced deeply what was wrong with that system, and did everything they could to bring about change from within the system.

Authentic prophets spoke the truth face-to-face with power, to powerful men and women whom the prophets knew intimately, frequently from their own position of power.

And often, the prophets were in the employ of those whom they challenged!

Finally, I offer a word on our own "prophetic" efforts to bring about change in the Church. I will be forever grateful to the late Jesuit Cardinal Avery Dulles for having instilled these ideas in my mind and heart years ago. The then Father Dulles said that reformers ought to speak prophetically. This may well be true, provided that the nature of prophecy be correctly understood. Father Dulles said that St. Thomas Aquinas made an essential distinction between prophecy as it functioned in the Old Testament and as it functions within the Church. The ancient prophets were sent for two purposes: "To establish the faith and to rectify behaviour." In our day, Father Dulles continued, "the faith is already founded, because the things promised of old have been fulfilled in Christ. But prophecy which has as its goal to rectify behaviour neither ceases nor will ever cease."

How do we speak the Word of God with authority today? How do we use our authority to further the Kingdom of God? How are our words, gestures, messages and lives prophetic today, in the Church and in the world?

Healing the Fevers of Life

Job 7:1-4, 6-7;
I Corinthians 9:16-19, 22-23;
Mark 1:29-39

The centrepiece of the stone ruins of the village of Capernaum on the Sea of Galilee's northwest shore is the black octagonal church of the *Panis Vitae* (Bread of Life), built directly above what is believed to be Simon Peter's house, the setting for today's Gospel story (Mark 1:29-39). One of my mentors and teachers, the late Passionist Father Carroll Stuhlmueller, once told me that the real centrepiece of Capernaum should be a huge memorial statue dedicated to the mothers-in-law of the world!

Try for a moment just to imagine the setting of this day in the life of Jesus. The newly constituted group of disciples who had left their nets, boats, hired servants, and even their father, to follow the Lord (1:16-20) are delighted in his presence. Jesus' words and actions completely overpower evil. His personality is so compelling and attractive. Leaving the synagogue where an evil spirit has been overcome, Jesus and his disciples walk only a few feet before encountering further evils of human sickness, prejudice and taboo. We read: "And the whole city was gathered around the door" (1:33-34). What a commotion!

In Mark's Gospel, the very first healing by Jesus involves a woman. He approaches Simon's mother-in-law as she lay in bed with fever. He takes her by the hand and raises her to health (1:31). Such actions were unacceptable for any man

---

– let alone someone who claimed to be a religious figure or leader. Not only does he touch the sick woman, but also he then allows her to serve him and his disciples. Because of the strict laws of ritual purity at that time, Jesus broke this taboo by taking her by the hand, raising her to health, and allowing her to serve him at table.

Peter's mother-in-law's response to the healing of Jesus is the discipleship of lowly service, a model to which Jesus will repeatedly invite his followers to embrace throughout the Gospel and which he models through his own life. Some will say that the purpose of today's Gospel story is to remind us that this woman's place is in the home. That is not the purpose of the story. The mother-in-law's action is in sharp contrast to that of her son-in-law, Simon, who calls to Jesus' attention the crowd that is clamouring for more healings (1:37) but does nothing, himself, about them.

In Mark's Gospel stories of the poor widow (12:41-44), the woman with the ointment (14:3-9), the women at the cross (15:40-41), and the women at the tomb (16:1), women represent the correct response to Jesus' invitation to discipleship. They stand in sharp contrast to the great insensitivity and misunderstanding of the male disciples. The presence of Jesus brings wholeness, holiness and dignity to women. How often do our hurtful, human customs prevent people from truly experiencing wholeness, holiness and dignity?

Job's test

In the Old Testament reading from Job (7:1-7), Job doesn't know it yet, but he is part of a "test" designed between Satan and God. Prior to today's verses, Job has endured immense suffering and loss. He knows that the shallow theological explanations of his friends are not God's ways; but still, he is at a loss to understand his own suffering. Job complains of hard labour, sleepless nights, a dreadful disease and the brevity of his hopeless life. For Job, all of life is a terrible fever! How often do we experience "Job" moments in our own life as our "fevers" burn away?

The healing of Simon's mother-in-law proclaims Jesus' power to heal all sorts of fevers. Around the year 400 A.D., St. Jerome preached on today's Gospel text in Bethlehem: "O that he would come to our house and enter and heal the fever of our sins by his command. For each and every one of us suffers from fever. When I grow angry, I am feverish. So many vices, so many fevers. But let us ask the apostles to call upon Jesus to come to us and touch our hand, for if he touches our hand, at once the fever flees" (*Corpus Christianorum*, LXXVIII 468).

With Jesus, healing of mind and body becomes a clear sign that the Kingdom of God is already present. Jesus' healing Word of power reaches the whole person: it heals the body and even more important, it restores those who suffer to a healthy relationship with God and with the community.

May we pray with confidence the words of Cardinal John Henry Newman's Sermon on Wisdom and Innocence: "May he support us all the day long, till the shades lengthen, and the evening comes, and the busy world is hushed, and the fever of life is over, and our work is done. Then in his mercy may he give us a safe lodging, and a holy rest, and peace at the last."

Finally, it is important to recognize what Jesus did after he healed the woman in today's story. He took time away to strengthen himself through prayer. Do we do the same in the midst of our busy worlds in which we live, in the midst of the burning fevers of life and the burdens of our daily work?

May these first moments of Jesus' ministry in Mark's Gospel teach us to recognize the goodness which God brings into our lives, but also that this goodness is not ours to horde for ourselves. The healing power of Jesus is still effective today – reaching out to us to heal us and restore us to life.

Let Us Not Fear the Sepulchres of This Earth

SIXTH SUNDAY IN ORDINARY TIME

Leviticus 13:1-2, 45-46;
1 Corinthians 10:31-11:1;
Mark 1:40-45

The first reading for this Sunday outlines the harsh laws for people with skin diseases usually labelled correctly or incorrectly as a form of leprosy (Leviticus 13:1-2; 45-46).

Throughout history, few diseases have been as dreaded as the horrible affliction known as leprosy. It was so common and severe among ancient peoples that God gave Moses extensive instructions to deal with it as evidenced in chapters 13 and 14 from Leviticus. The belief that only God could heal leprosy is key to understanding today's miracle that proves Jesus' identity.

Leprosy in the Bible appears in two principle forms. Both start with discolouration of a patch of skin. The disease becomes systemic and involves the internal organs as well as the skin. Marked deformity of the hands and feet occur when the tissues between the bones deteriorate and disappear.

In Jesus' time, lepers were forced to exist outside the community, separated from family and friends and thus deprived of the experience of any form of human interaction. We read in Leviticus 13:45-46 that lepers were to wear torn clothes, let their hair be disheveled, and live outside the camp. These homeless individuals were to cry "Unclean, unclean!" when a person without leprosy approached them. Lepers suffered both the disease and ostracism from society. In the end, both realities destroy their victims' lives. One may indeed wonder which was worse: the social ostracism experienced or the devastating skin lesions.

Mark 1:40 tells us that the leper appears abruptly in front of Jesus: "begging him, and kneeling." The news about Jesus' miraculous powers has gotten around, even to the reviled and outcast leper. "If you choose, you can make me clean," the leper tells Jesus. In even approaching Jesus, the leper has violated the Levitical code. By saying, "If you choose, you can make me clean," the leper not only indicates his absolute faith in Jesus' ability to cleanse him of his disease, but also actually challenges Jesus to act. In the ancient Mediterranean world, touching a leper was a radical act. By touching the reviled outcast, Jesus openly defied Levitical law. Only a priest could declare that someone was cured of the skin disease. As required by ancient law, Jesus sent the man to a priest for verification. Even though Jesus asked him not to, the man went about telling everyone of this great miracle.

My encounter with lepers

I had never encountered leprosy until I was pursuing my graduate studies in Scripture in the Holy Land. In 1992, I was invited by the Religious Sisters of the Sacred Heart to go down to Egypt from Jerusalem and spend several weeks teaching and preaching Scripture – first in Cairo, then down (or up!) the Nile River into Upper Egypt. We visited many of the very poor Christian villages where the sisters and other religious worked among the poorest of the poor. That journey remains engraved in my memory, for the remarkable women religious encountered along the way, and for the horrible human situations of suffering that we witnessed.

When we arrived in one of the Egyptian villages along the Nile, one of the sisters took me outside the central part of town, to an area where lepers and severely handicapped people were kept, in chains, in underground areas hidden away from civilization. It was like entering tombs of the living dead. Their lot was worse than animals. The stench was overpowering, the misery shocking, and the suffering incredible.

I descended into several hovels, blessed the people with my best Arabic and said some prayers with each person. The sister accompanying me said: "Simply touch them. You have no idea what the touch means, when they are kept as animals and monsters."

I laid hands on many of these women and men and touched their disfigured faces and bodies. Tears streamed down my face as the women and men and several children shrieked at first then wept openly. They reached out to hug and embrace me. Then we all shared bottles of Coca-Cola! Those unforgettable days, deep in the heart of Egypt, taught me what the social and physical condition of lepers must have been at the time of Jesus. There was not much difference between then and now.

As we read the story of Jesus among the outcasts, let us recall with gratitude the lives of three remarkable people in our Catholic tradition who worked with lepers and dared to touch and embrace those who were afflicted with that debilitating disease.

First, St. Damien of Molokai (Joseph De Veuster) who was born in Belgium in 1840. Joseph entered the Congregation of the Sacred Hearts at the age of 20 and was sent as a missionary to the Hawaiian Islands. He took the name of Damien. After nine years of priestly work, he obtained permission in 1873 to labour among the abandoned lepers on Molokai. Becoming a leper himself in 1885, Damien died in April 1889, a victim of his charity for others. He was beatified in 1994 by Blessed John Paul II, and canonized by Pope Benedict XVI on October 11, 2009.

With St. Damien, let us pray that we not fear the sepulchres of this earth. He descended into the lepers' colony of Molokai – then considered "the cemetery and hell of the living" – and from the first sermon embraced all those unfortunate people saying simply: "We lepers." And to the first sick person who said, "Be careful, Father, you might get my disease" he replied, "I am my own, if the sickness takes my body away God will give me another one."

Second, Blessed Sister Marianne Cope (1838–1918), was a mother to Molokai lepers. In the 1880s, Sister Marianne, as superior of her congregation of the Sisters of St. Francis in Syracuse, NY, responded to a call to assist with the care of lepers on the island of Molokai, Hawaii. She worked with Father Damien and with the outcasts of society as they were abandoned on the shores of the island, never to return to their families.

In the late 19th and early 20th century, about 10% of the Hansenites (people with leprosy) on Molokai and the Peninsula of Kalaupapa were Buddhists. Many practiced the native, indigenous religions of the Polynesian Islands. Some were Protestant and some were Catholic. Sister Marianne loved them all and showed her selfless compassion to those suffering from Hansen's disease. People of all religions of the islands still honour and revere Father Damien and Mother Marianne who brought healing to body and soul.

Be not afraid

Finally, let us recall with gratitude Blessed Teresa of Calcutta (1910-1997), who was never afraid to see and touch the face of Jesus in the distressing disguise of the poorest of the poor.

Mother Teresa wrote: "The fullness of our heart comes in our actions: how I treat that leper, how I treat that dying person, how I treat the homeless. Sometimes it is more difficult to work with the street people than with the people in our homes for the dying because they are peaceful and waiting; they are ready to go to God.

"You can touch the sick, the leper and believe that it is the body of Christ that you are touching, but it is much more difficult when these people are drunk or shouting to think that this is Jesus in His distressing disguise. How clean and loving our hands must be to be able to bring that compassion to them!

"We need to be pure in heart to see Jesus in the person of the spiritually poorest. Therefore, the more disfigured the image of God is in that person, the greater will be our faith and devotion in seeking Jesus' face and lovingly ministering to Him."

Most people will never encounter lepers. Nor will we know what it means to be completely ostracized by society. But there are other forms of leprosy today, which destroy human beings, kill their hope and spirit, and isolate them from society. Who are the modern lepers in our lives, suffering with physical diseases that stigmatize, isolate and shun, and cut others off from the land of the living? What are the social conditions today that force people to become the living dead, relegating them to cemeteries and dungeons of profound indignity, poverty, despair, isolation, violence, sadness, depression, homelessness, addiction and mental illness?

Let us not fear the sepulchres of this earth. Let us enter those hovels and bring a word of consolation and a gesture of healing to others. In the words of Blessed Teresa of Calcutta: "The more repugnant the work, the greater should be our faith and cheerful devotion. That we feel the repugnance is but natural but when we overcome it for love of Him we may become heroic."

To What Lengths Are We Willing to Go to Encounter Jesus?

SEVENTH SUNDAY IN ORDINARY TIME

Isaiah 43:18-19, 20-22, 24-25;
2 Corinthians 1:18-22;
Mark 2:1-12

Healing stories in the Gospels are never simply a reversal of physical misfortune. God works through miracles, through political forces, social action, intrigue, personal and societal chaos and daily, ordinary living to pick us up from where we have fallen and redirect us along right pathways.

Many aspects of Jesus' early ministry in Mark's Gospel are woven together in today's colourful story of the healing of the paralytic man. The story ends a whole series of healing miracles that began and ended in Capernaum (1:21-2:12). For reasons unknown, Mark tells us that Jesus had relocated his ministry to this fishing village on the northwest shore of the Sea of Galilee. It was from there that Jesus called five of the disciples.

Today's story (Mark 2:1-12) makes explicit what has been implied in preceding weeks: In healing the sick and casting out demons, Jesus is manifesting God's forgiveness of his people's sins. Sin is often equated with sickness in Scripture (see Psalm 103:3). And today's Psalm (41) reads like a foretelling of the Gospel scene – the man is helped on his sickbed, healed of his sins, and made able to stand before the Lord forever.

The Via Maris, a major highway, ran through Capernaum from the seacoast to Damascus and on to the east. Yet it was far enough away from Tiberias, the new, predominantly Gentile city where in 25 A.D. Herod Antipas had set up his capital. Capernaum also had a mixed population of fishermen, farmers, skilled artisans, merchants, tax collectors, etc. It is always important to recall that Jesus established the base of his ministry, not in some remote, back woods area, nor in sleepy Nazareth, but here in a very "cosmopolitan" town that was located at an important geographical, cultural and religious crossroads.

Strategic location

This strategic location also gave Jesus access to nearby villages and to the hill country to the north and west where he could carry on his ministry among receptive listeners without too much interference from political and religious authorities. This gives us an important insight into the identity and mission of Jesus.

I can just imagine Jesus seated under the roof of this small house in Capernaum. The crowd gathered around him was so great that no one could approach him. Two of a group of four men had chutzpah! They were persistent, bold and creative and decided that there were other ways to reach Jesus.

They climbed up on the roof and removed the tiles. Another stood on the ground receiving the tiles passed down from above. He made sure that the tiles would not be broken or stolen! After the whole event, he probably saw to it that the tiles were put back in place, appeasing some of the upset of the owner and neighbours after all that commotion! The fourth man stood beside their paralyzed and dazed friend, as he lay on his stretcher. This poor man, accustomed to immobility, was now filled with fear and frustration, yet deep down inside he could finally taste hope.

When Jesus was interrupted in his teaching by the abrupt intrusion from above, he saw first hand the faith of the paralyzed man's friends. Verse 10 of Mark's story goes to the heart of this moving Gospel account: "But so that you may know that the Son of Man has authority on earth to forgive sins."

When the man walked away cured of his illness, everyone was amazed. With the eyes of faith, the paralytic and his friends can see what the scribes cannot – Jesus' divine identity. The scribes, experts in the Jewish law, were appalled at what they regarded as pure blasphemy. They knew that God alone forgives sins. Jesus appears to be claiming equality with God. Today's story turns on this recognition. The scene marks the first time in the Gospels that Jesus commends the faith of a person or persons who come to him (see Matthew 9:2; Luke 5:20). Mark relates today's incident to further his theme that Jesus only very gradually revealed who he really was: the Messiah or the Christ, the Son of God.

Health care debate

Finally, let us try to apply the Gospel stories of healing and health of the past weeks to our present situations of healing and public health care in many parts of the world. I am thinking especially of the role of the Church in issues of the availability of health care for all people. There are some who say that the Church and her ministers have nothing to say about the matter! Any Church leader who dares speak out is simply written off as "one clad in the armour of religious righteousness," or a foolish person who "condemns capitalism and adopts the posture of socialism." There are those who reduce the health care crisis to a simple matter of socialism vs. capitalism in a free market, wealthy society, such as ours in Canada.

Churches do indeed have something to add to this debate. The Catholic Church has been a health care provider since her earliest years, and knows something about caring for large numbers of the sick and dying. It is a major part of her *raison d'être*.

One of the risks of privatized health care systems, if not very carefully managed and supervised, would result in a much higher quality of medical care for those who could afford to pay for it, and a much lower level of care to those who are simply unable to afford it. While the "front of the line" syndrome may be a bonus in certain circumstances, when it comes to health care, it can cause havoc and great injustice in societies around the world.

Let us recall the words of Blessed John Paul II in his 1991 encyclical letter *Centesimus Annus*, written on the 100th anniversary of *Rerum Novarum* (a major Church teaching on capital and labor by Pope Leo XIII): "In spite of the great changes which have taken place in the more advanced societies, the human inadequacies of capitalism and the resulting domination of things over people are far from disappearing." Is this not the crux of the current economic crisis in the world today?

Authentic health care is that which springs from a communal vision, one that is concerned with the health and well being of individuals, societies and entire populations. Such a model respects the human dignity of the individual as well as fostering a sense of community and trust. This model flows from a Christian, biblical and universal vision that is totally committed to the sacred dignity of human life, from the earliest moments to the final moments, from womb to tomb. The Church must continue to be a strong, clear voice for healing, health and life in the contemporary world. It is our mission and vocation that finds its roots in the healing ministry of Jesus.

Do we share the paralytic man's faith in today's Gospel? Do we have the chutzpah, creativity, perseverance and persistence of his friends to bring someone to Christ? To what lengths are we willing to go to encounter Jesus? How much are we willing to sacrifice so that our friends, too, might hear his saving word and experience the Lord's healing touch and presence?

Jesus Gives New Direction to the History of Salvation

EIGHTH SUNDAY IN ORDINARY TIME

Hosea 2:14b, 15b, 19-20
2 Corinthians 3:1-6
Mark 2:18-22

Jesus forges a new relationship with us

Today's Gospel (Mark 2:18-22) offers us another story in a series of encounters in Mark's Gospel between Jesus and people who don't understand why his rules seem different from what they are used to. In response to the question "Can the wedding guests fast (19)?", Jesus uses the marriage or bridal metaphor to express a new relationship of love between God and his people. Jesus also used the image of the garment that can't be patched any longer, and the used, fragile wine container that can't be used for new wine.

Jesus teaches that trying to assimilate the Pharisaic practice of fasting, or of extending the discipline of John's disciples beyond the arrival of the bridegroom, would be as useless as sewing a piece of unshrunken cloth on an old cloak or pouring new wine into old wineskins Both actions would result in the loss of both the cloth and the wine (21-22).

Attachment to externals

Jesus told his hearers that their attachment to an external sign, to something changeable, to a discipline, a habit, a fixed vision of themselves could interfere with their ability to truly see God. In his very person, Jesus is the inauguration of a new and joyful messianic time of fulfillment. Something old has passed; something new is at hand. Jesus wished to inaugurate a new age, to give new direction to the history of salvation. He used metaphors of new life that springs from the eternal and merges with the desire for change and novelty.

Jesus' bias for the new

Jesus' teaching about the incompatibility of old and new reveals a clear bias for that which was new. At the same time, today's Gospel about future fasting and about preserving the old garment warns against the easy assumption that everything old must be bad and everything new must be good. From the very beginning, the Church has always taken on rejuvenated forms drawn deeply from its profoundly Jewish roots. One vivid example of this is the Church's use of the Psalms in communal and private worship and prayer. Another well-known example is the discipline of fasting. Jesus does not deny the practice of fasting, but renews it in its forms, times and contents.

Fasting, in itself, is something good and laudable; it reflects fundamental religious attitudes: reverence before God, acknowledgment of one's sins, resistance to the desires of the flesh, concern for and solidarity with the poor. But we also know that fasting can be done for the wrong reasons and thus become very ambiguous.

Jesus and young people

Jesus began his ministry and the work of founding the Church when he was about thirty years old. He chose a group of young people – inexperienced, unprofessional, very impressionable, to be with him at the very beginnings of the Church. With their cooperation he wished to inaugurate a new age and to give new direction to the history of salvation. These young people were to be the new wine in new wineskins.

Each time the Church reaches out to young people, believes in them, empowers them and entrusts to them big dreams and hopes, the Church invests in its future. To introduce young people to Jesus Christ, to help them love the Church, to form them in prayer, devotion and worship is something very good, necessary, beautiful and hopeful. At the same time, the Church recognizes that many young people today are deeply afflicted and broken by the problems of our age: abandonment, anxiety, the marginalization of God from daily life; disappointments, anguish, fear and the lack of love. For these very reasons the Church must make a priority to walk with young people on their journeys.

Pope Benedict's connection with young people

Pope Benedict XVI has connected very well with young people throughout his Pontificate. He has never pandered to them, nor attempted to water down the Christian message when he speaks with young people. During his memorable visit to Malta and Gozo in particular, Pope Benedict spoke with young people on Sunday April 18, 2010. The questions put to the Pope by a group of young Maltese youth, and the Holy Father's encouraging response to them, puts today's Gospel into practice in a vivid way. Allow me to quote from Pope

Benedict's address to the young people of Malta and Gozo, gathered at the Valletta waterfront.

"...God loves every one of us with a depth and intensity that we can hardly begin to imagine. And he knows us intimately; he knows all our strengths and all our faults. Because he loves us so much, he wants to purify us of our faults and build up our virtues so that we can have life in abundance. When he challenges us because something in our lives is displeasing to him, he is not rejecting us, but he is asking us to change and become more perfect. That is what he asked of Saint Paul on the road to Damascus. God rejects no one. And the Church rejects no one. Yet in his great love, God challenges all of us to change and to become more perfect.

It is easy, when we are young and impressionable, to be swayed by our peers to accept ideas and values that we know are not what the Lord truly wants for us. That is why I say to you: do not be afraid, but rejoice in his love for you; trust him, answer his call to discipleship, and find nourishment and spiritual healing in the sacraments of the Church."

The above words express so well the thrust of today's Gospel: be rooted in the rich heritage of our Christian tradition but do not be afraid to set out in to the deep, to become something new, to move toward the future with hope, conviction and courage. When our roots are planted firmly in the heart of God and in the tradition of the Church, we will bear much fruit for the future. Young people are the new wine for the life of the Church. Friendship with Jesus Christ will keep young people and the Church forever alive and young.

Letters of recommendation

In today's second reading (2 Corinthians 3:1-6) Paul alludes to certain preachers who pride themselves on their written credentials. They seem to be reproaching Paul for not possessing similar credentials and compel him to spell out his own qualifications. The Corinthians themselves should have performed this function for Paul. Since he is forced to find someone or something that can recommend him, Paul points to them: their very existence constitutes his letter of recommendation (1-2).

The mention of "letters of recommendation" generates a series of metaphors in which Paul plays on the word "letter". The Corinthian community is Paul's letter of recommendation (2 Corinthians 3:2a). The Corinthians themselves are a letter engraved on his affections for all to see and read (3:2b). They are a letter from Christ that Paul merely delivers (3:3a). They are a letter written by the Spirit on the tablets of human hearts (3:3b). Paul's confidence is grounded in his sense of God-given mission (2 Corinthians 2:17).

Legacy of the Second Vatican Council

When Pope Benedict XVI held his first meeting with the Roman Curia in December 2005, he offered a long analysis of the legacy left by the Second Vatican Council. In that very important talk, he clearly stated his purpose of "freeing the Second Vatican Council from a particular interpretation of being a "rupture" with the past and a "new beginning.""

Benedict said in that address: "The hermeneutic of discontinuity risks ending in a split between the pre-conciliar

Church and the post-conciliar Church". The correct interpretation of Vatican Council II, in the view of Benedict XVI, is this: "... the hermeneutic of reform, of renewal in the continuity of the one subject-Church which the Lord has given to us. She is a subject which increases in time and develops, yet always remaining the same, the one subject of the journeying People of God."

More than just a "year in review," this papal address is essential to understand what Benedict is offering the Church through his Pontificate. There are still many people in the Church today who consider the Second Vatican Council to have been a rupture with the tradition of the Catholic Church. While some consider this rupture to be the Council's principal victory, others identify if with the Council's disastrous legacy.

Preserving the Unity of the Church

When he convened the Second Vatican Council, Blessed John XXIII affirmed in his opening address on October 11, 1962: "the Council wishes to transmit the doctrine, pure and integral, without any attenuation or distortion.... This sure and unchangeable doctrine, to which faithful obedience is due, must be explored and presented in the manner required by our era. The substance of the *depositum fidei*, or the truths contained in our venerable doctrine, is one thing, while the way in which these are expressed, though always with the same sense and meaning, is another."

One of the most important duties and responsibilities of the Successor of Peter and Vicar of Christ is to preserve the unity of the Church. Benedict, in particular, feels deeply responsible for unity, and cares for those who still today find themselves outside of ecclesial communion, but also of those who find themselves in a state of tension within it, and he invites all to a reciprocal openness within the unity of the same faith... that same unity and faith which inspired Blessed John XIII to convene the Council, and moved and animated Paul VI, John Paul I and Blessed John Paul II in their heroic efforts to give flesh and blood to the Second Vatican Council.

Our True Sabbath is Jesus Christ

Deuteronomy 5:12-15
2 Corinthians 4:6-11
Mark 2:23 – 3:6

The Jewish understanding of Sabbath lies at the heart of both the first reading from Deuteronomy 5:12-15 and today's Gospel (Mark 2:23-3:6). The history of the Sabbath in law and tradition suggests the notion of a pause from the routine of daily living in order to direct body, mind and heart to the dimension of the Holy.

In the first scene of today's Gospel, Jesus and his disciples are passing through a grain field on the Sabbath day. Some of the disciples are seen by the Pharisees to be picking heads of grain. The Pharisees challenge Jesus as to why his followers are doing something unlawful on the Sabbath (24). In response to their challenge, Jesus defends the action of his disciples based on the story found in 1 Samuel 21:2-7 in which an exception is made to the regulation of Leviticus 24:9 because of the hunger of David and his men. In the story from 1 Samuel, it was the priest Ahimelech, father of Abiathar, who gave the bread to David.

The healing of the man with a withered hand

The second scene presents us with a miracle story (3:1-6) that includes a controversy. The difference between this miracle

---

story and others is that in today's incident, the onlookers, instead of expressing amazement at the healing, are filled with hostility. When Jesus tells the man with a withered hand, "Stand up out in the middle!" he literally breaks the tranquility of the Sabbath and challenges his audience about the real meaning of the Sabbath law. What is striking is that the hostility of Jesus' opponents does not manifest itself through speech but rather through their "watching in order to accuse him" (2). Jesus is aware of this hostility and confronts it head on. The hardness of heart expressed by Jesus' opponents is already well known in this Gospel. The language used to describe Jesus' attitude toward defenders of the Sabbath law is unambiguous; to place religious scrupulosity above concern for human need is not pleasing to God.

The silence of the audience to this miracle is deafening. The people really say that they are more interested in their customs rather than in one of their own flesh and blood who is suffering and alienated because of his infirmity. They are more eager to destroy Jesus than to restore the man's withered hand. To observe the Sabbath is not only to rest and worship but also to do good, to save life, to make life whole, both our own and that of our neighbor. The Sabbath is a time to be refreshed, revitalized, reawakened and renewed. It provides opportunities to be with self, with others and with God in an atmosphere of peace and repose. The Sabbath, which was made for the celebration and preservation of life, becomes an occasion for malicious hostility that results in death, even the execution of the Lord of the Sabbath.

Jesus' approach to Jewish tradition

Jesus is an observant Jew who prays and celebrates the pre-scribed Jewish prayers and feasts. Yet he approaches the Jewish tradition in a new way. This is clearly evidenced in his position on the purity regulations (Mark 7); a new under-standing of the Ten Commandments in his Sermon on the Mount (Matthew 5:17–48); his approach to the cleansing of the temple (Matthew 21:12–13 and parallel passages), which anticipates the demise of the stone temple and proclaims the new temple and a new form of worship "in spirit and truth" (John 4:24). Therefore his question: "Is it lawful to do good on the Sabbath rather than to do evil?" places the matter in the broader theological context outside the argumentation of the scribes.

Jesus heals the man with the withered hand in the sight of all and reduces his opponents to silence. In the midst of all of this, opposition to him was mounting because people saw him as a one who violated the Sabbath. The conspiracy between religious and political leaders to do away with Jesus (6) represents the first explicit reference in Mark's Gospel to Jesus' death. In the controversy over plucking grain and heal-ing on the Sabbath, Jesus points opponents and disciples beyond them both to the wholeness of life under his own lordship.

Discovering the stillness and peace of the Sabbath

This week I leave you with three reflections on the meaning of the Sabbath. The first is by the late Rabbi Abraham Joshua Heschel, whose writings had a great influence on my own understanding of Judaism and the Old Testament. In his book *I Asked for Wonder: A Spiritual Anthology* (New York: Crossroad, 1998 Samuel Dresner, editor). Rabbi Heschel wrote:

"In the tempestuous ocean of time and toil there are islands of stillness where [we] may enter a harbor and reclaim [our] dignity. The island is the seventh day, the Sabbath, [when] we try to become attuned to holiness in time. It is a day on which we are called upon to share in what is eternal in time, to turn from the results of creation to the mystery of creation; from the world of creation to the creation of the world...

Six days a week we live under the tyranny of things. Six days a week we wrestle with the world, wringing profit from the earth; on the Sabbath we especially care for the seed of eternity planted in the soul. Six days a week we seek to dominate the world; on the seventh day we try to dominate the self. The world has our hands but, our soul belongs to Someone Else."

The second quote is from St. Augustine's *Confessions* (13:35-37):

"O Lord God grant us peace, for all that we have is your gift. Grant us the peace of repose, the peace of the Sabbath, the peace which has no evening. For this worldly order in all its beauty will pass away. All these things that are very good will come to an end when the limit of their existence is reached. They have been allotted their morning and evening. But the seventh day is without evening and the sun shall not set upon it, for you have sanctified it and willed that it should last forever. In that eternal Sabbath you will rest in us. Just as now you work in us."

The third quote is from #18 of Pope John Paul II's Apostolic Letter "Dies Domini" of May 31, 1998.

From the Sabbath to Sunday

"Because the Third Commandment depends upon the remembrance of God's saving works and because Christians saw the definitive time inaugurated by Christ as a new beginning, they made the first day after the Sabbath a festive day, for that was the day on which the Lord rose from the dead. The Paschal Mystery of Christ is the full revelation of the mystery of the world's origin, the climax of the history of salvation and the anticipation of the eschatological fulfillment of the world. What God accomplished in Creation and wrought for his People in the Exodus has found its fullest expression in Christ's Death and Resurrection, though its definitive fulfillment will not come until the Parousia, when Christ returns in glory. In him, the "spiritual" meaning of the Sabbath is fully realized, as Saint Gregory the Great declares: "For us, the true Sabbath is the person of our Redeemer, our Lord Jesus Christ." This is why the joy with which God, on humanity's first Sabbath, contemplates all that was created from nothing, is now expressed in the joy with which Christ, on Easter Sunday, appeared to his disciples, bringing the gift of peace and the gift of the Spirit (cf. Jn 20:19-23). It was in the Paschal Mystery that humanity, and with it the whole creation, "groaning in birth-pangs until now" (Rom 8:22), came to know its new "exodus" into the freedom of God's children who can cry out with Christ, "Abba, Father!" (Rom 8:15; Gal 4:6). In the light of this mystery, the meaning of the Old Testament precept concerning the Lord's Day is recovered, perfected and fully revealed in the glory which shines on the face of the Risen Christ (cf. 2 Cor 4:6). We move from the "Sabbath" to the "first day after the Sabbath", from the seventh day to the first day: the *dies Domini* becomes the *dies Christi!*

Questions for reflection this week

What is my own experience of "joyful rest" on Sunday? What are some of the difficulties I have in celebrating "Sunday"?

Are there any elements of the Jewish Sabbath that can help us to celebrate better Sunday as the Lord's Day?

What are some practical applications of the Sabbath to our own celebration of the Sunday?

What is the role of the Word of God in the Sunday celebration of the Eucharist?

The Kingdom Requires of Us to Do God's Will

Genesis 3:8-15
2 Corinthians 4:13 – 5:1
Mark 3:20-35

Today's Gospel story of the unbelieving scribes from Jerusalem who attributed Jesus' power over demons to Beelzebul (Mark 3:20-35) is inserted within the story of the arrival of Jesus' relatives. "Beelzebul" is a Canaanite divine name used here for the prince of demons. There are a number of references in the New Testament that try to establish a link between Jesus and Satan (Matthew 9:34; 10:25; 12:24, 27; John 7:20; 8:48, 52). These references referred not only to his lifetime, but probably indicated as well the tensions that existed between the Church and the synagogue. When Jesus said that Satan cannot cast out Satan (23b), he was saying that any entity divided against itself cannot stand, be it a kingdom, household or even Satan himself. Jesus has no kinship with Satan, but is his dreaded enemy.

Family ties

In the middle of the controversy, Jesus learns that his mother, brothers, and sisters have arrived (32). Throughout Jesus' earthly life, two groups felt themselves particularly close to him: first, his immediate family circle in Nazareth that thought they had lost him to the Twelve; and second, the group of the Twelve, his spiritual family. There were many

---

moments of tension and even alienation among the two groups. Both were blind to his true identity.

Jesus teaches his blood ties that his disciples are key to himself and his new ministry. Nevertheless this new group was a threat to blood relations (33-35). When certain members of Jesus' own family say that he is beside himself, they are also implying that he is possessed by a devil. That is the explicit response of the scribes who arrived from Jerusalem: "He is possessed by Beelzebub."

Jesus' family had ample reasons to think he was eccentric, or "beside himself," because his life revolved around another centre than that of his immediate relatives or of the people of his time. For Jesus, that centre is indicated in verse 35: it is doing the will of God. To do God's will is what the kingdom requires; family ties are secondary. The good news of the Gospel, with all its promise and demands, is that whoever does the will of God is not only the brother, sister, and mother of Jesus, but by that very fact is also his or her own true and deepest self.

The unpardonable sin against the Holy Spirit

The spirit that works in Jesus, by which he cast out demons, is the Holy Spirit of God. Today's Gospel text also contains the mysterious reference to the sin or blasphemy against the Holy Spirit (29). Why is blasphemy against the Holy Spirit unpardonable? Blasphemy does not consist in offending against the Holy Spirit with words; it means rather the refusal to accept the salvation that God offers to us through the Holy Spirit, working through the power of the crucified Christ.

When Jesus says that blasphemy against the Holy Spirit cannot be forgiven either in this life or in the next, it is because the non-forgiveness is linked to non-repentance, to the radical refusal to be converted. Only those who set themselves up against forgiveness are excluded from it.

When we close ourselves up in sin, thus making impossible our conversion, and consequently the forgiveness of sins, which has little importance for us, we enter a state of spiritual loss and destruction. To blaspheme against the Holy Spirit does not allow an escape from our self-imposed imprisonment to the cleansing and purification of consciences and the forgiveness of sins.

Doing the will of God

Jesus' new centre is to do the will of God. This is the kingdom's requirement. The will of God is first of all the comprehensive plan of God for the universe and history. It is the marvelous plan through which the Father, "destined us for adoption as his children through Jesus Christ, according to the good pleasure of his will" (Ephesians 1:5). The same expression "thy will be done" can refer also to any singular expression of the will of God. This "will" must be done first of all by God; it is God who fulfills his plan of salvation for the world.

Far from meaning some kind of passive, helpless abandonment to fate or circumstance, the "will of God" surpasses our wildest imagination and dreams, and reveals God's immense, providential, merciful care for each and every one of us. To allow God's will to be done in us requires a conscious, decided "yes" or "fiat" on our part, and a sweet and sometimes bittersweet surrender so that something great may happen in us, through us, because of us and even in spite of us.

In his programmatic homily at the inauguration of his Petrine Ministry on April 24, 2005, Benedict XVI said: "Dear friends! At this moment there is no need for me to present a programme of governance. ...My real programme of governance is not to do my own will, not to pursue my own ideas, but to listen, together with the whole Church, to the word and the will of the Lord, to be guided by Him, so that He himself will lead the Church at this hour of our history."

Imagine Joseph Ratzinger, now Benedict XVI, one of the greatest theologians and minds of the Church, announcing to the Church and the world that he has come not to do his own will, but to listen, together with the whole Church, to the word and the will of the Lord, to be guided by the Lord, so that the Lord himself will lead the Church at this hour of our history! What powerful words to be taken to heart for each of us!

The saints are eccentrics

How many times have we thought that the saints are merely "eccentrics" that the Church exalts for our imitation; people who were so unrepresentative of and out of touch with the human scene? It is certainly true of all those men and women who were "eccentric" in its literal sense: they deviated from the centre, from usual practice, the ordinary ways of doing things, the established methods. Another way of looking at the saints is that they stood at the "radical centre." Not measured or moderate, the saint's response to God's extravagant love is equally immoderate, marked by fidelity and total commitment. G. K. Chesterton said: "[such] people have exaggerated what the world and the Church have forgotten".

The reality that explained all reality

In today's second reading from Paul's second letter to the community in Corinth (4:13-5:1), Paul proclaims his faith, affirming life within himself despite death. Paul imagines God presenting him and them to Jesus at the parousia and the judgment. In verses 16-18, Paul explains the extent of his faith in life. Life is not only already present and revealing itself but will outlast his experience of affliction and dying: it is eternal. For Paul the dying and rising of Jesus Christ was the reality that explained all reality, that revealed the true face of God. The God of Jesus Crucified was revealed, not in the external appearances of power and splendor, but in the marvel of what appears to be human weakness and frailty.

Reconciliation and Penance

In light of today's Gospel, read #17 of Pope John Paul II's 1984 Post Synodal Apostolic Exhortation "Reconciliation and Penance."

"In another passage of the New Testament, [namely in St. Matthew's Gospel], Jesus himself speaks of a 'blasphemy against the Holy Spirit' that 'will not be forgiven' by reason of the fact that in its manifestation, it is an obstinate refusal to be converted to the love of the Father of mercies.

"Here of course it is a question of external radical manifestations: rejection of God, rejection of his grace and therefore opposition to the very source of salvation – these are manifestations whereby a person seems to exclude himself voluntarily from the path of forgiveness. It is to be hoped that very few persist to the end in this attitude of rebellion or even defiance of God. Moreover, God in his merciful love is greater than our hearts, as St. John further teaches us, and can overcome all our psychological and spiritual resistance. So that, as St. Thomas writes, 'considering the omnipotence and mercy of God, no one should despair of the salvation of anyone in this life.'

"But when we ponder the problem of a rebellious will meeting the infinitely just God, we cannot but experience feelings of salutary 'fear and trembling,' as St. Paul suggests. Moreover, Jesus' warning about the sin 'that will not be forgiven' confirms the existence of sins which can bring down on the sinner the punishment of 'eternal death.'

"In the light of these and other passages of sacred Scripture, doctors and theologians, spiritual teachers and pastors have divided sins into mortal and venial. St. Augustine, among others, speaks of letalia or mortifera crimina, contrasting them with venialia, levia or quotidiana. The meaning which he gives to these adjectives was to influence the successive magisterium of the church. After him, it was St. Thomas who was to formulate in the clearest possible terms the doctrine which became a constant in the church.

"In defining and distinguishing between mortal and venial sins, St. Thomas and the theology of sin that has its source in him could not be unaware of the biblical reference and therefore of the concept of spiritual death. According to St. Thomas, 'in order to live spiritually man must remain in communion with the supreme principle of life, which is God, since God is the ultimate end of man's being and acting. Now sin is a disorder perpetrated by the human being against this life-principle. And when through sin, the soul commits a disorder that reaches the point of turning away form its ultimate end God to which it is bound by charity, then the sin is mortal; on the other hand, whenever the disorder does not reach the point of a turning away from God, the sin is venial.' For this reason venial sin does not deprive the sinner of sanctifying grace, friendship with God, charity and therefore eternal happiness, whereas just such a deprivation is precisely the consequence of mortal sin.

"Furthermore, when sin is considered from the point of view of the punishment it merits, for St. Thomas and other doctors mortal sin is the sin which, if unforgiven, leads to eternal punishment; whereas venial sin is the sin that merits merely temporal punishment (that is, a partial punishment which can be expiated on earth or in purgatory)."

The Slow Progress in the Growth of God's Kingdom

ELEVENTH SUNDAY IN ORDINARY TIME

Ezekiel 17:22-24
2 Corinthians 5:6-10
Mark 4:26-34

The growth of plants, trees, flowers and grass, takes place very quietly and slowly, without our knowing. This growth permeates three of the four readings for this Sunday (Ezekiel 17:22-24, Psalm 92, Mark 4:26-34). Let us look at each of three readings then apply the plant images to the growth of God's kingdom in our midst.

Today's first reading from Ezekiel (17:22-24) is part of a lengthy allegory that combines fables from nature with concrete historical judgments, thus enabling the prophet to include the promise of future restoration in the historical framework of Judah's own experience. In the midst of Israel's great exile, Ezekiel knows that God does the unexpected – bringing low the high tree and making high the low. The great cedar represents the king of Judah, and the other trees are the kings of the surrounding nations. God will plant on Mount Zion in Jerusalem a young, tender sprig from the top of the same cedar. This is referring to the final king or messiah who will rise up from the house of David. This king will be enthroned in Jerusalem, atop the highest mountain of Israel (2 Samuel 7:13). Many other nations will come and find refuge under this new kingdom.

The God of Isarel always does the unexpected – bringing low the high tree and making high the low. God makes desert areas bloom and makes what may be superficially blooming wither (Ezekiel 17:24). God restores broken hearts and decimated hopes. Though the prophet Ezekiel's words referred at first to the hopes of ancient Israel, they still resound in our midst today. Even though the worldly dynasty of David would disappear, David's hopes would be fulfilled in a way far more glorious than he ever imagined!

We believe that the full realization of God's kingdom is found in Jesus of Nazareth, Son of Abraham and Son of David, who came to establish the kingdom in our midst. God's kingdom in Jesus grows in a hidden, mysterious way, independently of human efforts. The prophet Ezekiel's words stir our hearts and minds, and remind us of God's constant fidelity, especially when growth seems delayed or even impossible: "I the Lord have spoken, and I will do it" (17:24).

The just shall grow as tall as palms…

Psalm 92 is a psalm of praise extolling God's providence. Two dominant images of this Psalm are the cedar tree and the date palm. While the date palm can bear fruit, it lacks the lasting strength and stamina of the cedar. The cedar is mighty, but it cannot bear fruit. In biblical lands, the palm tree and the towering cedar of Lebanon suggest strength, justice, righteousness and beauty. Both the date palm and the cedar are planted deliberately in the house of the Lord. It is there, in the Sanctuary of God's Law, that they have their roots; it is from there that they derive all their vigor and strength. Both trees are presented as models for those who wish to live lives of righteousness and justice, planted firmly in God's presence.

Our homeland is the Lord

St. Paul builds on the the theme of Ezekiel's prophecy as he speaks about the mystery of our union with Christ's death and resurrection (2 Corinthians 5:6-10). Paul faces the fear of his own death and admits his difficulty at wanting to be "at home in the body/away from the Lord" or "away from the body/at home with the Lord." His confidence flows from his faith. In this life, we are separated from Christ. For this reason Paul would prefer death, "to be away from the body and at home with the Lord." At present we are citizens in exile, far away from our home. The Lord is the distant homeland, believed in but unseen (7). Paul affirms his confidence by contrasting what is of permanent value with what is only passing. Paul drives home the point that the sufferings of the present are not a valid criterion of apostleship because the true home of all believers is elsewhere.

So too with us – God is mysteriously drawing us towards our heavenly homeland. From this earthly home we prepare for our heavenly home; heaven is constantly calling us forward, instilling within us a deep longing to be with the Lord while we are still in the flesh here below. Paul's message speaks to us today: it is only from this earthly home that we will learn and prepare for the heavenly home; the way that we live our lives here and now with the Lord will be a very good indication of how we will spend our eternity with Him.

The assurance of the harvest

In today's well-known Gospel story of the sower, Jesus announces the fulfillment of Ezekiel's hopes, though with a kingdom even more unexpected than Ezekiel could ever imagine. This new kingdom would not be rooted in a geographical or political reality, but rather in human hearts. In today's parable of the sower, Mark (4:26-34) links two of Jesus' parables, featuring the image of a growing seed to speak of the kingdom of God. In the parable of the seed growing of itself (26-29), Mark contrasts the relative inactivity of the farmer with the assurance of the harvest. The sower need only do only one thing: wait for the crop to mature and then reap the harvest. Only Mark records the parable of the seed's growth (26-29). Sower and harvester are the same. The emphasis is on the power of the seed to grow of itself without human intervention (27). Mysteriously it produces blade and ear and full grain (28). Thus the kingdom of God initiated by Jesus in proclaiming the word develops quietly yet powerfully until it is fully established by him at the final judgment (29).

The mustard seed

The second parable is better known. Jesus uses the mustard seed to show the beginnings of the kingdom, exaggerating both the smallness of the mustard seed and the size of the mustard plant. The mustard seed is really not the smallest seed and the plant is only bush, not a tall tree. Jesus used this image to show that the kingdom will grow and flourish even though its beginnings seem very small and insignificant. The seed in Jesus' hand is tiny, simple and unimpressive. Yet the kingdom of God is like that.

From these small seeds will arise the great success of the kingdom of God and of God's Word. Since the harvest symbolizes the last judgment, it is likely that the parable also addresses the burning issue of slow progress in the growth of God's kingdom, especially when that growth was hindered by persecution, failure or sinfulness. Patience is called for in the face of humble beginnings. Jesus reassures the crowd that growth will come; it is only at the harvest that the farmer reappears. The growth of God's kingdom is the result of God's power, not ours. Like the tiny mustard seed, the kingdom of God is something that grows from a tiny beginning.

The Lord uses the vivid image of the mustard seed to speak about our faith. When we have faith, the Lord will accomplish great things in us. Whenever and wherever we take ourselves and our efforts too seriously, seeking by our plans and programs to "bring forth the kingdom of God," we will go away frustrated and sad. We must never forget that it is the Lord who sows, the Lord who waters, the Lord who reaps the harvest. We are merely servants in the vineyard. Let us beg the Lord to bless the desires he has planted deep in our hearts. As the mustard seed grows into a tree of shelter for birds, may our families and faith communities be signs of the kingdom where every person in our communities is protected, respected and loved.

The silent and vigorous growth of the Church

I was very struck by Pope Benedict XVI's use of the mustard seed imagery in his interview with journalists aboard the Papal flight to Madrid, Spain for the World Youth Day on August 18, 2011. The Holy Father was asked how the fruits of the World Youth Days can be ensured in the future? Do World Youth Days effectively produce fruits that last longer than the momentary bursts of enthusiasm? Pope Benedict responded to the questions with these words:

"God always sows in silence. The results are not immediately apparent in the statistics. And the seed the Lord scatters on the ground with the World Youth Days is like the seed of which he speaks in the Gospel: some seeds fell along the path and were lost; some fell on rocky ground and were lost, some fell upon thorns and were lost; but other seeds fell on good soil and brought forth abundant fruit.

"It is exactly like this with the sowing of the WYDs: a great deal is lost – and this is human. To borrow other words from the Lord: the mustard seed was small, but it grew and became a great tree. And with yet other words: of course, a great deal is lost, we cannot say straight away that there will be an immense growth of the Church tomorrow. God does not act in this way. However, the Church grows in silence and vigorously. I know from other World Youth Days that a great many friendships were born, friendships for life; a great many experiences that God exists. And let us place trust in this silent growth, and we may be certain, even if the statistics do not tell us much, that the Lord's seed really grows and will be for very many people the beginning of a friendship with God and with others, of a universality of thought, of a common responsibility which really shows us that these days do bear fruit."

To those words, I say Amen! Alleluia!

Questions for reflection this week

1. When was the last time that God has worked in your life, bringing about the most unexpected result?

2. What are the necessary conditions for the Word of God to be heard?

3. When have I been frustrated with the growth of God's kingdom? Why?

4. What has been my experience of World Youth Days and other great programs and activities of the Church?

It Took 40 Days ...

ASH WEDNESDAY

Joel 2:12-18;
2 Corinthians 5:20–6:2;
Matthew 6:1-6, 16-18

On Ash Wednesday the Church begins her great Lenten journey with Jesus on the road to Jerusalem. For centuries, Lent has been a very intense spiritual journey and experience for the followers of Jesus Christ.

Why are there 40 days in Lent? It took 40 days for sinfulness to drown in the flood before a new creation could inherit the earth. It took 40 years for the generation of slaves to die before the freeborn could enter the Promised Land. For 40 days Moses, Elijah and Jesus fasted and prayed to prepare themselves for a life's work.

Lent invites us to turn from our own selves, from our sin, to come together in community. Self-denial is the way we express our repentance. Self-denial is threefold, advises Matthew's Gospel.

We pray: "Go into your room and shut the door and pray to your Father who is in secret."

We fast: "so that your fasting may be seen not by others but by your Father."

We give alms: "Beware of practising your piety before people in order to be seen by them ... so that your alms may be done in secret, and your Father who sees in secret will reward you."

Through the Lenten exercise of prayer, fasting and alms-giving, we spring-clean our lives, sharpen our senses, put tomorrow in its place and treasure the day at hand.

One of the three Lenten practices open to most misinterpretation today is that of fasting. Fasting has become an ambiguous practice. In antiquity, only religious fasting was known; today, political and social fasting exists (hunger strikes), health and ideological fasting (vegetarians), pathological fasting (anorexia), aesthetic fasting (the cult of the body – believing that thinner is better). There is, above all, a fast imposed by necessity: that of millions of human beings who lack the indispensable minimum and die of hunger.

These fasts in themselves have nothing to do with religious or aesthetic reasons. In aesthetic fasting at times one can even "mortify" the vice of gluttony only to obey another capital vice, that of pride or vanity. Fasting, in itself, is something good and advisable; it translates some fundamental religious attitudes: reverence before God, acknowledgment of one's sins, resistance to the desires of the flesh, concern for and solidarity with the poor. As with all human things, however, it can fall into "presumption of the flesh." Remember the words of the Pharisee in the temple: "I fast twice a week" (Luke 18:12).

Lent is a time for us to discover the reasons for the pious practices, disciplines and devotions of our Catholic Christian tradition. What have we done with the important Lenten practice of fasting? If Jesus were here to speak to disciples of today, what would he stress most? We regard as more important the need to "share bread with the hungry and clothe the naked"; we are in fact ashamed to call ours a "fast," when what would be for us the height of austerity – to be on bread and water – for millions of people would already be an extraordinary luxury, especially if it is fresh bread and clean water.

In his message for Lent 2009, Benedict XVI wrote: "At the same time, fasting is an aid to open our eyes to the situation in which so many of our brothers and sisters live. In his First Letter, St. John admonishes: 'If anyone has the world's goods, and sees his brother in need, yet shuts up his bowels of compassion from him – how does the love of God abide in him?' Voluntary fasting enables us to grow in the spirit of the Good Samaritan, who bends low and goes to the help of his suffering brother.

"By freely embracing an act of self-denial for the sake of another, we make a statement that our brother or sister in need is not a stranger. It is precisely to keep alive this welcoming and attentive attitude towards our brothers and sisters that I encourage the parishes and every other community to intensify in Lent the custom of private and communal fasts, joined to the reading of the Word of God, prayer and almsgiving. From the beginning, this has been the hallmark of the Christian community, in which special collections were taken up, the faithful being invited to give to the poor what had been set aside from their fast. This practice needs to be rediscovered and encouraged again in our day, especially during the liturgical season of Lent."

Fasting helps us not to be reduced to pure "consumers"; it helps us to acquire the precious "fruit of the Spirit," which is "self-control," it predisposes us to the encounter with God. We must empty ourselves in order to be filled by God. Fasting creates authentic solidarity with millions of hungry people throughout the world. But we must not forget that there are alternative forms of fasting and abstinence from food. We can practice fasting from smoking and drinking. This not only benefits the soul but also the body. There is fasting from violent and sexual pictures that television, movies, magazines and Internet bombard us with daily as they distort human dignity. There is the fasting from condemning and dismissing others – a practice so prevalent in today's Church.

"See, now is the acceptable time; see, now is the day of salvation!" We need Lent to help us recognize that our identity and mission are rooted in Jesus' dying and rising. Prayer, fasting and almsgiving are the pillars of the Lenten journey for Christians.

Lent is a time to fast from certain things, but also a time to feast on others. Fast from discontent, anger, bitterness, self-concern, discouragement, laziness, suspicion, guilt. Feast on gratitude, patience, forgiveness, compassion for others, hope, commitment, truth, and the mercy of God. Lent is just such a time of fasting and feasting!

The Ways of the Desert

Genesis 9:8-15;
1 Peter 3:18-22;
Mark 1:12-15

Does anyone really look forward to Lent? What is it about Lent that excites us? What aspects of the Lenten journey test us? The Scriptural readings for this season are carefully chosen so as to replay salvation history before our very eyes.

Let us begin with Jesus in the desert – the Gospel for the first Sunday of Lent. The desert sun and the pangs of hunger and thirst conjured up the demon for him. Mark presents Jesus wrestling with the power of Satan, alone and silent in the desert wastes. Mark's version of the temptations of Jesus does not mention three temptations, nor does it say that Jesus fasted. Mark's whole focus is on presenting the temptations of Jesus as part of the great struggle between good and evil, between God and Satan.

Jesus' desert experience raises important questions for us. What are some of the "desert" experiences I have experienced in my life? What desert experience am I living through right now? When and how do I find moments of contemplation in the midst of a busy life? How have I lived in the midst of my own deserts? Have I been courageous and persistent in fighting with the demons? How have I resisted transforming my own deserts into places of abundant life?

In Matthew and Luke there is an ongoing conversation, as the prince of evil attempts to turn Jesus aside from the faith and integrity at the heart of his messianic mission. But if Israel had failed in the desert, Jesus would not. His bond with his Father was too strong for even the demons of the desert to break.

In the first temptation in the desert, Jesus responds to the evil one, not by denying human dependence on sustenance (food), but rather by putting human life and the human journey in perspective. Those who follow Jesus cannot become dependent on the things of this world. When we are so dependent on material things, and not on God, we give in to temptation and sin.

God's in charge

The second temptation deals with the adoration of the devil rather than God. Jesus once again reminds the evil one that God is in control. This is important for us to hear and believe, especially when our own temptations seem to overpower us, when everything around us might indicate failure, shadows, darkness and evil. It is God who is ultimately in charge of our destiny.

In the third temptation, the devil asks for a revelation or manifestation of God's love in favour of Jesus. Jesus answers the evil one by saying that he doesn't have to prove to anyone that God loves him.

Temptation is everything that makes us small, ugly, and mean. Temptation uses the trickiest moves that the evil one can think up. The more the devil has control of us, the less we want to acknowledge that he is fighting for every millimeter of this earth. Jesus didn't let him get away with that. At the very beginning of his campaign for this world and for each one of us, Jesus openly confronted the enemy. He began his fight using the power of Scripture during a night of doubt, confusion and temptation. We must never forget Jesus' example, so that we won't be seduced by the devil's deception.

We meet God in the midst of our deserts of sinfulness, selfishness, jealousy, efficiency, isolation, cynicism and despair. And in the midst of the desert we hear what God will do if we open our hearts to him and allow him to make our own deserts bloom. The ways of the desert were deep within the heart of Jesus, and it must be the same for all who would follow him.

Moriah, Tabor, Calvary:
Darkness Can Be Radiant

SECOND SUNDAY OF LENT

Genesis 22:1-2, 9-13, 15-18;
Romans 8:31b-35, 37;
Mark 9:2-10

Moriah. Sinai. Nebo. Carmel. Horeb. Gilboa. Gerizim. Mount
of Beatitudes. Tabor. Hermon. Zion. Mount of Olives. Calvary.
Golgotha. Mountains are often used in the Bible as the
stages of important encounters between God and his people.
Though we may have never visited the lands of the Bible, we
are all familiar with these biblical mountains and the great
events of our salvation history that took place there.

Today's Old Testament and Gospel reading take place
on two important biblical mountains – Mount Moriah and
Mount Tabor. Both readings give us profound insights into
our God and his Son, Jesus, who is our Saviour. First let
us consider the story of the sacrifice of Isaac by his father
Abraham as portrayed in Genesis 22:1-19. The story is called
the *Akedah* in Hebrew (Anglicization of the Aramaic word
for "binding") and it easily provokes scandal for the modern
mind: What sort of God is this who can command a father to
kill his own son?

How many pagan voices were assailing Abraham at this
moment? What would a contemporary father do if he were
to be called on to sacrifice his only son to God? He would
be thought mad if he even considered it – and unfaithful to

God as well. What a poignant story indeed! "Take your son, your only son Isaac, whom you love ... and offer him there as a burnt offering. ... So Abraham rose early in the morning." Because Abraham listened to the Lord's messenger, his only son's life was spared. The binding of Isaac, then, is a symbol of life, not death, for Abraham is forbidden to sacrifice his son.

What happens on Mount Moriah finds an echo in what happens atop Mount Tabor and Mount Calvary in the New Testament: The mounts Moriah, Tabor and Calvary are significant places of vision in the Bible. For on these peaks, we see a God who never abandons us in our deepest despair, terror and death. God is with us through thick and thin, through day and night.

These mountains teach us that it is only when we are willing to let go of what we love most and cherish most in this life, to offer it back to God, the giver of all good gifts, that we can ever hope to receive it back in ways we never dreamed of or imagined. Only then will we experience resurrection, healing, consoling light and new life.

We can only speculate on what lies behind the story of the Transfiguration – one of the Gospel's most mysterious and awesome visions (Mark 9:2-10; Matthew 17:1-9; Luke 9:28-36). Peter, James and John had an overwhelming experience with the Lord on Mount Tabor. Following the night of temptation and preceding the blackness of Golgotha, the glorious rays of the Transfiguration burst forth. Before their eyes, the Jesus they had known and with whom they walked became transfigured. His countenance was radiant; his garments streaming with white light. At his side, enveloped in glory, stood Moses, the mighty liberator, who had led Israel out of slavery, and Elijah, the greatest of Israel's prophets.

Jesus needed the light and affirmation of the mountain-top experience in his own life. In the midst of his passion predictions, he needed Mount Tabor, to strengthen him as he descended into the Jordan Valley and made his way up to Jerusalem. For every disciple since, it is the same. Those who follow Jesus must ascend the mountain to catch a glimpse of the mystery of God's presence in our world and in our lives.

And yet Mark's story of Jesus transfigured reminds us that gazing in contemplation is not enough. The disciples are told to listen to Jesus, the Beloved of God, and then return to their daily routine down in the valley.

The awesome Gospel story of the Transfiguration gives us an opportunity to look at some of our own mountaintop experiences. How have such experiences shed light on the shadows and darkness of life? What would our lives be without some of these peak experiences? How often do we turn to those few but significant experiences for strength, courage and perspective? How has the mountaintop experience enabled us to listen more attentively to God's voice – a voice calling us to fidelity and authenticity in our belief? When we're down in the valley we often can't see Christ's glory.

The most consoling message of the Transfiguration is perhaps for those who suffer, and those who witness the deformation of their own bodies and the bodies of their loved ones. Even Jesus will be disfigured in the passion, but will rise with a glorious body with which he will live for eternity and, faith tells us, with which he will meet us after death.

So many voices assail us that we find it difficult to listen to God's voice. Before light envelops us, we need to go through darkness. Before the heavens open up, we need to go through the mud and dirt. We must experience both mountains – Tabor and Golgotha – in order to see the glory of God. The Transfiguration teaches us that God's brilliant life included death, and there is no way around it – only through it.

It also reminds us that the terrifying darkness can be radiant and dazzling. During moments of transfiguration, God penetrates the hardened, incredulous, even disquieting regions within us, about which we really do not know what to do, and he leaves upon them the imprint of his own face, in all its radiant and dazzling glory and beauty.

A Burning Love for the Father's House

THIRD SUNDAY OF LENT

Exodus 20:1-17 **or** *20:1-3, 7-8, 12-17;*
1 Corinthians 1:18, 22-25;
John 2:13-25

For use with RCIA, Exodus 17:3-7;
Romans 5:1-2, 5-8;
John 4:5-42 **or** *4:5-15, 19b-26, 39a, 40-42*

In the Scripture readings for the Third Sunday of Lent (Year B), I would like to focus our reflection on two powerful images present in the texts: that of Jesus purifying Jerusalem's Temple, and St. Paul's message of the cross of Jesus Christ. Both the purifying action of Jesus and Paul's understanding of the cross can be of tremendous help to us as we grow in our knowledge and love of Jesus Christ this Lenten season.

John's account of Jesus' cleansing of the temple is in sharp contrast to the other Gospel accounts of this dramatic story. In the Synoptic Gospels, this scene takes place at the end of the "Palm Sunday Procession" into the holy city. With the people shouting out in triumph, Jesus entered into the temple area, not to do homage but to challenge the temple and its leaders. He overturned the tables of the moneychangers and upset the stalls of those selling birds and animals for the sacrifice. What a teaching moment this was! Jesus quoted from the Scriptures: "My house shall be called a house of prayer for all the nations ... but you have made it a den of robbers" (Mark 11:17, Isaiah 56:6-7, Jeremiah 7:11).

In the Fourth Gospel, the cleansing of the temple takes place at the beginning of Jesus' ministry and not at the beginning of the events of the last days of Jesus' life. The startling words and actions of Jesus in the temple, whether they are from the Synoptic accounts or John's account, took on new meaning for later generations of Christians. "Take these things out of here! Stop making my Father's house a marketplace!" The temple was not a commercial centre or shopping mall but rather a holy place of the Father. Like the prophets before him, Jesus tried to awaken the hearts of his people.

Jesus' disciples recall him saying in the temple the words of Psalm 69:9: "It is zeal for your house that has consumed me." I have often understood this verse to mean: "I am filled with a burning love for your house." When the magnificent Temple of Jerusalem had been destroyed by the Romans, and both Jews and Christians grieved at its loss, the followers of Jesus recalled this incident in the temple. Now they could see new meaning in it; it was a sign that the old temple was finished but a new temple was to be built. This new temple would not be of stone and wood and gold. It would be a living temple of holy people (I Peter 2:4-6; Ephesians 2:19-22).

Extreme Jesus

One intriguing aspect of today's Gospel story is the portrait of an angry Jesus in the temple-cleansing scene that gives way to two extremes in our own image of the Lord. Some people wish to transform an otherwise passive Christ into a whip-cracking revolutionary.

Others would like to excise any human qualities of Jesus and paint a very meek, bland character, who smiled, kept silent and never rocked the boat. The errors of the old extreme, however, do not justify a new extremism.

Jesus was not exclusively, not even primarily, concerned with social reform. Rather, he was filled with a deep devotion and burning love for his Father and the things of his Father. He wanted to form new people, created in God's image, who are sustained by his love, and bring that love to others. Jesus' disciples and apostles recognized him as a passionate figure – one who was committed to life and to losing it for the sake of truth and fidelity.

Have we given in to these extremes in our own understanding of and relationship with Jesus? Are we passionate about anything in our lives today? Are we filled with a deep and burning love for the things of God and for his Son, Jesus?

Message of the cross

In writing to the people of Corinth, Paul was addressing numerous disorders and scandals that were present. True communion and unity were threatened by groups and internal divisions that seriously compromised the unity of the Body of Christ. Rather than appealing to complex theological or philosophical words of wisdom to resolve the difficulties, Paul announces Christ to this community: Christ crucified. Paul's strength is not found in persuasive language, but rather, paradoxically, in the weakness of one who trusts only in the "power of God" (I Corinthians 2:1-4).

In St. Paul's First Letter to the Corinthians (1:18, 22-25), we hear "The message about the cross is foolishness to those who are perishing, but to us who are being saved it is the power of God." For St. Paul, the cross represents the centre of his theology: To say cross means to say salvation as grace given to every creature.

Paul's simple message of the cross is scandal and foolishness. He states this strongly with the words: "For the message about the cross is foolishness to those who are perishing, but to us who are being saved it is the power of God. God decided, through the foolishness of our proclamation, to save those who believe. For Jews demand signs and Greeks desire wisdom, but we proclaim Christ crucified, a stumbling-block to Jews and foolishness to Gentiles ...."

The "scandal" and the "foolishness" of the cross are precisely in the fact that where there seems to be only failure, sorrow and defeat, precisely there is all the power of the boundless love of God. The cross is the expression of love and love is the true power that is revealed precisely in this seeming weakness.

St. Paul has experienced this even in his own flesh, and he gives us testimony of this in various passages of his spiritual journey, which have become important points of departure for every disciple of Jesus: "He said to me, 'My grace is sufficient for you, for power is made perfect in weakness'" (2 Corinthians 12:9); and even "God chose what is low and despised of the world, things that are not, to reduce to nothing things that are" (1 Corinthians 1:28).

The Apostle to the Gentiles identifies himself to such a degree with Christ that he also, even in the midst of so many trials, lives in the faith of the Son of God who loved him and gave himself up for his sins and those of everyone (cf. Galatians 1:4; 2:20).

Today, as we contemplate Jesus' burning love for the things of his Father, and the saving mystery of his cross, let us pray these words:

O God, whose foolishness is wise
    and whose weakness is strong,
by the working of your grace in the disciplines of Lent
cleanse the temple of your Church
    and purify the sanctuary of our hearts.
May we be filled with a burning love for your house,
and may obedience to your commandments
absorb and surround us along this Lenten journey.
We ask this through Jesus Christ, the man of the cross,
your power and your wisdom,
the Lord who lives and reigns with you in the unity
    of the Holy Spirit,
God for ever and ever. Amen.[2]

---

2 See the prayer for the Third Sunday of Lent in Peter J. Scagnelli, *Prayers for Sundays and Seasons* (Chicago: Liturgy Training Publications, 1996), 34.

Nicodemus' Search for the "Soul of Theology"

Fourth Sunday of Lent

2 Chronicles 36:14-17a, 19-23;
Ephesians 2:4-10;
John 3:14-21

For use with RCIA, 1 Samuel 16:1b, 6-7, 10-13;
Ephesians 5:8-14;
John 9:1-41 **or** *9:1, 6-9, 13-17, 34-38*

The Gospel for the Fourth Sunday of Lent (Year B) features a nocturnal conversation between two important religious teachers: on the one hand a notable "teacher of Israel" named Nicodemus, and on the other, Jesus whom this Nicodemus calls a "teacher from God."

Nicodemus came to Jesus at night. His prominent role and position in the national cabinet called the Sanhedrin made him the custodian of a great tradition. He was expected by many to be a national expert on God!

It is important to provide some background for the Gospel passage for this Sunday. The conversation between Jesus and Nicodemus is one of the most significant dialogues of the New Testament and his coming to Jesus secretly at night suggests the darkness of unbelief. The whole visit and conversation are shrouded in ambiguity and the Johannine penchant for strong contrasts such as darkness and light can be seen in this highly symbolic story.

Jesus speaks to Nicodemus of the need to experience the presence of God and offer oneself to him. Knowing God is much more than a gathering of theological information and data about him. In speaking about being born again from above, Jesus does not mean that one must reenter the mother's womb for a second time; but Jesus refers to a rebirth, which the Spirit of God makes possible.

Lifted up

In today's Gospel text, Jesus tells Nicodemus, and all who will hear this story in future generations, that the Son of Man must be lifted up on a pole so that people may gaze upon him and find healing and peace. During Israel's sojourn in the desert, the people were afflicted by a plague of serpents. Moses raised up a serpent on a stake, and all who gazed upon it were restored to health. Both the bronze serpent and Jesus crucified symbolize human sinfulness. When Jesus is "raised up," it is not only his suffering on the cross that is intimated. The Greek word used for "raised up" has a double meaning: both a physical lifting up from the ground, as in the crucifixion, and the spiritual lifting up which is an exultation.

What lesson does Nicodemus teach us today? He alerts us to what happens when we buy into a system and try to "master" theology, scripture, tradition, rules and regulations. He teaches us that courses in religion and theology are no substitute for faith and conviction. For Nicodemus, God is much more than information and data – God is first and foremost a friend, a lover, a Lord and a Saviour, who patiently waits for us by day, and even by night. Rather than approaching Scripture as something to master, we must allow the Word of God to master us.

We know nothing more about Nicodemus, except that months afterward, he is able to postpone the inevitable clash between Jesus and the Sanhedrin. Later on, Nicodemus assists Joseph of Arimathea in retrieving the broken body of the dead Jesus.

Nicodemus and the Synod

I cannot help but read the story of Nicodemus in light of the Synod of Bishops at the Vatican on the Word of God in the Life and Mission of the Church. I had the privilege of serving as the Vatican's English language media attaché for the Synod of Bishops in October 2008 in Rome. The experience was a rich retreat steeped in Scripture and the documents of the Second Vatican Council.

At the synod, the Holy Father and the bishops of the world addressed the present impasse in Scriptural studies, often caused by the atomization and dissection of the Scriptures and a lack of integration of biblical studies with faith, the liturgy and lived spirituality. If Biblical texts are read and taught only for their historical and philological accuracy or inaccuracy, we fail to read the Bible as a book of faith that is the privileged possession of a living, breathing, praying community. We run the risk of selectivist and relativist interpretations of God's Word.

Over the past 18 years of lecturing in Scripture at the Graduate School of Theology of the University of St. Michael's College in Toronto, Canada, numerous students confided in me that their Scripture courses were "without a soul," divorced from the reality of the Church and unrelated to her liturgical life. Their simple yet revealing comments pointed toward one of the significant themes evoked during the Synod of Bishops on the Word of God.

On October 14, 2008, Benedict XVI shared some profound reflections on this very topic. In his brief, crystal-clear address to the whole assembly at the Vatican, the Pope touched upon one of the important themes that emerged in spades during this synod. When Catholic biblical exegesis is divorced from the living, breathing community of faith in the Church, exegesis is reduced to historiography and nothing more. The hermeneutic of faith disappears. We reduce everything to human sources and can simply explain everything away. Ultimately, we deny the One about whom the Scriptures speak, the One whose living presence lies underneath the words.

Referring to *Dei Verbum*, the Dogmatic Constitution on Divine Revelation, the Pope reaffirmed unequivocally the importance of the historical-critical method that finds its roots in John 1:14, the Word becoming flesh. Nothing that can help us understand the Biblical text should be excluded as long as the purpose of the different approaches and their limits are kept clear.

All the while the Pope was speaking, the New Testament figure of Nicodemus was on my mind, as well as numerous other personalities who were led by Jesus beyond theories, systems, structures into the encounter with the living Lord who is the Word among us. Nicodemus certainly had an endless amount of knowledge and learning, and he developed a great system of religion in which God is categorized and analyzed.

Jesus does not say that this is evil or even undesirable. He simply says that it is not enough.

Ever since my years of study at the Pontifical Biblical Institute in Rome, I have carried this little prayer of St. Bonaventure in my pocket. The words are from his *Itinerarium Mentis in Deum* inviting Christians to recognize the inadequacy of "reading without repentance, knowledge without devotion, research without the impulse of wonder, prudence without the ability to surrender to joy, action divorced from religion, learning sundered from love, intelligence without humility, study unsustained by divine grace, thought without the wisdom inspired by God."

Those words serve as a measure and guide for each of us, as we study theology and the Word of God, and allow the Word to master us. May our knowledge, learning, science and intelligence humbly lead us into an encounter, by day and by night, with Jesus Christ, the ultimate goal of our journey.

Gazing Upon the Face of Jesus

Jeremiah 31:31-34;
Hebrews 5:7-9;
John 12:20-33

For use with RCIA, Ezekiel 37:12-14;
Romans 8:8-11;
John 11:1-45 **or** *11:3-7, 17, 20-27, 33b-45*

The Fifth Sunday of Lent (Year B) invites us to fix our gaze upon Jesus, the model priest of suffering, compassion and human solidarity.

First, let us consider John's Gospel story from Chapter 12 – a fitting climax to Jesus' public ministry. It is the last official act before the events of his passion next Sunday. There are Gentiles, non-Jews, who seek Jesus out for the first time. They do not come simply to catch a glimpse of him, to have some general audience with him, but rather to "see" him. In John's Gospel, "seeing" Jesus is believing in him. How simple yet how stunning a request: "Sir, we wish to see Jesus" (John 12:21)!

Throughout the entire Scriptures, men and women have longed to see God, to gaze upon God's countenance, beauty and glory. How many times in the Psalms do we ask to see the face of God? "Make your face shine upon your servant" (Psalm 119:135). Not only do we beg to see God's face, but we are told to look for it. "Seek my face," the Lord urges in our hearts (cf. Psalm 27:8).

But we cannot seem to find the face we are told to look for. Then the laments begin: "Do not hide your face from me" (Psalm 102:2). "Why do you hide your face from me?" (Psalm 88:14). "How long will you hide your face from me?" (Psalm 13:2). We beg, we seek, but we cannot find God's face. Then we are distraught. Moses, speaking as friend-to-friend, asked to see God's face. But God said to him, "You cannot see my face; for no one shall see my face and live" (Exodus 33:20).

When we ask in the Psalms to see God's face, we are really asking to see God as God truly is, to gaze into the depths of God. In the last chapter of the last book of the Scriptures, it is written: "They will see his face" (Revelation 22:4). We see God's face revealed to us in the person of Jesus of Nazareth. How often do we long to "see" the face of Jesus? Where are we seeking his face today? What do we do when we finally "see" the face of Jesus?

Garden of suffering

The author of the Letter to the Hebrews is filled with the thoughts and theology of Paul and John, but he also contemplates Jesus' agony in the garden in relation to temple sacrifices and the priesthood according to the Hebrew Scriptures. The Old Testament never dreamed of requiring the high priest to make himself like his brothers and sisters, but was preoccupied on the contrary with separating him from them. An attitude of compassion toward sinners appeared to be incompatible with the priesthood of the Old Covenant. Furthermore, no text ever required that the high priest should be free from all sin.

Hebrews 5:7-9 presents us with a different type of priesthood – one of extraordinary compassion and solidarity. In his days on earth, Jesus shared our flesh and blood, crying out with prayers and silent tears. Jesus has been tested in all respects like us – he knows all of our difficulties; he is a tried man; he knows our condition from the inside and from the outside – only by this did he acquire a profound capacity for compassion. That is the only kind of priesthood that makes a difference, and that matters, then and now.

What does this image of Jesus teach us today? Far from creating an abyss between Jesus Christ and ourselves, our own daily trials and weaknesses have become the privileged place of our encounter with him, and not only with him, but with God himself. The consequence is that from now on, not one of us can be bowed down under a painful situation without finding that Christ is, by that very fact, at our side. Jesus was "heard because of his 'reverence' or his 'pious submission.'" And we are given the consolation that we, too, will be heard because of our own persistence in prayer, our reverence before God and our pious submission to his will for us.

Blessed John Paul II's agony

We read in today's Gospel passage that the Greeks address themselves first to Philip, who is from the village of Bethsaida on the Sea of Galilee: "Philip went and told Andrew; then Andrew and Philip went and told Jesus" (John 12:22). To see Jesus, one must be led to him by an apostle. The testimony of those who lived with him, at his side, shows him to us and we cannot do without this testimony.

We need the apostolic writings, especially the Gospels, handed down to us by tradition, of which our parents, priests, deacons, teachers, catechists, preachers and other believers are witnesses and bearers of the Good News. How important and necessary it is to recognize those key people in our lives who are living witnesses and links to the tradition and the Good News about Jesus Christ! One such person for millions of people throughout the world was Karol Wojtyla, the man we now know as Blessed Pope John Paul II.

The world witnessed the agony and passion of this Successor of Peter in a most public way. As we commemorate the anniversary of Blessed John Paul II's death on April 2, I cannot help but recall those moving days and see how much he revealed to us the face of God and the image of Jesus crucified.

One of the most powerful lessons he taught us in the twilight of his Pontificate was that everyone must suffer, even the Vicar of Christ. Rather than hide his infirmities, as most public figures do, he let the whole world see what he went through. In the final act of his life, the athlete was immobilized, the distinctive, booming voice silenced, and the hand that produced voluminous encyclicals no longer able to write. Yet nothing made Blessed John Paul II waver, even the debilitating sickness hidden under the glazed Parkinsonian mask, and ultimately his inability to speak and move. Many believe that the most powerful message he preached was when the words and actions failed.

One of the unforgettable, silent, teaching moments of those final days took place on Good Friday night 2005, while the Pope, seated in his private chapel in the Vatican, viewed the television coverage of the *Via Crucis* from Rome's Colosseum. At the station commemorating the death of the Lord, a television camera in the papal chapel showed the Pope embracing a cross in his hands with his cheek resting against the wood. His accepting of suffering and death needed no words. The image spoke for itself.

Several hours before his death, Pope John Paul's last audible words were: "Let me go to the house of the Father." In the intimate setting of prayer, as Mass was celebrated at the foot of his bed and the throngs of faithful sang below in St. Peter's Square, he died at 9:37 p.m. on April 2. Through his public passion, suffering and death, this holy priest, Successor of the Apostles, and Servant of God, showed us the face of Jesus in a remarkable way.

The Passion of Jesus Is Our Reason for Hope

PALM SUNDAY

Isaiah 50:4-7;
Philippians 2:6-11;
Mark 14:1–15:47 **or** *15:1-39*

For use at the Blessing of the Palms,
Mark 11:1-10 **or**
John 12:12-16

The Passion, suffering, death and resurrection of the Lord are the very themes that unite us as a Christian people and a Church during Holy Week.

This year on Palm Sunday, we listen attentively to Mark's Passion story of Jesus' final days and hours on earth. It is a story of striking contrasts. As we hear anew this moving story, Jesus' passion penetrates the numbness of our lives. This week in particular, we have a privileged opportunity to learn from what happened to Jesus and discover not only the identity of those who tried, condemned and killed him long ago, but also what killed Jesus and what vicious circles of violence, brutality, hatred and jealousy continue to crucify him today in his brothers and sisters of the human family.

Zooming in on Mark's Passion narrative

Mark's account (Mark 11:1-10) of Jesus' entry into Jerusalem is the most subdued version of the event in the New Testament. For some reason the evangelist places much emphasis on the donkey in this account. It was the custom for pilgrims to enter

Jerusalem on foot. Only kings and rulers would "ride" into the city – most often on great steeds and horses and in ostentatious processions, in order to make their presence known. Jesus, a different kind of king, chooses to ride into the city, not on a majestic stallion but on the back of a young beast of burden.

By being led through the city on the back of a lowly donkey, Jesus comes as a king whose rule is not about being served but serving. His kingdom is not built on might but on compassion and generous service. The donkey Jesus mounts sends us back to the words of the ancient prophet, Zechariah, who foretold this scene five centuries before: "Rejoice greatly, O daughter Zion! Shout aloud, O daughter Jerusalem! See, your king comes to you; triumphant and victorious is he, humble and riding on a donkey . . . "

In Mark's jarring Passion story, we witness the anguish of Jesus who has been totally abandoned by friends and disciples. Jesus is resigned to his fate. He makes no response to Judas when he is betrayed by him or to Pilate during his interrogation. In Mark, Pilate makes no effort to save him, as the Roman procurator does in the other three Gospels.

As he does throughout his Gospel, Mark depicts the utter failure of the disciples to provide any support to Jesus or to even understand what is happening. The enigmatic, young male disciple who flees naked into the night when Jesus is arrested is a powerful symbol in Mark's Gospel of his followers who initially left family and friends behind to follow Jesus. Now that the heat is on, they leave everything behind to flee from him.

When we remember the events of that first Holy Week – from the upper room to Gethsemane, from Pilate's judgment seat to Golgotha, from the cross to the empty tomb, Jesus turns our world and its value system upside down. He teaches us that true authority is found in dedicated service and generosity to others; greatness is centred in humility; the just and loving will be exalted by God in God's good time.

Viewing Mark's Passion through the lenses of fidelity

In Mark's passion narrative when Jesus is in Bethany visiting Simon the Leper, an anonymous woman breaks open her alabaster jar of costly perfumed oil, and anoints Jesus' head in a royal way (14:3-9). As the fragrance of the oil fills the room, those with Jesus are shocked at the woman's extravagant gesture. But Jesus defends her as she had performed an act of true fidelity and love. Jesus tells those around him: "she has anointed my body beforehand for its burial" (14:8). For this, Jesus promises, she would be remembered wherever the Gospel would be preached (14:9). This woman is the only one apart from the Mother of Jesus to be so greatly honoured.

While his male disciples and apostles clearly manifest a bold track record of failure, betrayal and abandonment, this anonymous woman embodies boldness, courage, love and fidelity. What an example! Though she may not fully understand the significance of her symbolic and prophetic act of anointing him, nor the timeliness of her action, she only desires simply to be with him and to express to him lavish love and attention.

Is this not what each of us is called to do during Holy Week in particular? Is it not to love Jesus and to be attentive to him throughout the final tragic movements of the symphony of his earthly life, and in the midst of all of the setbacks, failures and betrayals of our own lives? Our lives must be like the woman's jar of expensive ointment poured out so lavishly on the Lord in the final moments of his life on earth.

Who, if not the condemned Saviour?

At the conclusion of the Stations of the Cross at Rome's Colosseum on Good Friday night in the Jubilee Year 2000, Blessed John Paul II spoke these moving and powerful words:

"Who, if not the condemned Saviour, can fully understand the pain of those unjustly condemned?

"Who, if not the King scorned and humiliated, can meet the expectations of the countless men and women who live without hope or dignity?

"Who, if not the crucified Son of God, can know the sorrow and loneliness of so many lives shattered and without a future?"

What a Saviour we have! He truly understands our human condition. He walks with us and shares our sorrows, loneliness and suffering. How do we respond to such outlandish love and genuine solidarity? Passion Sunday invites us to put on what Paul calls the "attitude of Christ Jesus" (Philippians 2:6-11) in his passion and death: to "empty" ourselves of our own interests, fears and needs for the sake of others. May we reach out to heal those who are hurting and comfort the despairing around us despite our own denials and betrayals.

During the moving liturgies of Holy Week, we are given the special grace to carry on, with joy and in hope, despite rejection, humiliation and suffering. In this way, the Passion of Jesus becomes a reason for hope and a moment of grace for us all as we seek the reign of God in our own lives – however lonely and painful that search may be. Holy Week gives us the consolation and the conviction that we are not alone.

The Bare Facts and Bare Feet of the Last Supper

Holy Thursday

Exodus 12:1-8, 11-14;
I Corinthians 11:23-26;
John 13:1-15

Both the Jewish and Christian traditions view eating and feasting as more than simply an opportunity to refuel the body, enjoy certain delicacies, or celebrate a particular occasion.

Eating and feasting became for both traditions, encounters with transcendent realities and even union with the divine. In the New Testament, so much of Jesus' own ministry took place during meals at table. Some say that you can eat your way through the Gospels with Jesus!

Jesus attends many meals throughout the four Gospels: with Levi and his business colleagues, with Simon the Pharisee, with Lazarus and his sisters in Bethany, with Zacchaeus and the crowd in Jericho, with outcasts and centurions, with crowds on Galilean hillsides, and with disciples in their homes.

It is ultimately during the final meal that Jesus leaves us with his most precious gift in the Eucharist. The Scripture readings for Holy Thursday root us deeply in our Jewish past: celebrating the Passover with the Jewish people, receiving from St. Paul that which was handed on to him, namely the Eucharistic banquet, and looking at Jesus squarely in the face as he kneels before us to wash our feet in humble service. Instead of presenting to us one of the synoptic Gospel stories of the "institution" of the Eucharist, the Church offers us the disturbing posture of the Master kneeling before his friends to wash their feet in a gesture of humility and service.

Just imagine the scene! As Jesus wraps a towel around his waist, takes a pitcher of water, stoops down and begins washing the feet of his disciples, he teaches his friends that liberation and new life are won not in presiding over multitudes from royal thrones nor by the quantity of bloody sacrifices offered on temple altars but by walking with the lowly and poor and serving them as a foot washer along the journey.

On this holy night of "institution," as Jesus drank from the cup of his blood and stooped to wash feet, a new and dynamic, common bond was created with his disciples and with us. It is as though the whole history of salvation ends tonight just as it begins – with bare feet and the voice of God speaking to us through his own flesh and blood: "You should do as I have done to you" (John 13:15). The washing of the feet is integral to the Last Supper. It is John's way of saying to Christ's followers throughout the ages: "You must remember his sacrifice in the Mass, but you must also remember his admonition to go out and serve the world."

At the Last Supper, Jesus teaches us that true authority in the Church comes from being a servant, from laying down our lives for our friends. His life is a feast for the poor and for sinners. It must be the same for those who receive the Lord's body and blood. We become what we receive in this meal and we imitate Jesus in his saving works, his healing words, and his gestures of humble service. From the Eucharist must flow a certain style of communitarian life, a genuine care for our neighbours, and for strangers.

Finally, the celebration of the Eucharist always projects us forward just as we profess the memorial acclamation after the consecration at Mass: "When we eat this Bread and drink this Cup, we proclaim your Death, O Lord, until you come again."

The transforming power of a meal

Each year around Holy Thursday, I try to make time to watch one of my favourite "Eucharistic" movies: *Babette's Feast*. It is based on a story of the opening of the hearts of a small, puritanical community on the coast of Norway by the generosity of a French refugee cook. The movie, directed by Gabriel Axel, received the Academy Award in 1986 for Best Foreign Film and is a faithful adaptation of Isak Dinesen's 1958 short story *Babettes gæstebud*. It has been called "a cinematic icon of the Eucharist" because it explores love and generosity in the context of a meal and the meal's ability to transform lives.

Here is the plot of the movie. In 19th-century Denmark, two adult sisters live in an isolated village with their father, who is the honoured pastor of a small Protestant church that is practically a sect unto itself. Although they each are presented with a real opportunity to leave the village, the sisters choose to stay with their father, to serve him and their church. After some years, a French woman refugee, Babette, arrives at their door, begs them to take her in, and commits herself to work for them as maid/housekeeper/cook. Babette arrived with a note from a French singer who had passed through the area some time before, fallen in love with one of the sisters, but left disappointed. The note commends Babette to these "good people," and offhandedly mentions that she can cook.

During the intervening dozen years, Babette cooks very plain and simple meals to which the sisters are accustomed.

In the 12th year of her service to this family, Babette wins the French lottery, a prize of 10,000 francs. At the same time, the sisters are planning a simple celebration of the 100th anniversary of their father, the founder of their small Christian sect. They expect Babette to leave with her winnings, but instead, she surprises them by offering to cook a meal for the anniversary. Although the sisters are secretly concerned about what Babette, a Catholic and a foreigner, might do, the sisters allow her to go ahead. Babette uses just the tiniest opening, a modest celebration, to cook up a storm and wreak havoc in the lives of the sisters, and with their community, by such outrageous generosity.

God is ever ready, looking for the smallest opening, in a sense praying that we will grant him the joy of accepting his offer! Life in Christ begins with the tiniest move on our part, just the hint of an opening, and then God steps in and overwhelms us in response. When we accept, God takes over in the kitchen, raining down upon us grace upon grace. The finest French delicacies are nothing compared to the gifts God has to bestow upon us, especially in the ultimate gift of himself in the Eucharist.

In the end, Babette's feast produced some amazing effects. The community had become reconciled with each other. The dinner guests at Babette's feast encountered the divine and received fulfillment through the experience of the physical act of eating. *Babette's Feast* is a masterpiece that can help us to explore divine generosity with the image of a meal, its transforming quality, its gestures of humble, loving service, and its fruits of reconciliation and forgiveness that take place around the table. No wonder why this film reminds me of the other meal that took place in an Upper Room in Jerusalem centuries before.

Embracing the True Science of the Cross

Good Friday

Isaiah 52:13–53:12;
Hebrews 4:14-16; 5:7-9;
John 18:1–19:42

Each year on Good Friday we read the Passion according to St. John. Throughout this hauntingly moving narrative, there is an emphasis on Jesus' sovereignty even in death.

As we contemplate the mystery of Jesus crucified, we learn in his suffering and dying how vast a person he was among us. We are invited to realize the tragedy of Jesus' death in the context of our own trials, sorrows, and deaths. Jesus' cross is a message, a word for us, a sign of contradiction, a sign of victory, and we gaze upon the cross and respond in faith to the message of life which flows from it, a message which brings us healing and reconciliation.

As the cross is held high in our midst, in some strange and mysterious way, we look upon it and find strength and hope in the midst of our own struggles.

Ecce Homo

Jesus crucified is the symbol of what humankind does to goodness – we kill it. It is not evil that we are afraid of but goodness. In John's Passion story, Pontius Pilate presents Jesus to the people with the words: *Ecce Homo* – Behold the Man (19:5). What an incredible expression to describe the paradoxical person and mission of God's own son!

Ecce Homo – in whom humanity was so well integrated that he was fully human and is truly a model for each of how we must be fully human in order to be authentically holy.

Ecce Homo – who lived for others, healing them, restoring them and loving them to life.

Ecce Homo – who had the courage to choose women as disciples and close friends in his day.

Ecce Homo – who claimed to have a unique, personal relationship with the God of Israel whom he called *Abba*.

Ecce Homo – who came into the world as the sinless one, the perfect one, the just one, the holy one, and his fellow human beings killed him. In the end, we destroy and kill the perfect human being, the very one that we have so longed for and loved.

From the very beginning of our lives, we are darkened with this self-destructive force, this primordial sin of being blind to human goodness. Is that not part of what we mean when we speak of original sin: the endless capacity within the human flesh for self-destruction and self-hatred?

In his death, Jesus turns us outward

In the Synoptic Gospels, Jesus is torn from the midst of his family, disciples and friends, and they don't ever get a chance to see him again until he is raised from the dead. But things are different in John's Gospel where Jesus does get a chance to say good-bye, at least to his mother and one of his male disciples, who are gathered at the foot of his cross. Before he dies on the cross, Jesus commits his beloved disciple to his mother's care and his mother to that disciple's care. "Here is your son! Here is your mother!" Jesus turns us outward toward people to whom we are not physically related, identifying these people as our spiritual mothers, fathers, sisters or brothers.

Through his death, Jesus breaks down the barriers between people and creates a new family by the power that flows from his death for humanity. Even the bowing of his head at the moment of death can be interpreted as a nod in their direction. Out of Jesus' death comes life for his followers.

The Science of the cross

On Good Friday, let us remember a Jewish woman, Edith Stein, who loved the cross and embraced its contradiction and mystery throughout her own life. There is a marvellous, life-size, bronze sculpture Edith Stein in the centre of the German city of Cologne, close to the archdiocesan seminary. The sculpture depicts three Edith Steins at the three critical moments of her life. The first moment presents Edith as the young Jewish philosopher and professor, a student of Edmund Husserl. Edith is presented deep in meditation and a Star of David leans against her knee.

The second depiction of the young woman shows Edith split in two. The artist shows her face and head almost divided. She moved from Judaism to agnosticism and even atheism. Hers was a painful search for the truth.

The third representation is Edith as Sister Teresa Benedicta of the Cross, and she holds in her arms the crucified Christ: "Teresa blessed by the Cross" as her name indicates. She moved from Judaism, through atheism, to Christianity.

In her biography, we find a poignant moment from the critical period in her life, in Breslau, when she was moving beyond Judaism. Before her official entrance into the Carmel of Cologne, she had to face her Jewish mother. Her mother said to her daughter: "Edith, You can be religious also in the Jewish faith, don't you think?"

Edith responded: "Sure, when you have never known anything else."

Then her mother desperately replied: "And you, why did you know him? I don't want to say anything against him; certainly he was a very good man; but why did he become God?"

The last weeks at home and the moment of separation were very painful. It was impossible to make her mother understand even a little. Edith wrote: "And yet I crossed the threshold of the Lord's house in profound peace."

Like Edith Stein, we encounter Jesus and his cross, and we have known something else. We have met Someone else: the Man of the cross. We have no alternative but to go to him.

After Edith had entered the Cologne Carmel, she continued to write her great work on the cross: *Kreuzwissenschaft* – the science of the cross. From Cologne she and her sister Rosa were deported to Echt in Holland and then rounded up with other Jews only to be sent to Auschwitz where she and her sister were burned to death by the evil Nazi regime on August 9, 1942.

On Good Friday we gather together as the Christian community to "behold the man" – *Ecce Homo* – and to gaze upon Jesus, who took upon himself all of our sins and failings so that we could experience peace and reconciliation with the One who sent him. If we have not truly encountered and embraced the Man of the cross our efforts are in vain. The validity of all of our efforts is determined by our embracing Jesus and his cross each day, by allowing the Paschal Mystery to transfigure our lives.

The cross of Jesus teaches us that what could have remained hideous and beyond remembrance is transformed into beauty, hope and new life. On Good Friday, may the cross be our true science, our comfort in time of trouble, our refuge in the face of danger, our safeguard on life's journey, until the Lord welcomes us to our heavenly home. Let us continue to mark ourselves daily with the sign of the cross, and be ever mindful of what we are truly doing and professing with this sign:

"In the Name of the Father"
We touch our minds because we know
So little how to create a world of justice,
    peace and hope.

"In the Name of the Son"
We touch the centre of our body
To bring acceptance to the fears and pain
Stemming from our own passage through death to life.

"In the Name of the Spirit"
We embrace our heart
To remember that from the centre of the Cross of Jesus,
God's vulnerable heart
Can bring healing and salvation to our own.

Between the Sadness of the Cross and the Joy of Easter

HOLY SATURDAY

Genesis 1:1–2:2; Genesis 22:1-18;
Exodus 14:15-31, 15:20, 1;
Isaiah 54:5-14; Isaiah 55:1-11;
Baruch 3:9-15, 32–4:2;
Ezekiel 36:16-17a, 18-28;
Romans 6:3-11;
Mark 16:1-8

Holy Saturday is a day of grief and mourning, of patient waiting and hoping. With Mary and the disciples, we grieve the death of the most important member of our Christian community. The faith of Mary and the disciples was strongly challenged on that first Holy Saturday as they awaited the resurrection.

When the full impact of the death of friends and loved ones fully hits us, it has the potential to stun, dull, and crush the human heart. It can immobilize us from action and thought. If we are people without faith and hope, the experience of confusion, grief and loss has the potential to kill us.

Today we reflect on that period of confusion and silence, between the sadness of the cross and the joy of Easter. From the bewilderment of Jesus' disciples to the great faith of Mary, we examine our own lives in light of the great "Sabbath of Time" and draw courage from Mary's example to face the future with deep hope, patience, love and interior peace.

At the end of this long day of waiting, we celebrate the mother of all liturgies, a true feast for the senses. The Church gathers in darkness and lights a new fire and a great candle that will make this night bright for us. We listen to our ancient Scriptures: stories of creation, Abraham and Isaac, Moses and Miriam and the crossing of the sea, poems of promise and rejoicing, and the story of the empty tomb. We see, hear, taste, feel the newness of God in Jesus Christ, risen from the dead. In the "Mother of all liturgies" the past and present meet, death and life embrace and life is triumphant; we reject evil and renew our baptismal promises to God.

On Holy Saturday, many of us are far too busy with Easter preparations to reflect on the significance of this day. We do not take the necessary time to grieve, ponder and enter into the mind and heart of Mary and the disciples on that first Holy Saturday.

I am very grateful to one of my good friends and Basilian confrères, Father Robert Crooker, CSB, who taught me years ago about the mystery and meaning of Holy Saturday. Father Crooker is a retired professor of Canon Law from our Basilian University of St. Thomas in Houston, Texas. Though now in his 80s, this priest is a great example of one who has remained "evergreen" in his faith, spirituality, outlook and love of the Church. He is one of those special persons with whom one can discuss the deepest spiritual and religious matters in simple, profound, wise and always hopeful ways.

Father Crooker sent me the following text back in 1990, which I have read on every Holy Saturday since. His words can help us appreciate more deeply the significance of this great day of watching and waiting.

—◊—

Our Lady's Sabbath
By Father Robert Crooker, CSB

I've read your book now, Luke, and even though
you asked me to correct or amplify
those parts about the days before my son
began to teach and preach in Galilee,
not one word of it would I change. But oh,
the memories it stirred! I never tire
of thinking back on all he did and said,
and weighing it anew within my heart.

Even the things that you had learned from me
came to me with new force. A case in point:
I told you when we found him in the Temple,
we did not understand, Joseph and I,
the word he spoke to us, how he must be
about his Father's business; but now
it seems to me that everything he said
was full of deeper meanings than we grasped,
and only on the Last Day shall we know
all that he meant.

You know Elizabeth
said to me at our visit, "Blest is she
who has believed." The more I think on that,
the plainer it becomes that my belief
is dearer than my motherhood itself.

(You also wrote how Jesus told that woman,
the one who called the womb that bore him happy,
that happier are they who hear God's word
and keep it.) True indeed it was that day
the Mighty One had done great things for me,
but greater yet are those he has done since,
although in ways so hidden and sublime
no human words can tell, even to one
so docile to his Spirit as are you!

And so it was, my thoughts turned as I read
to something that you scarcely touched upon:
the Sabbath when my son lay in the tomb
(of which you say no more than that we kept
the rest according to the Law's command).
That was the day the Spirit poured on me
such gifts of faith and hope as to surpass,
if such may be, the very ones he gave
at Pentecost in tongues of holy fire.

When we had buried Jesus' body, John
insisted that I not go to my home,
but come to spend the Sabbath rest with him.
We said but little to each other there,
and if we sought to speak our voices failed.
And yet, for all the grief that pierced
my heart that night, there was a certitude
and peace beyond expression that I would
have shared with him, so desolate he seemed,
had I but found the words. (My son himself
was much like that the day that Joseph died:
we sat, he held my hand, we wept together,

yet almost nothing did he find to say.
I wondered, later, that he chose to speak
so much to Martha at her brother's tomb,
more than to me at Joseph's death – but then
my Joseph has to wait for the Last Day
to rise, and so the case was not the same.)

Mary and Martha had, of course, told me
the words he spoke as he prepared to call
their brother from his grave, especially
that phrase so deeply graven in their minds:
"I am the resurrection and the life."
It was those very words that came to me
the afternoon I stood and watched him die:
I asked within myself, as once I had
to Gabriel long before, "How can this be?"
The answer was the same: with God all things
are possible. So, as I sat next day,
and weighed these words again within my heart,
even amid the darkness and the pain
they seemed to me most certain, and my soul
did magnify my Savior God the more.

Do not misunderstand: I knew not then
just how it all would happen on the morrow.
But when they went with spices to the tomb,
I sensed within that it would not be right
for me to go along and seek him there.
In all the wild confusion of that day,
I stayed at John's, and while they dashed about
with half-believed reports that he was risen,
he came himself to share with me his joy

and let me glimpse the blessed, glorious light
that radiated from his precious wounds.

Yet even then, I somehow could not touch:
he spoke to me as through some mystic veil
that hung between the mortal and the Risen.
(It was the same, I later heard, with Mary
of Magdala, who met him in the garden
beside the tomb.) When afterwards they told
of how he made poor Thomas feel his hands
and side, I wondered why it was that I,
who bore him in my womb and at my breast
had nurtured him, was not allowed to touch,
and others were.

      I've pondered that, and now
I see a reason for it: the Apostles
are sent to tell the world what they have heard
and seen and touched, but I was called to be
perfect disciple, steadfast in belief
even that day when he who is called "Rock"
was shaken, and had first to be restored
before he could confirm his brothers' faith.
Thus even in his rising he has left
his mother here to walk by faith, not sight,
until he shall return to take her home.
It will not be much longer now, I think,
before I share his glory to the full
and drink with great delight the joys that he
prepares for me.

The Sabbath is not kept,
these days, the way it was when I was young:
my son himself was never strict on that
the way my parents were, and now, of course,
his followers prefer to celebrate
the first day of the week, to mark the day
when he arose triumphant over death.
I know that this is right; yet all the same
I love to keep the holy rest each week,
and recollect with awe and thankfulness
the graces of that blest but dreadful day
when I, alone unshaken, held within
my heart the faith of God's new Israel.

The Silence and Courage of the Resurrection Witnesses

Acts 10:34a, 37-43;
Colossians 3:1-4 **or** *1 Corinthians 5:6b-8;*
John 20:1-18 **or**
Luke 24:13-35

Easter is the promise that death will visit each of us. But more important, it is the assurance that death is not the last word. The Resurrection of Jesus prompts us to recall, from the darkest moments of grief to life's smallest trials, how much God comforts us and gives us the strength to persevere. The Easter mysteries give us a new identity and a new name: we are saved, redeemed, renewed; we are Christian, and we have no more need for fear or despair.

Through the powerful Scripture readings of the Triduum, and especially the Gospels of the Easter Vigil and Easter morning, we catch glimpses of just what resurrection means. How can we give expression to the conquest of death and the harrowing of hell? We must honestly admit to ourselves that there are no words. Therefore we turn to the experiences of the women at the tomb in Mark's Resurrection account and to Mary Magdalene, witness of the Risen Lord, to find images and words to describe what has happened.

The Silence of the Women

Mark's Gospel text for the Easter Vigil (16:1-8) leaves us more than perplexed. We read that after discovering Jesus' tomb to

Easter Sunday   147

be open and empty and hearing the angelic message about the resurrection and a future meeting with him in Galilee, the women "went out and fled from the tomb, for terror and amazement had seized them; and they said nothing to anyone, for they were afraid."

Is it possible that Mark's Gospel can really end with 16:8? Early Christian editors, puzzled by such a shocking ending, supplied two more conventional endings for the Gospel; the longer of these is printed in most bibles as Mark 16:9-20. Nevertheless, the question lingers: What can we say about a resurrection story in which the risen Jesus, himself never appears? How could Mark differ so much from Luke's masterful resurrection chapter (24) or John's highly developed portraits of the first witnesses of the resurrection (20-21)?

Rather than dismiss the strangeness of Mark's ending, let us reflect carefully on what Mark's Gospel offers us. First of all, we never see the Risen Jesus, himself. We are offered instead a rather haunting scene. It is early morning, still dark, and the women arrive at the tomb for a near impossible task. The tomb is already opened and they are greeted by someone from heaven who commissions them: "Go, and tell his disciples and Peter that he is going ahead of you to Galilee; there you will see him, just as he told you" (16:7).

The fear and trembling that accompanies the women prevents them from telling anyone about what they have seen. Of what are they afraid? By remaining silent, are they disobeying the message of the angel to "Go and tell ..."? What are we to make of the silence of the women?

Mark's resurrection account is constructed to unsettle us – to undo the ease that makes us forget that the call to discipleship is the call to the cross. Throughout the entire Gospel, we are invited to view our lives in the shadow of the cross.

The women go to the tomb, drawn unconsciously by the powerful and enticing mystery of God about to be revealed to them. They flee from the tomb (16:8) shocked by the awesome message of Jesus' resurrection. Faced with this rather incredible news of the resurrection of the crucified Jesus, the silent and fearful flight of the women is not only understandable but also highly appropriate.

Is it not also the same for you and for me? When faced with the awesome power of God at work in our lives, raising those dead parts back to life and restoring our dashed hopes and crushed spirits, a response of silence and fear, wonder and awe, is also understandable and at times appropriate – even for us.

The Witness of Mary Magdalene

Mary Magdalene, Mary of Bethany (sister of Martha and Lazarus), and the unnamed penitent woman who anointed Jesus' feet (Luke 7:36-48) are sometimes understood to be the same woman. From this, plus the statement that Jesus had cast seven demons out of Mary Magdalene (Luke 8:2), has risen the tradition that Mary Magdalene had been a prostitute before she met Jesus. But in reality we know nothing about her sins or weaknesses. They could have been inexplicable physical disease, mental illness, or anything that prevented her from wholeness in mind and body.

Mary Magdalene is mentioned in the Gospels as being among the women of Galilee who followed Jesus and his disciples, ministered to him, and who, according to each of the evangelists, was present at his crucifixion and burial, and went to the tomb on Easter Sunday to anoint his body.

Jesus lived in an androcentric society. Women were property, first of their fathers, then of their husbands; they did not have the right to testify; they could not study the Torah. In this restricting atmosphere, Jesus acted without animosity, accepting women, honoring them, respecting them, and treasuring their friendship. He journeyed with them, touched and cured them, loved them and allowed them to love him.

In our Easter Sunday Gospel (John 20:1-18), we peer once again into the early morning scene of sadness as Mary Magdalene weeps uncontrollably at the grave of her friend, Jesus. We hear anew their conversation: "Woman, why are you weeping? Whom are you seeking?" "… Sir, if you have carried him away, tell me where you have laid him, and I will take him away." Jesus said to her, "Mary!" She turned and said to him in Hebrew, *Rabbouni!* which means, Teacher. … "Do not hold on to me, because I have not yet ascended to the Father. But go to my brothers and say to them, 'I am ascending to my Father and your Father, to my God and your God.'" Mary Magdalene came, announcing to the disciples, "I have seen the Lord," and that he had said these things to her (John 20:15-18).

Because of her incredible message and mission, Mary Magdalene was fittingly called *Apostola Apostolorum* (Apostle to the Apostles) in the early Church because she was the first to see the Risen Lord, and to announce his Resurrection to the other apostles.

For Jesus, women were equally as able as men to penetrate the great religious truths, live them and announce them to others. There is no secret code about this story, which is still astonishingly good news more than 2,000 years later. Alleluia, Alleluia, Alleluia!

Allowing the Presence of the Risen Jesus
to Make a Difference

SECOND SUNDAY OF EASTER OR DIVINE MERCY SUNDAY

Acts 4:32-35;
1 John 5:1-6;
John 20:19-31

There is a proverb that says: "When the heart is not applied, hands can't do anything." It seems as if this were written for Thomas the Apostle in today's very familiar Gospel story that provides us with an archetypal experience of doubt, struggle and faith.

John's second appearance of the Risen Lord to the disciples is both intense and focused. It is evening, the first day of the week, and the doors were bolted shut. Anxious disciples are sealed inside. A suspicious, hostile world is forced tightly outside. Jesus is missing. Suddenly, the Risen One defies locked doors, blocked hearts, and distorted vision and simply appears. Jesus reaches out ever so gently to the broken and wounded Apostle. Thomas hesitatingly put his finger into the wounds of Jesus and love flowed out. How can you hear this story without thinking of Caravaggio's magnificent painting of this scene?

Who is this Thomas? He, along with many of the other male disciples, stood before the cross, not comprehending. Thomas' dreams were hanging on that cross and his hopes had been shattered. Over the years I have come to see Thomas as truly one of the greatest and most honest lovers of Jesus, not the eternal sceptic, nor the bullish, stubborn personality that the Christian tradition has often painted. I have never enjoyed being called "doubting Thomas" when I was growing up, simply because I liked to ask questions! I used to secretly hope that I was named after Aquinas, More, Becket or Villanova. But my mother insisted that it was the Apostle they chose for me!

Thomas' struggle and ours

What do we do when something to which we have totally committed ourselves is destroyed before our very eyes? What do we do when powerful and faceless institutions suddenly crush someone to whom we have given total loyalty. And what do we do when our immediate reaction in the actual moment of crisis is to run and hide, for fear of the madding crowds? Such were the questions of most of the disciples, including Thomas, who had supported and followed Jesus of Nazareth for the better part of three years.

The doubting Thomas within each of us must be touched. We are asked to respond to the wounds first within ourselves then in others. Even in our weakness, we are urged to breathe forth the Spirit so that the wounds may be healed and our fears overcome. With Thomas we will believe, when our trembling hand finally and hesitantly reaches out to the Lord in the community of faith. The words addressed to Thomas were given to us: "Blessed are those who have not seen and yet have come to believe!"

Long ago St. Gregory the Great said of Thomas the Apostle: "If, by touching the wounds on the body of his master, Thomas is able to help us overcome the wounds of disbelief, then the doubting of Thomas will have been more use to us than the faith of all the other apostles."

Centuries after Thomas, we remain forever grateful for the honesty and humanity of his struggle. Though we know so little about Thomas, his family background and his destiny, we are given an important hint into his identity in the etymology of his name in Greek: Thomas (Didymous in Greek) means "twin". Who was Thomas' other half, his twin? Maybe we can see his twin by looking into the mirror. Thomas' other half is anyone who has struggled with the pain of unbelief, doubt and despair, and has allowed the presence of the Risen Jesus to make a difference.

Divine Mercy is not an option!

Over the past few years, I have listened to not a few liturgists and pastoral ministers complaining about the fact that this Sunday was given a new name by the Pope, Blessed John Paul II in the Jubilee Year 2000. Officially called the Second Sunday of Easter after the liturgical reform of Vatican II, now, by Decree of the Congregation for Divine Worship and the Sacraments, the name has been changed to: "Second Sunday of Easter, or Divine Mercy Sunday."

The Pope made the surprise announcement of this change in his homily at the canonization of St. Maria Faustina Kowalska on April 30, 2000. On that day he declared: "It is important then that we accept the whole message that comes to us from the Word of God on this Second Sunday of Easter, which from now on throughout the Church, will be called 'Divine Mercy Sunday.'"

What do the visions of a Polish nun have to do with Thomas the Apostle's encounter with the Risen Lord? Do we have to 'force' a link between Divine Mercy and the Gospel story of Thomas and the Risen Jesus? The answer to the first question is: "Everything!" and to the second: "No!"

Clearly, the celebration of Divine Mercy Sunday does not compete with, nor endanger the integrity of the Easter Season, nor does it take away from Thomas' awesome encounter with the Risen Lord. Divine Mercy Sunday is the Octave Day of Easter, celebrating the merciful love of God shining through the whole Easter Triduum and the whole Easter mystery.

The connection is more than evident from the scripture readings for this first Sunday after Easter. At St. Faustina's canonization, Blessed Pope John Paul II said in his moving homily: "Jesus shows his hands and his side (to the Apostles). He points, that is, to the wounds of the Passion, especially the wound in his heart, the source from which flows the great wave of mercy poured out on humanity."

The Meaning of the Day

Divine Mercy Sunday is not a new feast established to celebrate St. Faustina's revelations. In fact it is not about St. Faustina at all! Rather it recovers an ancient liturgical tradition, reflected in a teaching attributed to St. Augustine about the Easter Octave, which he called "the days of mercy and pardon," and the Octave Day itself "the compendium of the days of mercy."

The Vatican did not give the title of "Divine Mercy Sunday" to the Second Sunday of Easter merely as an "option," for those dioceses who happen to like that sort of thing! This means that preaching on God's mercy is not just an option for this Sunday. To fail to preach on God's mercy this day would mean largely to ignore the prayers, readings and psalms appointed for that day, as well as the title "Divine Mercy Sunday" now given to that day in the Roman Missal.

Several years ago, when I, too, was finding difficulty in seeing the internal links between the Second Sunday of Easter, my patron saint, Thomas, and Sr. Faustina's revelation for this day, I came across this wonderful quote by St. Bernard (Canticle 61, 4-5: PL 183, 1072): "What I cannot obtain by myself, I appropriate (usurp!) with trust from the pierced side of the Lord, because he is full of mercy.

"My merit, therefore, is God's mercy. I am certainly not poor in merits, as long as he is rich in mercy. If the mercies of the Lord are many (Psalm 119:156), I too will abound with merits. And what about my justice? O Lord, I will remember only your justice. In fact, it is also mine, because you are for me justice on the part of God."

Then the light went on for me. From that moment onward, I no longer regret being named after this Thomas and not the others! Thomas' encounter with the Risen Lord gave me a whole new perspective on the meaning of mercy.

And that has made all of the difference.

Luke's Resurrection Symphony
in 4 Movements

THIRD SUNDAY OF EASTER

Acts 3:13-15, 17-19;
1 John 2:1-5;
Luke 24:35-48

I often consider Chapter 24 of Luke's Gospel to be a Resurrection Symphony in four brilliant movements.

The first movement is the story of the women at the tomb, which ends with Peter's visit to the tomb to check it (v 1-12). The second movement tells the great story of the two disciples on the road to Emmaus, culminating in their learning that the Lord had also appeared to Peter (v 13-35). The third movement is the appearance of the Lord to his disciples at a meal, ending with their commissioning by Jesus (v 36-49). And the fourth movement – Jesus' ascension into heaven (v 50-52).

The most well-known of these stories is the Emmaus episode that begins in verse 13. It serves as a transition between the events of the Passion and discovery of the tomb and the appearance tradition. It is different from the other resurrection appearances because the Lord disappears at the moment of recognition. The Emmaus narrative (24:13-35) serves as a bridge between the empty tomb (24:1-12) and Jesus' self-revelation to his apostles (24:36ff.) immediately following the Emmaus disciples' meal, their recognition of Jesus, and hasty return to Jerusalem.

Cleopas and his companion are going away from the locality where the decisive events have happened, toward a little village of no significance. They did not believe the message of the Resurrection, due to the scandal of the cross. Puzzled and discouraged, they are unable to see any liberation in the death, the empty tomb, or the message about the appearances of Jesus to the others. In their eyes, either the mission of Jesus had entirely failed, or else they, themselves, had been badly deceived in their expectations about Jesus.

As the two downtrodden disciples journeyed with Jesus on that Emmaus road, their hearts began to gradually catch fire within them as they came to understand with their minds the truth about the suffering Messiah. At the meal in Emmaus, they experienced the power of the Resurrection in their hearts. The solution to the problem of these two disciples was not a perfectly logical answer.

Emmaus at the Synod

The most frequently quoted Gospel story at the October 2008 synod on the Word of God was undoubtedly Luke's account of the disciples on the road to Emmaus (Luke 24:13-35). Cited by cardinals, bishops, experts and special guests in many of the presentations coming from every corner of the earth, the Emmaus story proved once again to be a great model or paradigm for catechesis, teaching, Bible study and above all for Christian living.

The journey motif of the Emmaus story (and one can say of the entire synod on the Word of God) is not only a matter of the distance between Jerusalem and Emmaus, but also of the painful and gradual journey of words that must descend from the head to the heart; of a coming to faith, and a return to a proper relationship with the stranger who is none other than Jesus the Lord.

Eating and drinking with Jesus

The Gospel for the Third Sunday of Easter (Year B) is the continuation of the Emmaus story – how God always leads people into an experience of community and table fellowship (Luke 24:36-48). There are several aspects of the story – the appearance of Jesus among the startled and frightened disciples (v 36-43) and the words about the fulfillment of Scripture and commissioning of the disciples (v 44-48). Many elements that were present in the Emmaus story are made more explicit. The Lukan stories also represent the Risen Lord as the One who receives hospitality and food from the disciples. Only after the disciples have extended an invitation to the Stranger to remain with them is it possible for full recognition to take place. They were unable to fully recognize him on the road, but they did recognize him in the breaking of the bread.

Table fellowship reveals the depth of humanity. The touching, human scene of Jesus taking bread and fish and eating it with his disciples drives home the fact that ghosts don't eat – humans do – and it reassures the disciples that the Risen Lord is truly in their midst. No theological or dogmatic assertion will prove this to them. Rather, the striking humanity of Jesus, at table, will finally convince them that he is alive.

In spite of the testimony from the women and the two travellers, the disciples still could not believe their eyes when

Jesus appeared before them. Only Jesus could validate the experience and supply its proper understanding. Jesus would first prove their experience was no hoax. Like the appearance to Thomas in John's Gospel, Jesus showed his wounds and challenged his followers to "touch" him. The experience of the Risen Lord was tactile. Jesus has substance, unlike a ghost. Unlike John 20, Jesus showed his followers his hands and feet (not his hands and side). Luke inferred that Jesus had been nailed in his feet.

The real heart of the story, however, is not the meal but the quality of the appearance or vision. Jesus appeared as a living, solid form. The Holy and Divine could be found in the tangible. Holiness was not only a matter of ecstasy, touching the transcendent, while leaving the world behind. God reached his people through his creation, not in spite of it. This insight became the foundation of the Church's self-awareness as the Body of Christ. It also grounded worship in the Church as sacramental. The believer encounters the Risen Christ through the bodily senses. His followers saw, touched, and heard the Risen One. We see, hear, and touch Christ today through the sacraments, through shared witness and service to others.

The Eucharist is a summary of Jesus' life, a call to lay down one's life for others. The breaking of bread is also a powerful sign of unity. When we break bread, it is a means of sharing in the body of Christ. Paul says, "Because there is one bread, we who are many are one body, for we all partake of the one bread" (I Corinthians 10:16-17).

It is not only that the person sharing the cup and the broken bread establishes a union with Christ: A further union is established through the "partaking" of the same loaf – the union between all the members of the celebrating community. The unity expressed here is not just a matter of human conviviality; it is a gift given in the breaking of bread, a sharing in the body of Christ. The Eucharist makes the members of the body celebrate their oneness, a oneness experienced on three levels: one in Christ, one with each other, and one in service to the world.

The sacramental encounter of young people with Christ

Allow me to share a final thought with you about eating and drinking with Jesus.

During the synod on the Word of God, one of the memorable interventions was made by Salesian Father Pascual Chávez Villanueva, president of the Union of Superiors-General and Rector of the Salesian Society of St. John Bosco. Father Pascual, whose Salesian Congregation has a special charism for working with young people, offered the Emmaus story as model of bringing the Word of God closer to the world of youth. He drew our attention to the fact that young people today share very few things with the two disciples on the road but perhaps nothing as much as the frustration of their dreams, the fatigue in their faith and the disenchantment in discipleship.

"Young people need a Church that meets them there where they are. Arriving to Emmaus, the disciples still did not recognize the person of Jesus. What Jesus was unable to do in accompanying them, conversing with them, interpreting the Word of God, he accomplished with the Eucharistic gesture.

An education in faith which forgets or postpones the sacramental encounter of young people with Christ is not a secure, efficient way to find him."

Those final words have remained with me. How do we teach young people the importance of the sacraments in their own lives? How do we provide opportunities for young people to encounter Christ? Do we not open the door to this importance and foster such encounters by beginning with simple table fellowship with young people?

It is often the very ordinary moments of table fellowship that bring about the realization that we are human, loving, loveable and genuinely interested in others, their tribulations, their hopes and their futures. Table fellowship does indeed reveal the depth of humanity, and the depth of compassion. It is a springboard to adult faith, and to a living encounter with the Risen Lord who wishes to share his own life with us each day. Stay with us, Lord!

Jesus, the Beautiful and Noble Shepherd

FOURTH SUNDAY OF EASTER

Acts 4:7-12;
1 John 3:1-2;
John 10:11-18

In the Bible and in the ancient Near East, "shepherd" was a political title that stressed the obligation of kings to provide for their subjects. The title connoted total concern for and dedication to others. Tending flocks and herds is an important part of the Palestinian economy in biblical times. In the Old Testament, God is called the Shepherd of Israel who goes before the flock (Psalm 68:7), guides it (Psalm 23:3), leads it to food and water (Psalm 23:2), protects it (Psalm 23:4), and carries its young (Isaiah 40:11). Embedded in the living piety of believers, the metaphor brings out the fact that God shelters the entire people.

In Psalm 23, the author speaks of the Lord as his shepherd. The image of shepherd as host is also found in this beloved psalm. Shepherd and host are both images set against the background of the desert, where the protector of the sheep is also the protector of the desert traveller, offering hospitality and safety from enemies. The rod is a defensive weapon against wild animals, while the staff is a supportive instrument; they symbolize concern and loyalty.

The New Testament does not judge shepherds adversely. They know their sheep (John 10:3), seek lost sheep (Luke 15:4ff.), and hazard their lives for the flock (John 10:11-12).

The shepherd is a figure for God himself (Luke 15:4ff.). The New Testament never calls God a shepherd, and only in the parable of the lost sheep (Luke 15:4ff.; Matthew 18:12ff.) does the comparison occur. Here God, like the rejoicing shepherd of the parable, takes joy in the forgiveness and restoration of the sinner. The choice of the image reflects vividly the contrast between Jesus' love for sinners and the Pharisees' contempt for them. It can be said that the Emmaus story in Luke's Gospel (24:13-35) is a continuation of Jesus' journey, his pursuit of wayward disciples which was already prefigured by the parable of the shepherd who went in search of lost sheep until he found them and returned them to the fold (15:3-7).

Confidence

On the Fourth Sunday of Easter, traditionally called Good Shepherd Sunday, we encounter the Good Shepherd who is really the beautiful or noble shepherd (in the Greek text) who knows his flock intimately. Jesus knew shepherds and had much sympathy for their lot and he relied on one of his favourite metaphors to assure us that we can place our confidence in him. For those who heard Jesus claim this title for himself, it meant more than tenderness and compassion; there was the dramatic and startling degree of love so great that the shepherd is willing to lay down his life for his flock.

Unlike the hired hand, who works for pay, the good shepherd's life is devoted to the sheep out of pure love. The sheep are far more than a responsibility to the good shepherd – who is also their owner. They are the object of the shepherd's love and concern. Thus, the shepherd's devotion to them is completely unselfish; the good shepherd is willing to die for the sheep rather than abandon them. To the hired hand, the sheep are merely a commodity, to be watched over only so they can provide wool and mutton.

The beauty of Jesus, our Good Shepherd, lies in the love with which he offers his life even unto death for each and every one of his sheep. In so doing, he establishes with each one a direct and personal relationship of intense love. Jesus' beauty and nobility are revealed in his letting himself be loved by us. In Jesus we discover the Father and his Son who are shepherds who care for us, know us and even love us in our stubbornness, deafness and diffidence.

Sometimes, it seems that followers are expected to put the needs of the leader first. The people are the means to an end: the leader's pleasure. Does it not often seem that shepherds are first, sheep last? The emphasis in today's readings is on the sheep and their welfare. The shepherd is the means to ensure the end: the well-being of the flock. Sheep are first, shepherds last. John's Gospel portrays Jesus as the life-giving shepherd.

Vocations

The Fourth Sunday of Easter is also the World Day of Prayer for Vocations. The readings are very fitting for as we beg the Lord of the harvest and of the Church to send more labourers into his vast vineyards. As a model of religious leadership, Jesus shows us that love can be the only motivation for ministry, especially for pastoral ministry. He also shows us that there must be no exclusiveness on the part of the religious leader.

If there are sheep outside the fold (even sheep excluded by the fold itself), the good shepherd must go fetch them. And they must be brought in, so that there will be one flock under one shepherd. The motivation for inclusion is love, not social justice, not ethical fairness, not mere tolerance, and certainly not political correctness or impressive statistics. Only love can draw the circle that includes everyone.

Shepherds have power over sheep. As we contemplate Jesus, the Good Shepherd, we call to mind everyone over whom we exercise authority – children, elderly parents, our coworkers and colleagues, people who ask us for help throughout the week, people who depend on us for material and spiritual needs. Whatever title we bear, the rod and staff we carry must be symbols not of oppression but of dedication. Today's readings invite us to ask for forgiveness for the times we have not responded to those for whom we care, and ask for the grace to be good shepherds. We fix our eyes anew on the Good Shepherd who knows that other sheep not of this fold are not lost sheep, but his sheep.

One final thought on shepherding. Anthropologists tell us that between the hunting and the farming stages of cultural development shepherds stood as people who existed in both worlds and tied them together. For that reason, shepherds appear in ancient myths and sagas as a symbol for the divine unity of opposites. What the ancient pagans hinted at, Christian faith has brought into a crisp reality with Jesus Christ as the great reconciler. He is the Good Shepherd, who has come into the centre of every great conflict in order to establish beauty, unity and peace.

May it be ever so for each person who strives to be a good shepherd today, in the Church and in the world. As we enter those places of conflict and tribulation in our own times, may the Lord use us as his instruments to establish beauty, nobility, unity and peace.

Making Our Home in Jesus

FIFTH SUNDAY OF EASTER

Acts 9:26-31;
1 John 3:18-24;
John 15:1-8

In John's Gospel (15:1-8) for the 5th Sunday of Easter, we have the image of the vine and its branches to express the relationship between Christ and his disciples. We should not be surprised that at one level it seems utterly simple, but that at other levels it fills us with a sense of mystery, awe, and beauty, always leaving us wanting more.

The branches of a vine have an intimate relationship with the vine, depending on it at all times and forming one living organism with it. The vine, which can be a bit foreign in northern climates, is natural for anyone in the Middle East, where many families possess a vine, a fig tree, or olive trees in their gardens.

Jesus tells his followers that he is the true vine, the real vine, and that they are the branches, whose task is to bear fruit by sharing his life: "I am the true vine, and my Father is the vinegrower. Abide in me as I abide in you. Apart from me you can do nothing. If you abide in me, and my words abide in you, ask for whatever you wish, and it will be done for you" (John 15:1, 4-5, 7).

While the images of Christ as king and lord, teacher, shepherd and judge, have their own importance in forming our perspective on how Christ relates to us, these images need to be balanced by such images as the vine, which integrate the disciple into the life of Christ and Christ into the life of the disciple in an intimate unity and closeness that the other images might not always convey.

Today's passage is one of the classic descriptions of authentic Christian spirituality. The image of the vine, while inviting us to a depth of spirituality, sets that personal quest within the larger context of the family of God, stretching through time from Abraham to the present day and beyond, and through space from the Middle East in the first century to the four corners of the earth today.

If Jesus is the vine, we are summoned to abide, to live, to make our home in him. The Gospel text of the vine challenges us: How do we maintain intimacy with the living God as we strive to be obedient to our vocation of bearing fruit for the world? What does it mean, to abide or dwell in the vine, to be intimately attached to Jesus?

Abiding in Jesus includes being part of the life of the Church, committed to the daily and weekly fellowship of his people, in mutual support, prayer, common worship, sacramental life, study and not least, work for the Gospel in the world. In every Eucharistic celebration we are drawn into that intimate fellowship both with Jesus himself and with each other at his table.

Authentic Christian spirituality is the personal knowledge of Jesus Christ given to us, as the vine gives its sap to the branches, so that we can be extensions of his work, his love, his fruit-bearing, his glorifying of the Father. That is the heart of the Eucharistic mystery.

And yet as soon as Jesus introduced the theme of the vine and the branches in the Gospel passage, he speaks of his Father, the vinedresser, doing two things that require a knife. Every branch that doesn't bear fruit, the Father removes, cuts away; and every branch that does bear fruit the Father prunes, so that it may bear more fruit.

The spirituality to which this Gospel passage invites us is not one of unbridled personal development, fulfilling all the potential we might discover within ourselves. As we follow Jesus and come to know him personally, we find him calling us to submit to the pruning-knife, to cut out some things from our lives that are good in themselves and that would even have had the potential to develop into fruit-bearing branches, in order that other things may flourish. Pruning is always a painful process. It is a form of loss or death. The vinedresser is never more intimately involved than when wielding the pruning-knife!

The call to abide in the vine is a call to a personal and intimate knowledge of Jesus himself, not an idea, but a living person. True disciples of Jesus are dependent on the inner presence and activity of Christ for the renewal and regeneration of their own life into one of faith and love. True disciples can only be effective in the regeneration of the lives of others when they are "plugged into Jesus," grafted onto his life, allowing his very presence to pulsate through their minds and hearts.

The images of vine and vineyard are brought together beautifully in that well-known passage from *Lumen Gentium*, No. 6, the Second Vatican Council's Dogmatic Constitution on the Church:

"The Church is a piece of land to be cultivated, the tillage of God. On that land the ancient olive tree grows whose holy roots were the Prophets and in which the reconciliation of Jews and Gentiles has been brought about and will be brought about. That land, like a choice vineyard, has been planted by the heavenly Husbandman. The true vine is Christ who gives life and the power to bear abundant fruit to the branches, that is, to us, who through the Church remain in Christ without whom we can do nothing."

To illustrate this dependency, this grafting on the Lord, let me share with you some profound words of a great woman of the Church, St. Teresa Benedicta of the Cross (Edith Stein) (1891-1942), Carmelite, martyr, co-patroness of Europe, and one who knew what it meant to be intimately connected to the Lord. They are taken from Chapter 6 of her *Essays on Woman* (ICS Publications).

"The notion of the Church as community of the faithful is the most accessible to human reason. Whoever believes in Christ and his gospel, hopes for the fulfillment of his promises, clings to him in love, and keeps his commandments must unite with all who are like-minded in the deepest communion of mind and heart. Those who adhered to the Lord during his stay on earth were the early seeds of the great Christian community; they spread that community and that faith which held them together, until they have been inherited by us today through the process of time.

"But, if even a natural human community is more than a loose union of single individuals, if even here we can verify a movement developing into a kind of organic unit, it must be still more true of the supernatural community of the Church. The union of the soul with Christ differs from the union among people in the world: It is a rooting and growing in him (so we are told by the parable of the vine and the branches) which begins in baptism, and which is constantly strengthened and formed through the sacraments in diverse ways. However, this real union with Christ implies the growth of a genuine community among all Christians. Thus the Church forms the Mystical Body of Christ. The Body is a living Body, and the spirit which gives the Body life is Christ's spirit, streaming from the head to all parts (Ephesians 5:23,30). The spirit which Christ radiates is the Holy Spirit; the Church is thus the temple of the Holy Spirit (Ephesians 2:21-22)."

This week, let us pray that our belonging to Christ be profound and real, going beyond all of the turbulence that exists on life's surface. May Christ's very life flow through us, building up the Body of Christ that is the Church.

Goodness and Friendship
Through the Ages

Acts 10:25-26, 34-35, 44-48;
1 John 4:7-10;
John 15:9-17

On this Sixth Sunday of Easter, I wish to offer some reflections on the first reading from the Acts of the Apostles (10:25-26, 34-35, 44-48), and then some thoughts on friendship flowing from John's Gospel (15:9-17) and Benedict XVI's teaching.

Christianity demands that the believer not only grasp intellectually the main tenets of the faith, but also act on them in daily life. The extraordinary story of Cornelius' conversion in today's first reading certainly illustrates this message. It is the longest individual narrative in the Acts of the Apostles. The theme of this narrative is divine compulsion: Peter is the least prepared to accept Cornelius into the Christian community, and he even refuses to admit him two times.

Peter had to be converted before he could convert Cornelius. Peter came to the realization that God's gifts were given to all those who listened to the Word of God. His question "Can anyone withhold the water for baptizing these people who have received the Holy Spirit just as we have?" (10:47) echoes the Ethiopian's question and Philip's response in the earlier story: "What is to prevent me from being baptized?" (8:36).

Peter's actions with Cornelius had far-reaching implications. Struck at once with the exceptional sincerity, hospitality and deep goodness of Cornelius and his household, Peter spontaneously exclaimed: "God has shown me that I should not call anyone profane or unclean. God shows no partiality."

That statement broke centuries of customs, and even of theology, that Israel alone was God's chosen people, separated from all other nations as God's very own (cf. Deuteronomy 7:6-8; Exodus 19:5-6). Peter had no choice but to baptize the household of Cornelius and he was criticized for his ecumenical approach, but responded to his critics: "Who was I that I could hinder God?" (11:17). When his critics heard these words, they were silenced and began to glorify God (11:18).

Paul, too, found the same spontaneous manifestation of the faith among the gentiles, and so made the exciting declaration: "We now turn to the Gentiles!" The controversy over the law was to linger for a long time, so that Paul dedicated to this topic his most comprehensive theological work: the Letter to the Romans.

I call you friends

In today's Gospel text from St. John (15:15), we hear the powerful words: "I do not call you servants any longer ... but I have called you friends." We are not useless servants but friends! The Lord calls us friends; he makes us his friends; he gives us his friendship.

Jesus defines friendship in two ways. There are no secrets between friends: Christ tells us everything he hears from the Father; he gives us his full confidence and, with confidence, also knowledge. He reveals his face to us, his heart. He shows his tenderness for us, his passionate love that goes to the folly of the cross.

If we were to name one of the most frequent and important themes of Benedict XVI's teaching and preaching over the past years, it would certainly be his invitation to be a friend of Jesus. He sounded this theme clearly during the Mass for the election of the Roman Pontiff in St. Peter's Basilica, before the conclave. "Adult and mature is a faith profoundly rooted in friendship with Christ. This friendship opens us to all that is good and gives us the measure to discern between what is true and what is false, between deceit and truth," he said.

I remember how moved I was as I listened to the Holy Father's homily at the beginning of the Petrine Ministry of the Bishop of Rome on April 24, 2005. Three times during that memorable homily, Benedict XVI spoke of the importance of "friendship" with Jesus: "The Church as a whole and all her pastors, like Christ, must set out to lead people out of the desert, towards the place of life, toward friendship with the Son of God, toward the One who gives us life, and life in abundance. (…)

"There is nothing more beautiful than to know him and to speak to others of our friendship with him. (…)

"Only in this friendship are the doors of life opened wide. Only in this friendship is the great potential of human existence truly revealed. Only in this friendship do we experience beauty and liberation."

Eight months later, in his Angelus address of January 15, 2006, Benedict XVI said: "Friendship with the Teacher guarantees profound peace and serenity to the soul, even in the dark moments and in the most arduous trials. When faith meets with dark nights, in which the presence of God is no longer 'felt' or 'seen,' friendship with Jesus guarantees that in reality nothing can ever separate us from his love" (cf. Romans 8: 39).

Again on August 26, 2007, the theme of friendship was front and centre: "True friendship with Jesus is expressed in the way of life: It is expressed with goodness of heart, with humility, meekness and mercy, love for justice and truth, a sincere and honest commitment to peace and reconciliation."

We might say that this is the "identity card" that qualifies us as his real "friends"; this is the "passport" that will give us access to eternal life. How do we understand the tremendous gift of friendship in our lives?

Matter of the heart

For many years, I have looked to the life and writings of Cardinal John Henry Newman (1801-1890) as a brilliant model of friendship. Newman truly speaks heart-to-heart – *cor ad cor loquitur* – a phrase that he chose as his personal motto. There was nothing superficial about Newman's way of relating to so many different people. He looked at them and loved them for who they were.

With the beatification of the beloved English Cardinal on September 19, 2010, it is good for us to consider some of Newman's understanding of friendship. Cardinal Newman had a great appreciation for the nobility of human virtues as evidenced in the literature and history of ancient Rome and Greece. At the same time the saints that he most admired – St. Paul, the ancient Church Fathers, his spiritual father St. Philip Neri, and St. Francis De Sales – could all be described as humanly attractive.

Newman had an extraordinary capacity and gift for friendship, which often translated into leadership. No one could describe Cardinal Newman as extroverted or light-hearted. We need only to glance at the many volumes of his letters and diaries, or look at the index of names in his auto-biographical works, to see that he shared deep friendships with hundreds of people throughout his life. This personal influence has been exerted very powerfully upon millions of people who have read his works and discovered what friend-ship really means.

Authenticity

I could not write about friendship without passing along a warning to countless women and men who search for it every day. The great popularity of online social networking sites such as MySpace and Facebook merits careful attention, reflection and scrutiny. It has been said that if Facebook were a country, it would be the eighth most populated nation worldwide!

We must carefully ask several questions: What is it doing for us?

These tools help to bring people together and improve social networks. For example, homebound, infirm, chronic-ally ill and elderly people can connect with a community of others in the same situation and new bonds of solidarity are born.

But there are also related questions: What is it doing to us? What is it doing to our sense of social boundaries? To our sense of individuality? To our friendships?

Friendship in these virtual spaces is quite different from real time friendship. Friendship is a relationship that involves the sharing of mutual interests, reciprocity, trust, and the revelation of intimate details over time and within specific contexts. True friendship depends on mutual revelations, and can only flourish within the boundaries of privacy and modesty.

On social networking sites, however, there is a concept of public friendship which is not the friendship spoken of by Jesus in the Gospel, nor Benedict XVI in his wonderful writings, nor Cardinal Newman in his letters. The distance and abstraction of our online friendships and online relationships can lead to a kind of systemic desensitization as a culture if we are not wise, prudent and attentive to these new realities.

We expose everything, but are we feeling anything?

Such friendships, or rather acquaintances, are quite different from the *cor ad cor loquitur* so ardently desired and experienced by Jesus with his disciples, or by an impetuous Peter, a Roman official named Cornelius, a British Cardinal named John Henry and a German Pope named Benedict XVI who have modeled their lives on the Good Shepherd and faithful friend to every human being.

Fulfilling the Gospel Dream

ASCENSION OF THE LORD

Acts 1:1-11;
Ephesians 1:17-23 **or** *Ephesians 4:1-13* **or** *4:1-7, 11-13;*
Mark 16:15-20

The angels' words to the "men of Galilee" in the first reading from the Acts of the Apostles for the Feast of the Ascension of the Lord (1:1-11) are painfully blunt and leave little room for misinterpretation: "Why do you stand here looking up at the skies? This Jesus who has been taken from you will return, just as you saw him go up to the heavens."

Jesus' disciples are given a last bit of instruction. "Don't keep trying to stare into the future. Don't be overly concerned about which hour he will come back." We must not stand idly staring up into the heavens and moaning about the past, about which we can do nothing, except to bury it deeply in God's hands and heart! The Lord will be glorified, and it follows that his disciples will also share in his glory.

As Jesus disappeared, he didn't simply dissolve into thin air. On the day of his Ascension, one might conclude that Jesus removed himself into a new form of divine exclusion. The case is exactly the opposite. In God, Jesus is "here" in a new and very specific way. Only in his physical separation from the historical scene can his spiritual union with all the world for all time be complete. Jesus left the world one day in order to be available to all people throughout all time. He had to dissolve bonds he had made with his friends, in order to be available for everybody. In Jesus, the future has already begun!

The Ascension according to Mark's account

There are similarities in the reports of Jesus' Ascension found in the Synoptic Gospels – Mark, Matthew, and Luke. In each case, Jesus assigns his disciples the task of proclaiming the gospel message to the entire world.

In the Gospels of Mark and Matthew, the disciples are sent by Jesus to baptize and to preach. In Luke's Gospel, however, the commission to baptize is not found. Instead, Jesus directs the disciples to return to Jerusalem to await the fulfillment of his promise to send them the Holy Spirit. Only the Gospels of Mark and Luke actually report Jesus' ascension into heaven. Matthew's Gospel concludes with Jesus' promise to remain with his disciples forever.

The Ascension Gospel text for this year (Mark 16:15-20) is taken from the conclusion of the Gospel of Mark. Mark's concluding chapter contains several irregularities obvious to many readers. On Easter Sunday morning in this Year B, we heard proclaimed the story of the discovery of the empty tomb by the women, and the fright and fear that accompanied these first Resurrection witnesses. Verse 8 comes to an abrupt conclusion as they flee in fright and tell no one what had transpired. This may very well be the original ending of Mark's Gospel, but it is also possible that the more complete ending has been lost.

Some manuscripts of Mark's Gospel include what scholars have termed the "Shorter Ending." This ending indicates that the women told their story to Peter's companions. A significant number of scholars believe that this ending is not original to Mark. They think that this ending was added by copyists who sought to resolve the original abrupt ending at Verse 8.

Other early manuscripts include a "Longer Ending" that scholars also believe was written by someone other than the Evangelist. Nonetheless, quotations from this "Longer Ending" are found in the writings of the early Church Fathers, and it was accepted at the Council of Trent as part of the canonical Gospel of Mark. Our Gospel for this year's celebration of the Feast of the Ascension is taken from this "Longer Ending."

Even if this ending to Mark's Gospel was written by someone other than the Evangelist, in the commission that Jesus gives to his disciples, there are elements that are quite typical of Mark's Gospel. The signs that will accompany belief in Jesus are as distinct as the action performed by Jesus during his ministry. Those who believe in Jesus will be empowered to do what Jesus himself has done.

During his ministry, Jesus sent his disciples to preach, to heal, and to drive out unclean spirits. Now they are sent again to do these things and more. From his place with God in heaven, Jesus helped his disciples, and he continues to help us as we try to live as his followers.

Only the Gospel of Mark notes that Jesus ascended to sit at the right hand of God. In noting this, Mark teaches that

Jesus' ascension affirms the glory Jesus received from God after his death and resurrection.

The desire for heavenly realities …

Just as the Risen Lord entrusted himself into the hands of such pathetic, broken people who were with him, he does the same to us. Our own brokenness and sinfulness are so overpowering at times that we forget that this incredible commissioning is possible, even for poor, weak, folks like us! How often do we marvel at the fact that Christ could truly inhabit us and act through our bodies, minds and hearts, and yes, even through the Church!

We know that we move toward heaven to the extent that we approach Jesus. We are assured that he hasn't ever stopped being present with us throughout all time. The mysterious feast of the Ascension reminds us that Christ accepts our lack of confidence in ourselves. He accepts the shadowy and dark areas of our humanity. He accepts our capacity for deceit, betrayal, greed and power. And having accepted us, he calls us, gives us the eternal commission to be his people, and sends us to serve him and love him, in spite of ourselves and because of ourselves. Blessed John Henry Cardinal Newman said it well long ago:

> "He calls us again and again, in order to justify us
>   again and again -
> and again and again, and more and more,
> to sanctify and glorify us.
> It were well if we understood this;
> but we are slow to master the great truth,

that Christ is, as it were,
walking among us, and by his hand, or eye, or voice,
bidding us follow him."

Let's get going and carry a piece of heaven into the world. This is the meaning of the Resurrection and the Ascension of our Lord, not one of divine abandonment of the human cause, but divine empowerment of the Gospel dream! May Christ's dying and rising move us to make God's glory dwell on earth. May our hope for the future inspire us in a respect for the present moment. May the desire for the heavenly realities not make us neglect our work on earth.

Set Free the Gifts of the Spirit

SOLEMNITY OF PENTECOST

Acts 2:1-11;
1 Corinthians 12:3b-7, 12-13
or Galatians 5:16-25;
John 20:19-23 or John 15:26-27; 16:12-15

Christian theology of the Holy Spirit is rooted in Judaism. The term Spirit translates the Hebrew word (*ruah*) and even in the pronunciation of it we detect God's wind and breath. The wind of God, the breath of God, the presence of God are all ways of referring to God's presence.

The expression "Holy Spirit" was used only seven times in the Old Testament, whereas the terms "Spirit of God" or "Spirit of the Lord" occurs 67 times in the Hebrew Scriptures. In the very first line of the book of Genesis 1:1, God's Spirit was gently hovering over the primordial waters waiting for the opportune moment of drawing order from that chaos.

Jesus, himself, uses the sensory image of the wind in the mysterious, nocturnal conversation with Nicodemus when he talks about the Spirit as the wind that blows where it wills (cf. John 3). This, then, is the Spirit's first function in the Scriptures: to be the mysterious presence of God in history, not reducible to human or earthly logic.

The second function of the Spirit in the Old Testament is that of putting things in order. The Genesis creation account (Chapter 1) reveals a descending Spirit upon this formless world and its descent produces the miracle of creation, the transformation of chaos into cosmos, of disorder into order, of anonymity into community.

The third function of the Spirit in the Old Testament is life-giver. In Genesis 2:7, we read: "The Lord God formed man from the dust of the ground, and breathed into his nostrils the breath of life; and the man became a living being." As a result of this divine breath, the human creature is transformed into a living being, no longer to be simply a creature but a partner made in the image and likeness of God, with whom and to whom God speaks and confides responsibility for the world.

The fourth function of the Holy Spirit is guide. We read in Isaiah 11: "The spirit of the Lord shall rest upon him, the spirit of wisdom and understanding, the spirit of counsel and might, the spirit of knowledge and fear of the Lord." The fear of the Lord is not something that terrorizes people but could be understood as our ability to say "wow," "awesome" before God's handiwork and God's creation.

The fifth function of the Spirit is healer, articulated so powerfully in the prophecy of Ezekiel 36:26-27 – "A new heart I will give you, and a new spirit I will put within you; and make you follow my statutes and be careful to observe my ordinances." The Spirit enters, recreates, restores to health and vanquishes sin.

The sixth function of the Holy Spirit is the universal principle. We read in Joel 2:28-29: "I will pour out my spirit on all flesh; your sons and your daughters shall prophecy … Even on the male and female slaves, in those days, I will pour out my spirit." The day will come when all humanity will be truly possessed by the spirit and that day will coincide with the eagerly awaited Messianic age of which the prophets speak. It was this principle that captivated Jesus' activity and ministry in a remarkable way.

The seventh function of the Holy Spirit takes place on the feast of Pentecost when the disciples were all filled with the Holy Spirit and began to speak in other tongues as the Spirit gave them utterance. The coming of the Holy Spirit signals the start of a world-wide mission for Christians beyond their geographic boundaries of Israel, first from Israel to Rome, and then from Rome then to the ends of the earth. It is a mission that overcomes human obstacles and has the Spirit as its driving force.

The Catholic Experience

The Holy Spirit makes the Christian experience truly Catholic and universal, open to all human experience. To be Catholic is to be universal and open to the world. Not only to Canada, North America, Europe or Asia, or a certain familiar part of the world or segment of society, but it must be open to all, to every single person. The mind of Christ is not intended to be a selective mentality for a few but the perspective from which the whole world will be renewed and redeemed. An insight like this, the universal scope of salvation did not however come easily and without much pain and confusion.

In fact, the whole of the New Testament can be understood precisely as the emergence of the Catholic, the universal, in Christian life. Christianity, had it not moved from where it was particular and small would have just been a small modification of the Jewish experience, a subset of Jewish piety that was still focused in and around Jerusalem and the restoration of a literal kingdom of Israel. The first two generations of Christians discovered that Christianity could not be just that. Because they had received the Holy Spirit, which is the universal principle, the Holy Spirit opened peoples' eyes to the universal import of the Christian truth and through the encounter with non-Jews who received the Holy Spirit.

The artists of the Middle Ages often contrasted the Tower of Babel with the "Tower" of the Upper Room. Babel symbolizes the divisions of people caused by sin. Pentecost stands for a hope that such separations are not a tragic necessity. The babbling mob of Babel compares poorly with the heartfelt unity of the Pentecost crowd. Babel was a mob. Pentecost was a community. A people without God lost the ability to communicate. A people suffused with the Spirit spoke heart to heart.

At Pentecost the full meaning of Jesus' life and message is poured into our hearts by the Spirit alive in the community. The New Testament seems to say that – for a fleeting moment – the nations of the earth paused from their customary strife and experienced a community caused by God. The brief and shining hour of Pentecost remains to charm and encourage us to this day.

World Youth Day

One of the finest teachings on the Holy Spirit in recent times took place in July, 2008 during the great vigil at World Youth Day in Sydney, Australia. The Saturday evening prayer vigil at the Randwick Racecourse on July 19 began in darkness, gradually illuminated by torches borne by dancers on the podium, representing the opening to the Holy Spirit.

"Tonight we focus our attention on how to become witnesses," Benedict XVI told the young people in his address. "You are already well aware that our Christian witness is offered to a world which in many ways is fragile. The unity of God's creation is weakened by wounds that run particularly deep when social relations break apart, or when the human spirit is all but crushed through the exploitation and abuse of persons. Indeed, society today is being fragmented by a way of thinking that is inherently shortsighted, because it disregards the full horizon of truth, the truth about God and about us. By its nature, relativism fails to see the whole picture. It ignores the very principles which enable us to live and flourish in unity, order and harmony".

Yet, the Pope went on, "such attempts to construct unity in fact undermine it. To separate the Holy Spirit from Christ present in the Church's institutional structure would compromise the unity of the Christian community, which is precisely the Spirit's gift! (…) Unfortunately the temptation to 'go it alone' persists. Some today portray their local community as somehow separate from the so-called institutional Church, by speaking of the former as flexible and open to the Spirit and the latter as rigid and devoid of the Spirit."

"Let us invoke the Holy Spirit: He is the artisan of God's works," the Pope concluded. "Let His gifts shape you! Just as the Church travels the same journey with all humanity, so too you are called to exercise the Spirit's gifts amidst the ups and downs of your daily life. Let your faith mature through your studies, work, sport, music and art. Let it be sustained by prayer and nurtured by the Sacraments. (…) In the end, life is not about accumulation. It is much more than success. To be truly alive is to be transformed from within, open to the energy of God's love. In accepting the power of the Holy Spirit you too can transform your families, communities and nations. Set free the gifts! Let wisdom, courage, awe and reverence be the marks of greatness!"

Come Holy Spirit!

We read in the Gospels "But the Advocate, the Holy Spirit, whom the Father will send in my name, will teach you everything, and remind you of all that I have said to you." (John 14:26). This act of reminding and recalling is stated very clearly in the *Catechism of The Catholic Church*, (No. 1099) "The Holy Spirit is the Church's living memory." On this great feast and birth of the Church, let us pray for the gift of memory, and for the courage to move from the empowering mystery of the Upper Room to the reality of daily life.

Come Holy Spirit, fill the hearts of your faithful
And kindle in us the fire of your Love!

Lord, send us your Spirit,
And renew the face of the earth...
The face of our Church, the face of our communities,
Our own faces, our own hearts. Amen.

God Puts Relationship and Community First

FEAST OF THE HOLY TRINITY

Deuteronomy 4:32-34, 39-40;
Romans 8:14-17;
Matthew 28:16-20

One of the important dimensions of our Trinitarian God is the community of love and persons modeled for us in the mystery of the Holy Trinity. For Christians, the Trinity is the primary symbol of a community that is held together by containing diversity within itself.

If our faith is based in this Trinitarian mystery that is fundamentally a mystery of community, then all of our earthly efforts and activities must work toward building up the human community that is a reflection of God's rich, Trinitarian life.

Today's Deuteronomy passage (4:32-34,39-40) is an excellent point of departure for probing the depths of the mystery of the Trinity. Consider for a moment Moses' words encouraging and exhorting the people of Israel: "From there you will seek the Lord your God, and you will find him if you search after him with all your heart and soul. In your distress, when all these things have happened to you in time to come, you will return to the Lord your God and heed him. Because the Lord your God is a merciful God, he will neither abandon you nor destroy you; he will not forget the covenant with your ancestors that he swore to them" (4:29-31). The whole passage speaks of the special relationship between God and Israel, linking the uniqueness of Israel's special vocation with the uniqueness of Israel's God.

Then in a series of rhetorical questions, Moses, knowing full well that the Lord alone is God, puts the people of Israel "on the stand," and asks them about this God of theirs: "Ask now about former ages, long before your own, ever since the day that God created man on the earth; ask from one end of heaven to the other: Has anything so great as this ever happened or has its like ever been heard of? Has any people ever heard the voice of a god speaking out of a fire, as you have heard, and lived? Or has any god ever attempted to go and take a nation for himself from the midst of another nation, by trials, by signs and wonders, by war, by a mighty hand and an outstretched arm, and by terrifying displays of power, as the Lord your God did for you in Egypt before your very eyes? To you it was shown so that you would acknowledge that the Lord is God; there is no other besides him" (4:32-35).

Matthew's commission

The majestic departure scene at the end of Matthew's Gospel (28:16-20) relates to us Jesus' final earthly moments and the great commission to the Church: "Go therefore and make disciples of all nations, baptizing them in the name of the Father and of the Son and of the Holy Spirit, and teaching them to obey everything that I have commanded you. And remember, I am with you always, to the end of the age" (19-20).

The great apostolic commission implies a service that is pastoral: "Go therefore and make disciples of all the nations";

liturgical: "baptizing them"; prophetic: "teaching them to obey everything that I have commanded you"; and guaranteed by the Lord's closeness, until the end of time. The scene gives a foretaste of the final glorious coming of the Son of Man (Matthew 26:64). Then his triumph will be manifest to all; now it is revealed only to the disciples, who are commissioned to announce it to all nations and bring them to believe in Jesus and obey his commandments. Since universal power belongs to the risen Jesus (Matthew 28:18), he gives the eleven a mission that is truly universal. They are to make disciples of all nations.

Baptism is the means of entrance into the community of the risen one, the Church. "In the name of the Father and of the Son and of the Holy Spirit": This is perhaps the clearest expression in the New Testament of Trinitarian belief. It may have been the baptismal formula of Matthew's church, but primarily it designates the effect of baptism, the union of those baptized with the Father, Son, and Holy Spirit.

Trinitarian language

The language of Father and Son is relational language, and reminds us that, for God, as for us, created in God's image, relationship and community are primary. God can no more be defined by what God does than we can. God is a Being, not a Doing, just as we are human beings, not human doings. This is a point of theology, but also, with all good theology, a practical point.

To define God's inner life in the Trinity in terms of God's activity leads to defining humans, created in God's image, in the same way. Those who choose to say, "In the name of the Creator, the Redeemer and the Sustainer" err in defining God by function and not by person. God is a living being who exists in intimate relationship with us.

Our God isn't immovable. God isn't alone. God is communication between the Father, the Son, and the Holy Spirit. This is the profound mystery that the liturgy for the feast of the Holy Trinity recalls: both the unspeakable reality of God and the manner in which this mystery has been given to us. The Trinity celebrates the peace and unity of the divine persons in whom the circular dance of love – *perichoresis* in Greek – continues. That unity is a dance of life and relationships, encompassing all aspects of human life.

We must constantly strive for this unity and peace of God, Jesus, and their life-giving Spirit, a peace that theological controversy never gives. Though theology is absolutely necessary, we would do well to pray more and love God more, than trying to figure out our Trinitarian God! The consolation is this: Complete understanding is not necessary for love.

Listen to St. Catherine of Siena's famous prayer from her Dialogue on Divine Providence:

"Eternal God, eternal Trinity, you have made the blood of Christ so precious through his sharing in your divine nature. You are a mystery as deep as the sea; the more I search, the more I find, and the more I find the more I search for you. But I can never be satisfied; what I receive will ever leave me desiring more. When you fill my soul I have an ever-greater hunger, and I grow more famished for your light. I desire above all to see you, the true light, as you really are."

Love can never outgrow its fascination with the puzzling aspects of the one loved. This is our approach to the Trinitarian mystery. We must love God more. On this feast, let us pray that we be caught up in the unifying and reconciling work of the Holy Spirit of God. The increasing glory of God is this progressive revelation of the Trinity.

Many times during our lives, we experience this revelation and God's Trinitarian presence through the depth of love, communication and relationship with other people. Our God is rich in relationships, communication and love for all people. This God models to us what the dynamic Trinitarian life is all about – communication, relationship and affection. The quality of our Christian life is based on imitation of the interior life of the Trinity.

The foundation of our Trinitarian faith is dialogue, communication and a "dance of life." Though we may struggle in understanding the Holy Trinity, we nevertheless take it into our very hands each time that we mark ourselves with the sign of the cross. Words once spoken over us at baptism become the words with which we bless ourselves in the name of the Trinity. Herein lies the meaning of this unique, one God in three Persons. I offer you this prayer for today's feast and the coming week:

Glory to you, Father,
Who by the power of your love,
Created the world and formed us in your own image
and likeness.

Glory to you, only begotten Son,
Who in your wisdom assumed our human condition
To lead us to the Kingdom.

Glory to you, Holy Spirit,
Who in your mercy sanctified us in baptism.
You work to create in us a new beginning each day.

Glory to you, Holy Trinity,
You always have been, you are and you always will be
Equally great to the end of the ages.

We adore you, we praise you, we give you thanks
Because you were pleased to reveal the depth
of your mystery
To the humble, to little ones.

Grant that we may walk in faith and joyful hope
until the day
When it will be ours to live in the fullness of your love
And to contemplate forever what we now believe
here below:
God who is Father, Son and Spirit! Glory to You!

May God's Holy Trinity – in unspeakable goodness and mystery – teach us and guide us in the life that is ours, and may we grow in "God's love [which] has been poured into our hearts through the Holy Spirit that has been given to us" (Romans 5:5).

Food and Drink for the Journey

Solemnity of the Body and Blood of Christ

Exodus 24:3-8;
Hebrews 9:11-15;
Mark 14:12-16, 22-26

Today's Gospel (Mark 14:12-16, 22-26) links Jesus' death with Israel's great feast of liberation, the Passover.

At the first Passover, the blood on the doorpost prevented the death of the firstborn. The bread broken at the Last Supper symbolizes the disciples' sharing in Jesus' self-offering. Drinking from the cup of his blood creates a new and dynamic common bond. Jesus' blood sanctifies and revitalizes each of us. The Eucharist has something that distinguishes it from every other kind of memorial. It is memorial and presence together, even if hidden under the signs of bread and wine.

Our Eucharistic Liturgy proclaims the one bond of life between God and his people. Just as blood that flows outward from the heart unites all the bodily members in one flow of life, so too are we united intimately with God through the precious body and blood of Jesus. The very nature of the Eucharist implies a bond with God and with the community. Our destinies are intertwined with God's own life. We cannot be loners, for blood is a common bond.

As we celebrate the Solemnity of the Body and Blood of the Lord this year, we realize two things: this feast is a daily one. Yet we set aside one day in the year to celebrate a feast of those feasts which we celebrate every day. Not only do we celebrate the bread and wine which become the body and blood of the Lord, we celebrate the new identity given to those who share among them Jesus' body and blood and then become what they eat and drink.

Faith in Jesus' resurrection can itself be an unproductive or dangerous ideology if it does not stimulate us actually to share bread with our brothers and sisters who are hungry. We are not engaging in social and political action but in sacramental celebration, a memorial or commemoration: the recollection of Jesus' life and death, in the conviction of faith of his resurrection as Lord, sitting in God's place of honour as the advocate of poor and oppressed people who have no bread. When we receive the Eucharist, we partake of the one who becomes food and drink for others. Each time we celebrate the Eucharist, do we realize that the Eucharistic Christ is really present as bread for the poor?

Christianity, Catholicism, the sacraments, especially the Eucharist, are not theological concepts, courses, things, ideas, passing fancies, symbols – they are a living person and his name is Jesus.

Quebec's Eucharistic congress

At many moments of crisis and turbulence in Christian history, the Lord confirmed his real presence in the Blessed Sacrament in some rather miraculous ways. Most of these Eucharistic miracles involved incidences in which the Host has "turned into human flesh and blood." The miracles in Bolsena and Orvieto in Italy quickly come to mind, and there is, of course, the well known Eucharistic miracle story from

Lanciano, Italy. Such stories seem to be far removed from our own experiences, and are often times quite hard to believe. In recent times such miracle stories have receded from the front burners of contemporary theology and spirituality and are often relegated to the realm of eccentric piety and devotion.

As Catholics we believe that the consecrated elements are the Body, Blood, Soul, and Divinity of our Lord, under the appearances of bread and wine. Therefore, Jesus, through the Eucharistic miracles, merely manifests his presence in a more tangible way. Some tell us that we don't really need the extraordinary manifestations to confirm what we already know and believe. They say that extraordinary miracles are not the essence of true Eucharistic piety, devotion and understanding.

I would like to reflect on an extraordinary Eucharistic event that deeply marked the Church in Canada and touched many parts of the world as well.

During the week of June 15-22, 2008, I rediscovered what extraordinary Eucharistic miracles are all about, only this time it wasn't in churches of old Europe. Along with 15,000 other people from throughout Canada and 75 other countries of the world, I saw the Eucharist come alive in a very powerful way in a hockey arena in Quebec City's Pepsi Coliseum during the 49th International Eucharistic Congress.

In his homily for the opening of the congress, the 84-year-old Slovakian Cardinal Jozef Tomko, papal legate to the event, said that "Jesus is the gift of God, he is the food that feeds us and fulfills us and allows us life in eternity. The Eucharist is a person, not an object, not a dead gift. Maybe we should ask not what is the Eucharist, but who is the Eucharist?" The answer to this question, Tomko said, is Jesus in the sacramental form of bread and wine "to indicate he wanted to become our food and sustain our life."

One of the very memorable and profound catechesis sessions of the Quebec congress was on the theme "The Eucharist, the Life of Christ in our Lives" given by Bishop Louis Tagle of Imus in the Philippines. Bishop Tagle spoke about Eucharistic adoration outside of Mass: "Beholding Jesus, we receive and are transformed by the mystery we adore. Eucharistic adoration is similar to standing at the foot of the cross of Jesus, being a witness to his sacrifice of life and being renewed by it."

Bishop Tagle pointed to the example of the Roman centurion who guarded Jesus on the cross as a "model of adoration." "We learn from the centurion to face Jesus, to keep watch over him, to behold him, to contemplate him. At first the centurion spent hours watching over Jesus out of duty but ended up contemplating him in truth. What did the centurion see? We can assume that he saw the horror of suffering that preceded Jesus' death. But I also believe that in Jesus, the centurion saw incredible love, love for the God who had failed to remove this cup of suffering from him, and love for neighbours."

The prelate concluded his powerful catechesis: "I wish that Eucharistic adoration would lead us to know Jesus more as the compassionate companion of many crucified peoples of today. Let us adore Jesus who offered his life as a gift to the Father for us sinners. Let us adore him for ourselves, for the poor, for the earth, for the Church and for the life of the world."

One day during the congress in Quebec, the daily rainfall compelled me to take a taxi to the Pepsi Coliseum. The young driver, an Algerian Muslim man, asked me from where I came and then spoke to me about the congress, having encountered so many of the delegates on the streets of Quebec City. When he learned that I was from English-speaking Canada, he lit up! "What are they giving you people to eat these days?" he asked me. I looked puzzled and asked him to explain and he did so in impeccable English! He said: "I have never seen so many happy people in Quebec City since I emigrated here 10 years ago. There has to be something in the food and drink. It must be awesome!"

Quebec's Eucharistic Congress was a privileged opportunity for Canada to re-actualize the historic and cultural patrimony of holiness and social engagement of the Church that draws its roots from the Eucharistic mystery.

In his 2003 encyclical letter *Ecclesia de Eucharistia* Blessed Pope John Paul II wrote: "The Eucharist builds the Church and the Church makes the Eucharist." The International Eucharistic Congress in Quebec City did just that.

Even the Wind and Sea Obey Him

TWELFTH SUNDAY IN ORDINARY TIME

Job 38:1-4, 8-11;
2 Corinthians 5:14-17;
Mark 4:35-41

There are many biblical passages that reveal the imagery of the angry sea. The Lord redeems his people from slavery in Egypt by turning the sea against the Egyptians (Exodus 15:8). Other times the roaring waves of the sea are tamed only after fierce struggles (Psalm 89, Isaiah 51:9-10). The sea mythology of the Old Testament underlies the first reading, psalm and Gospel for the 12th Sunday in Ordinary Time (Year B). In the Scriptures, the sea becomes a hostile, angry, dangerous area.

The question of Job is one asked by humanity throughout the ages: "Why do good, innocent people suffer?" Throughout the book, Job has been asking God to justify his actions, and God's response forms the key section of the whole book. Chapter 38 begins the next to the final section in this book, in which God finally answers the ultimatums hurled at the divine throne. God responds by firing questions at Job about creation, implying that Job cannot explain his suffering because God's response basically challenges Job's right to question the Almighty!

Today's small excerpt from the magnificent speech of God surrounds the Lord with the most awesome imagery. The Lord addressed Job out of the whirlwind and questioned him about the control of the ocean waves. "Where were you when I laid the foundation of the earth? Tell me, if you have understanding" (Job 38:4). Or "who shut in the sea with doors when it burst out from the womb?" (Job 38:8) The implied question is: If Job cannot understand God's providence for the sea and the powers of nature, how will he ever grasp divine care for humans? For the author of Job, power means service.

Psalm 107 points out the mercies of God as demonstrated in the fate of individuals, and provides some insights into the multiplicity of ways in which God's loving-kindness is displayed. The psalm speaks of a variety of dangers that confront believers: travel by land, imprisonment, sickness, and travel by sea. Consider the rich images used throughout this psalm: "stormy winds that lift up the waves of the sea" (107:25); "waves that mounted up to heaven then had their courage melt away" (107:26).

The storm and the waves hold people prisoners, and now that their own resources are at an end, they realize that the Lord alone can deliver them from the grasp of these elements. In desperation the people cry out, God intervenes and the people admit indebtedness. The transformation of the storm into a gentle breeze dramatizes the Lord's response to people in need. When the psalmist says that the waves of the sea were hushed, the Hebrew word used means not so much to be silent but rather to grow still. In fact, in biblical literature this word is used only here and in Jonah 1:11, 12 with reference to the calming down of the turbulent sea and in Proverbs 26:20 in connection with the cessation of contention.

Love at the centre

In today's second reading (2 Corinthians 5:14-17), Paul speaks of his love of Christ and his personal conviction of that love which is the central motivation in his ministry. The Greek phrase for "love of Christ" includes both our love for Christ and Christ's love for us, whereby Christ is both the object and subject of love. Only if Christ loves us first, by dying and rising, can we love in return. Because we share in his death and resurrection, we can no longer live for ourselves but are to live a new life of service in imitation of Christ. Paul also notes that he had to change his view of Christ and see him not from a merely human standpoint but in the light of revelation in the Spirit. If we see Christ from God's viewpoint, then we should view everyone from the same perspective. Paul then brings the passage to a climax, insisting that everyone who is in Christ is a new creation and that everything is new – "everything old has passed away; see, everything has become new!" (2 Corinthians 5:17). The power of God in Jesus is a reality, which, for our benefit, restrains itself so humbly and so completely, that we experience it as holy freedom – a freedom that removes fear and gives us the courage to act.

In the New Testament, the sea almost always represents a moment of conversion. It is along the sea that Jesus calls others to join him in his prophetic ministry and outreach to the poor and the sick. A sudden squall on the Sea of Galilee provides the crisis in today's Gospel story (Mark 4:35-41) that takes place after a full day of teaching for Jesus. The calming of the storm is also a great teaching moment for Jesus. When the disciples awake him, they address him as "Teacher."

Throughout the entire storm at sea, Mark insists on Jesus' calmness and rootedness in God. He is "in the stern, asleep on the cushion" (Mark 4:38), trusting in God, in contrast to the disciples, who are frightened. When they rebuke Jesus for sleeping, he rebukes them for their lack of faith. In Mark's account, both the disciples' words to Jesus and his responses to them are quite harsh. Matthew and Luke soften both statements, but here the disciples really rebuke Jesus – and his rebuke to them doesn't merely speak of "little faith" but of "no faith."

The calming of the storm reveals much to us, for as the first reading from Job has indicated, only God can control the wind and sea. Jesus does much more than quiet the storm waves roaring across the sea and tossing the boat from side to side or tipping it dangerously into the waters. Jesus shares God's control of the seas, emerging as the new creator, bringing peace and order out of the primordial chaos and establishing himself as Ruler over the new Kingdom of Israel.

Riding the waves

Besides indicating Christ's divine power over nature, the calming of the story suggests his power over evil – for the sea commonly symbolizes evil and chaos. The boat is already a symbol of the Church, so the story also challenges us to trust in Christ's power so that we can persevere through the storms that assail us as individuals and as a Church. Mark writes to his own community, which experiences chaos in the Lord's absence. It's almost as if the Lord is sleeping – uninvolved.

Jesus challenges this lack of faith and affirms his continuing presence with power.

A boat was a common symbol for the Church – here it is a symbol of a storm-tossed community crying out for help. Christ seems asleep and unconcerned, but he is in total control of the situation. The statement of peace recalls the greeting of the risen Christ. With Christ we pass through the raging sea and already share in his calm strength – even though like Job our questions may remain unanswered.

Today's readings clearly show that power must ultimately take the form of loving involvement. Who are the holders of power in our day-to-day experience? Power resides with parents, teachers, elected officials, Church leaders, and many others. The measure of genuine power is found in self-sacrifice. Parents give all for their children; teachers labour long hours for their students; pastors gladly spend themselves for their communities. The result of all this is new life for both the leader and the follower. Jesus gave his life in history's ultimate display of power and service. His life, especially in the midst of the storms, teaches us how to live in the midst of the storms of our own lives and times.

This week, let us take some time to reflect on the following questions that flow from our Scripture texts for the day: What are my deepest fears? How have I experienced God bringing order out of the chaos of my life? How is our Church storm-tossed today, and by what signs do we know that Jesus is fully in control of the situation?

Arise, Live and Love Again!

Wisdom 1:13-15; 2:23-24;
2 Corinthians 8:7, 9, 13-15;
Mark 5:21-43 or 5:21-24, 35-43

Last week we witnessed Jesus' divine power at work on the forces of nature (Mark 4:37-41). Today's Gospel stories reveal his power over disease and death.

In these powerful accounts, Jesus reminds us of the importance of faith. Nothing is possible without faith. On the way to Jairus' house (Mark 5), Jesus encounters interruptions, delays, and even obstacles along the road. The people in the passage transfer their uncleanness to Jesus, and to each Jesus bestows the cleansing wholeness of God. Let us consider for a moment each situation.

The hemorrhaging woman

Jesus' miraculous healing of this woman who had been hemorrhaging for 12 years is narrated in three of the four Gospels (Matthew 9:20-22; Mark 5:25-34; Luke 8:43-48). The law regarded three forms of uncleanness as serious enough to exclude the infected person from society: leprosy, uncleanness caused by bodily discharges, and impurity resulting from contact with the dead (Numbers 5:2-4). The woman in Mark 5 had a disease that made her ritually unclean (Leviticus 15:25-27). It would have excluded her from most social contact and worship at the temple. She desperately wanted Jesus to heal her, but she knew that her bleeding would cause Jesus to become ritually unclean under Jewish law.

Anyone who had one of the diseases was made unclean. Anything or anyone that one touched became unclean. Those who were unclean also suffered from estranged relationships with others and with God. Anything unclean was unfit or unworthy to be in the presence of a God who was holy. Those deemed unclean had to go through a rite of purification or cleansing in order to be welcomed back into society and into the presence of God.

The woman's bold invasion of Jesus' space, and her touching of Jesus' garment, thus making Jesus unclean, could have put him off. On the contrary, Jesus not only heals the woman, but also restores her relationships with others. When Jesus calls the woman "daughter," he established a relationship with one with whom he should not have a relationship.

Jairus' daughter

The very touching story of Jairus' daughter is "sandwiched" around the story about the hemorrhaging woman. Jairus was an elected leader of the local synagogue, responsible for supervising the weekly worship, operating the school, and caring for the building. Some synagogue leaders had been pressured not to support Jesus, but Jairus had not caved into that pressure. Jairus bowed before Jesus and uttered his anguished request for help: "My little daughter is at the point of death. Come and lay your hands on her, so that she may be made well and live." Jairus' gesture was a significant and daring act of respect and worship.

The story continues: Jesus, "took her by the hand, and said to her, 'Talitha cum,' which means, 'Little girl, get up!' And immediately the girl got up and began to walk about" (5:41-42). By calling her "little girl," he established the same kind of relationship with her as Jairus has with his daughter.

In each situation, Jesus' holiness transforms the person's uncleanness. The flow of blood is stopped. The woman is healed. The corpse comes back to life. The young girl gets out of bed. Jesus raises each person up to his level, making that individual worthy to be in the presence of God.

Jesus, the healer

In so many of the healing stories, Jesus manifests the power to give people health, healing and even to bring the dead back to life. Remember the young man of Nain in Luke 7 who had died. Jesus said, "Young man, I say to you, rise!" Luke reports that the "dead man sat up and began to speak."

Jesus responded to the cries of the leper who begged him, "If you choose, you can make me clean!" Moved with compassion, Jesus gave a word of command which was proper to God and not to a mere human being: "I do choose. Be made clean!" Mark wrote: "Immediately the leprosy left him, and he was made clean" (Mark 1:42). How can we forget the case of the paralytic who was let down through an opening made in the roof of the house, Jesus said, "I say to you, stand up, take your mat and go to your home" (cf. Mark 2:1-12).

Jesus' story continues in the Acts of the Apostles when we hear about people who "carried out the sick into the streets, and laid them on cots and mats, in order that when

Peter's shadow might fall on some of them as he came by" (Acts 5:15). These "wonders and signs" were performed by the apostles not in their own name, but in the name of Jesus Christ, and were therefore a further proof of his divine power.

Talitha cum

The story of Jairus' daughter not only speaks about the death of a child and the raising of that young girl back to life, but it also speaks about death of the heart and spirit, a disease that affects so many young people today.

Those powerful words – *Talitha cum* (Little girl, arise) – are not only addressed to this little girl in Mark's story, but also to many young people, perhaps to each one of us. How many young children live with fear and sadness because of divided family situations, tragedy and loss! How many young people are caught up in vicious cycles of death: drugs, abortion, pornography, violence, gangs and suicide?

Living in a big city such as Toronto, I have the opportunity of meeting many young people, and when I hear some of their stories of brokenness, sadness and despair, I realize how much work the churches must do to bring young people back to life.

Jesus continues today to resurrect those dead young people to life. He does so with his word, and also by sending them his disciples who, in his name, and with his very love, repeat to today's young people his cry: "*Talitha cum*," "young man, young woman, arise! Live again! Love again! You are loved!"

"Alive" in Darlinghurst

As I reflect on today's Gospel and Jesus' powerful words: *"Talitha cum,"* I recall vividly one of Benedict XVI's special moments during World Youth Day 2008 in Australia.

The Holy Father went to the University of Notre Dame's Sacred Heart chapel in Darlinghurst (Sydney) where he met young people with histories of drug addiction and other problems, who are following the "Alive" rehabilitation program. The Pope recalled Moses' words in the Old Testament: "'I set before you life or death, blessing or curse. Choose life, then, so that you and your descendants may live in the love of the Lord your God, (…) for in this your life consists."

"It was clear what they had to do," the Pope explained, "they had to turn away from other gods and worship the true God Who had revealed himself to Moses – and they had to obey his commandments. You might think that in today's world, people are unlikely to start worshipping other gods. But sometimes people worship 'other gods' without realizing it. False 'gods' (…) are nearly always associated with the worship of three things: material possessions, possessive love, or power."

"Authentic love is obviously something good," the Pope continued. "When we love, we become most fully ourselves, most fully human. But (…) people often think they are being loving when actually they are being possessive or manipulative. People sometimes treat others as objects to satisfy their own needs. (…) How easy it is to be deceived by the many voices in our society that advocate a permissive approach to sexuality, without regard for modesty, self-respect or the moral values that bring quality to human relationships!"

"Dear friends, I see you as ambassadors of hope to others in similar situations. You can convince them of the need to choose the path of life and shun the path of death, because you speak from experience. All through the Gospels, it was those who had taken wrong turnings who were particularly loved by Jesus, because once they recognized their mistake, they were all the more open to his healing message.

"Indeed, Jesus was often criticized by self-righteous members of society for spending so much time with such people. 'Why does your master eat with tax collectors and sinners?' they asked. He responded: 'It is not the healthy who need the doctor, but the sick ... I did not come to call the virtuous but sinners' (cf. Matthew 9:11-13).

"It was those who were willing to rebuild their lives who were most ready to listen to Jesus and become his disciples. You can follow in their footsteps, you too can grow particularly close to Jesus because you have chosen to turn back towards him. You can be sure that, just like the Father in the story of the prodigal son, Jesus welcomes you with open arms. He offers you unconditional love – and it is in loving friendship with him that the fullness of life is to be found."

I am sure that Jesus was smiling upon Benedict XVI and that wonderful gathering in Sydney last July. Jesus' words – *Talitha cum* – were heard once again Down Under as the Holy Father invited young people to rise up, to live and to love again.

A Unity Transcending All Differences

Sts. Peter and Paul

Acts 12:1-11;
2 Timothy 4:6-8, 17-18;
Matthew 16:13-19

Given the significance of the Solemnity of Sts. Peter and Paul, and the formal conclusion of the Year of St. Paul in 2008, I offered this special reflection for the June 29 feast.

Peter's journey was from the weakness of denial to the rock of fidelity. He gave us the ultimate witness of the cross. Paul's pilgrimage was from the blindness of persecution to the fire of proclamation. He made the Word of God come alive for the nations.

To be with Peter means to preserve the unity of the Christian Church. To speak with Paul is to proclaim the pure Word of God.

The passion of both was to proclaim the Gospel of Christ. Their commitment was to create a place for everyone in Christ's Church. Their loyalty to Christ was valid to death. Peter and Paul are for us a strong foundation; they are pillars of our Church.

The crucial question

Today's Gospel story (Matthew 16:13-19) is about affirmation, identity and purpose. Jesus and his disciples entered the area of Caesarea Philippi in the process of a long journey from their familiar surroundings. Caesarea Philippi, built by

Philip, was a garrison town for the Roman army, full of all the architecture, imagery, and lifestyles of Greco-Roman urban civilization. It was a foreign place to the apostles who were more familiar with towns and the lakeside.

Sexuality and violence ran rampant in this religious shrine town known for its worship of the Greek god Pan. In this centre of power, sophistication and rampant pagan worship, Jesus turns to his disciples and asks what people are saying about him. How do they see his work? Who is he in their minds? Probably taken aback by the question, the disciples dredge their memories for overheard remarks, snatches of shared conversation, opinions circulating in the fishing towns of the lake area. Jesus himself is aware of some of the stories about him. He knows only too well the attitude of his own town of Nazareth, and the memory probably hurts him deeply.

The disciples list a whole series of labels that people have applied to Jesus. And these names reveal the different expectations held about him. Some thought of him as fiery Elijah, working toward a real confrontation with the powers that be. Others considered him more like the long-suffering Jeremiah, concentrating more on the inner journey, the private side of life. Above all, the question asked of the disciples echoes through time as the classic point of decision for every Christian.

Everyone must at some point experience what happened at Caesarea Philippi and answer Jesus' provocative question, "But, who do you say I am?" What do we perceive to be our responsibilities and commitments following upon our own declaration of faith in Jesus?

Lightning strikes

In the year 35 AD, Saul appears as a self-righteous young Pharisee, almost fanatically anti-Christian. We read in Acts 7 that he was present, although not taking part, at the stoning of Stephen, the first martyr. It was very soon afterward that Paul experienced the revelation that transformed his entire life.

On the road to the Syrian city of Damascus, where he was going to continue his persecutions against the Christians, he was struck blind. Paul accepted eagerly the commission to preach the Gospel of Christ, but like many another called to a great task, he felt his unworthiness and withdrew from the world to spend three years in "Arabia" in meditation and prayer before beginning his mission.

His extensive travels by land and sea are recounted in his letters in the New Testament. Paul himself tells us he was stoned, scourged three times, shipwrecked three times, endured hunger and thirst, sleepless nights, perils and hardships; besides these physical trials, he suffered many disappointments and almost constant anxieties over the weak and widely scattered communities of Christians.

Legendary farewell

According to the ancient tradition, on the morning of June 29, Peter and Paul were taken from their common cell at Rome's Mamertine prison and separated. Peter was taken to Nero's Circus where he was crucified upside down, while Paul was taken east of Rome to the area now known as Tre Fontane. Artists through the ages have dwelt on their goodbye, often depicting the last embrace between the two friends.

The Golden Legend records their parting words:

Paul to Peter: "Peace be with you, foundation stone of the churches and shepherd of the sheep and lambs of Christ!"

And Peter to Paul: "Go in peace, preacher of virtuous living, mediator and leader of the salvation of the righteous!"

The connection between the two saints is also evident in their respective basilicas. Emperor Constantine built the first six Christian churches in Rome from 313 to 328, and among them were St. Peter's Basilica and St. Paul's Outside the Walls.

Five of the churches face east, as was common in orienting churches at the time. St. Paul's faces west, so that across the city, both basilicas watch over the sheep and lambs of Rome.

A text from St. John Chrysostom is very appropriate for this great feast. It comes from Chrysostom's homily on St. Paul's Letter to the Romans. After expressing his ardent desire to visit St. Paul's tomb in Rome and see there even the dust of St. Paul's body, St. John Chrysostom exclaims:

"Who could grant me now this to throw myself around the body of Paul and be riveted to his tomb and to see the dust of that body which completed what was lacking in Christ's afflictions; which bore the marks (of Christ) and sowed the Gospel everywhere ... the dust of that mouth through which Christ spoke. (...)

"Nor is it that mouth only, but I wish I could see the dust of Paul's heart too, which one should rightly call the heart of the world, the fountain of countless blessings and the very element of our life. (...) A heart which was so large as to take in entire cities and peoples and nations (...) which became higher than the heavens, wider than the whole world, brighter than the sun's beam, warmer than the fire, stronger than the adamant; letting rivers flow from it, (…) which was deemed to love Christ like no one else ever did.

"I wish I could see the dust of Paul's hands, hands in chains, through the imposition of which the Spirit was given, through which this divine letter (to the Romans) was written.

"I wish I could see the dust of those eyes which were rightly blinded and recovered their sight again for the salvation of the world; which were counted worthy to see Christ in the body; which saw earthly things, yet saw them not; which saw the things that are not seen; which knew no sleep, and were watchful even at midnight. (…)

"I wish I could also see the dust of those feet, Paul's feet, which ran through the world and were not tired, which were bound in stocks when the prison shook, which went through parts populated and uninhabited, which walked on so many journeys. (…)

"I wish I could see the tomb where the weapons of righteousness lay, the weapons of light, the limbs of Paul, which now are alive but in life were made dead (to sin), (…) which were in Christ's limbs, clothed in Christ, bound in the Spirit, riveted to the fear of God, bearing the marks of Christ" (St. John Chrysostom, "Homily 32 on the Epistle to the Romans," Migne, *Patrologia Graeca* 60, 678-80).

Build this Church

As ordinary men, Peter and Paul might have avoided each other from time to time. Peter was a fisherman from the Sea of Galilee and Paul a Greek-educated intellectual. But Jesus brought them together as a sign for his Church in which the entire spectrum of humanity would find a new place to call home. Together they worked to build the Church. Together they witnessed to Christ. Together they suffered the death of their Lord, death at murderous hands. Paul died by the sword and Peter was crucified head-down. They had a unity that transcended all differences. They teach us about the depth of Christian commitment. For Peter and Paul, insight into Jesus' true identity brought new demands and responsibilities.

In proclaiming the Year of St. Paul in June 2007, Benedict XVI invited each Catholic to hold up a mirror to his or her life and to ask, "Am I as determined and as energetic about spreading the Catholic faith as St. Paul was?" "Is spreading the faith both by example and by my conversations with friends, colleagues and acquaintances even a concern for me?" "What do I perceive to be my responsibilities following upon my own declaration of faith in Jesus?"

Is Not This the Carpenter,
the Son of Mary?

FOURTEENTH SUNDAY IN ORDINARY TIME

Ezekiel 2:3-5; 2:23-24;
2 Corinthians 12:7-10;
Mark 6:1-6

We know today's Gospel story well, perhaps too well! It would have been customary for Jesus to go to the synagogue each week during the Sabbath, and when his turn came, to read from the scriptures during the Sabbath service.

His hometown folks listened ever so attentively to his teaching because they had heard about the miracles he had performed in other towns. What signs would their hometown boy work on his own turf?

In today's story, Jesus startled his own people with a seeming rebuke that no prophet of God can receive honour among his own people. The people of Nazareth took offence at him and refused to listen to what he had to say. They despised his preaching because he was from the working class; a carpenter, a mere layman and they despised him because of his family. Jesus could do no mighty works in their midst because they were closed and disbelieving toward him.

If people have come together to hate and to refuse to understand, then they will see no other point of view than their own, and they will refuse to love and accept others. Does the story sound familiar to us? How many times have we found ourselves in similar situations?

Homecoming

We often think that Luke is the only evangelist who records Jesus' visit to Nazareth, "where he had been brought up" and that programmatic episode in the Nazareth synagogue (Luke 4:16). Mark and Matthew also refer to this episode, although without mentioning the name of the town, calling it simply "his hometown" or "his native place" (Mark 6:1; Matthew 13:54). There are, however, several differences between the story told by Luke and those of Mark and Matthew. In the Gospels of Mark and Matthew, people consider the humble origin of Jesus who was "the carpenter" (Mark 6:3), "the son of the carpenter" (Matthew 13:55) and use it to doubt the greatness of his mission. Luke, on the other hand, makes no mention of Jesus' humble origins.

In Mark, Jesus' visit to his hometown is found not at the beginning of his ministry, but after a long period of preaching the Gospel and healing, even after the talks on the parables (Mark 4:1-34) and the resurrection of Jairus' daughter (Mark 5:21-43). In Matthew, Jesus has also already pronounced his address on mission to the "Twelve Apostles" (10:2-42).

What was the meaning of the peoples' questions about Jesus in Mark's account (6:1-6) that forms this Sunday's Gospel? "'Where did this man get all this? What is this wisdom that has been given to him? What deeds of power are being done by his hands! Is not this the carpenter, the son of Mary, and the brother of James and Joses and Judas and Simon, and are not his sisters here with us?' And they took offense at him."

"Who do you think you are?" they seem to be asking him. Jesus sees that the questions about him correspond to a deeply possessive attitude: Is not this the carpenter, the son of Mary, and therefore one of us? You belong to us and therefore you must do for us all that you are able to do. We own you!

"A prophet is not without honour, except in his home-town and among his own kin, and in his own house." Jesus resists the possessive attitude manifested by his people. The people of Jesus' native place were suffering from a particular form of blindness – a blindness that sometimes affects us, too. Jesus refuses to place his extraordinary gifts at the service of his own people, putting strangers first.

Vision and heart

Today's Gospel shows how difficult it is for us to attain to a universal vision. When we are faced with someone like Jesus, someone with a generous heart, a wide vision and a great spirit, our reactions are very often filled with jealousy, selfishness, and meanness of spirit. His own people couldn't recognize the holiness of Jesus, because they had never really accepted their own. They couldn't honour his relationship with God because they had never fully explored their own sense of belonging to the Lord. They couldn't see the Messiah standing right beside them, because he looked too much like one of them. Until we see ourselves as people beloved of God, miracles will be scarce and the prophets and messengers who rise among us will struggle to be heard and accepted for whom they truly are.

In today's Gospel story, Mark tells us that Jesus was amazed at their unbelief. Listening to Jesus, his own people were initially filled with admiration in him and pride because of him. His message of liberation was marvellous. Then they recognize this young prophet as one of them and they say: "Is not this the carpenter, the son of Mary?"

The most severe critics are often people very familiar to us, a member of our family, a relative, or neighbour we rub shoulders with on a regular basis. The people of Nazareth refused to renounce their possessive attitude toward Jesus. When possessive love is obstructed it produces a violent reaction. This sort of reaction provokes many dramas of jealousy and passion. They took offence at him in Mark's account just as "all in the synagogue were filled with rage …" (Luke 4:28) and they sought to kill him (4:29) in Luke's version of the story. Refusal to open our heart can lead to such extremes.

Today's Gospel warns us to be on guard against certain attitudes that are incompatible with the example of Jesus: the human tendency to be possessive, and egoistic and small in mind and heart. We cannot forget that Jesus is the Saviour of the world (John 4:42), and not of the village, town, city or nation!

In order to approach and imitate Jesus, who is total beauty and uniqueness, the quality of magnanimity is necessary in our hearts and minds. The opposite and enemy of magnanimity is envy. Envy is that fault in the human character that cannot recognize the beauty and uniqueness of the other, and denies the other honour. Envy can no longer see because the eyes are "nailed shut," blinded to one's own beauty and the beauty in others. Envy inevitably leads to forms of violence and destruction, of self and of others. In order to approach and imitate Jesus, who is total beauty and uniqueness, the attitude of envy must be first acknowledged and then banished.

Magnanimity lets others be free, for the other person must become great enough to be an image of God's beauty. Magnanimity arouses the desire in each of us for the other to receive the greatest possible satisfaction and happiness that rightly belongs to the other! Magnanimity is capable of looking beyond itself, it can grant the other what oneself perhaps bitterly lacks, and can perhaps even rejoice in the other's goodness, greatness and beauty.

Let us pray that Jesus not be amazed at our own unbelief, but rather rejoice in our small, daily acts of fidelity to him and our service to our sisters and brothers. May the Lord grant us magnanimous hearts so that we may look far beyond ourselves and recognize the goodness, greatness and beauty of other people, instead of being jealous of their gifts. God's power alone can save us from emptiness and poverty of spirit, from confusion and error, and from the fear of death and hopelessness. The gospel of salvation is "great news" for us today.

Jesus Sends Us to Teach and Heal

Amos 7:12-15;
Ephesians 1:3-14 **or** *Ephesians 1:3-10;*
Mark 6:7-13

When the Gospels relate to us the call extended by Jesus to his young disciples and apostles, it is always done in a very compassionate way. Jesus looks upon those whom he calls; he loves them, challenges them and calls them to be something they could hardly fathom!

Today's Gospel (Mark 6:7-13) is about the formation of those who will eventually spread the Gospel to the ends of the earth. Mark sees the teaching and work of the apostles as an extension of Jesus' teaching and work. In Mark's story, the preparation for the mission of the Twelve is seen in the call of the first disciples to be fishers of men (Mark 1:16-20), then of the Twelve set apart to be with Jesus and to receive authority to preach and expel demons (3:13-19). Now they are given the specific mission to exercise that authority in word and power as representatives of Jesus during the time of their formation.

In Mark's call story, Jesus does not mention any prohibition to visit pagan territory and to enter Samaritan towns. These differences indicate a certain adaptation to conditions in and outside of Palestine and suggest in Mark's account a later activity in the Church. For the rest, Jesus required of his apostles a total dependence on God for food and shelter (cf. Mark 6:35-44; 8:1-9). Remaining in the same house as a guest (6:10), rather than moving to another offering greater comfort avoided any impression of seeking advantage for oneself and prevented dishonour to one's host. Why does Jesus tell the apostles to "travel light" with little or no provision? He wants his disciples to be dependent on him and not on themselves. He promises to work through and in each person called for his glory. The significance of shaking the dust off one's feet served as testimony against those who rejected the call to repentance.

Help or hindrance?

One of the frequent themes of Mark's Gospel is the ignorance of the disciples. When we read the whole Gospel, we realize that the disciples are as much a hindrance as a help to Jesus. They do not understand Jesus' words or support him in his mission. Repeatedly Jesus rebukes them for their inability to see and comprehend and for their hardness of heart. But when the disciples misunderstand Jesus and in other ways fail him, they are doing more than simply trying his patience. They are serving as agents of testing. As ones who "think the things of humans," rather than the things of God, they cannot comprehend that the straight and narrow path lying before Jesus must necessarily end at the cross. And so they act in ways that threaten to lead Jesus astray.

Many times we find ourselves asking, "Why did Mark portray the disciples in such a bad light?" But Mark's earliest readers would have focused not on Mark's literary strategies but on the events depicted in the narrative. They would have asked something like this: "What could it mean that the disciples whom we know as great leaders were so weak and acted so shamefully?" And the answer to that question would have been obvious: God had opened the eyes of the disciples, and had transformed them from ones who misunderstood and tested Jesus into worthy servants, even fearless leaders. There is hope for us! These famous call stories were remembered by Christians who knew the reality of their own weakness and failure, yet who also trusted in the presence of the Lord who triumphed over fear.

In Jesus' Name

What kind of authority and power does the Lord want us to exercise on his behalf? Jesus gave his apostles both the power and the authority to speak and to act in his name. He commanded them to do the works that he did: to cast out evil spirits, to heal, and to speak the word of God, the good news of the Gospel, which they received from Jesus. When Jesus spoke of power and authority he did something unheard of. He wedded power and authority with love and humility. The "world" and the "flesh" seek power for selfish gain. Jesus teaches us to use it for the good of our neighbour. Following Jesus is a risk, as every new way of life is. Each of us is called to teach as Jesus taught and to heal boldly and compassionately as he did.

Law, Prophets and Writings

In light of the first reading from the book of the prophet Amos (7:12-15) I would also like to offer some reflections on Jesus in relation to the Law, the Prophets, and the Writings of

---

the Old Testament. On the one hand, Jesus knows the Law perfectly and observes it with devotion. On the other hand, however, He shows himself perfectly free with regard to the Law. He wishes to give the authentic interpretation of the Law. He goes so far as to declare himself the new lawgiver, with an authority equal to that of God. He himself is the fulfillment of the Law (cf. Romans 10:4).

Jesus also shows that He is the genuine continuation of the prophets in his message and his life. Like them, He proclaims faith in the "God of Abraham, of Isaac, and of Jacob" (Matthew 22:32). He defends the rights of God and of the poor (cf. Matthew 11:20-24). On the other hand, Jesus does not hesitate to declare himself greater than all of them. He is superior to them, not only in the prophetic line, but He is the first, as the origin and source of all prophetic inspiration.

Jesus also presents himself as a fulfillment of the wisdom literature in the Old Testament. Jesus fulfills the Law and the Prophets by embodying this awareness in himself: He embodies the way and reforms it by the witness He gives throughout his life, and even in his death. There is a radical change in values, as if a new creation would emerge from a creation undergoing a major upheaval.

By his death, Jesus explains the apparent contradiction of these values in the wisdom literature, and opens the path which had seemed to become an impasse for humankind. For those who follow Jesus, and hopefully that is each one of us, we must walk in his footsteps, enduring all of his misunderstanding, suffering, and even death, in order to truly be his disciples.

The more we probe the depths of the very Scriptures which he fulfilled with his life, the more we will become like him.

Extended call

Spend some time this week reflecting on how the Lord has called you to be a disciple. In what ways have you felt the personal call of Christ? How does Christ make a difference in your life? What has his call demanded of you? What experiences or people in your life have been instrumental in deepening your faith? Is it possible to be a committed disciple of Jesus, yet still experience weakness and failure? In what ways can you, as a disciple of Jesus, share in his mission of teaching and healing today? To whom are you being sent, to teach and to heal?

Jesus,
the Compassionate Shepherd of God

SIXTEENTH SUNDAY IN ORDINARY TIME

Jeremiah 23:1-6;
Ephesians 2:13-18;
Mark 6:30-34

The themes of sheep and shepherding flow through the Scripture readings for the Sixteenth Sunday in Ordinary Time (Year B). The moving Gospel story of Jesus having compassion on the crowds that were "like sheep without a shepherd" helps us to focus on his ministry of teaching, reconciling and shepherding.

Literature of antiquity often referred to the person responsible for guiding a community as a shepherd. Likewise, the Old Testament frequently described the Lord himself as the shepherd of his people. Individuals invoked him as "my shepherd" (Psalm 23:1), and the community prayed to him as the "Shepherd of Israel" (Psalm 80:1).

In the New Testament, the image of the shepherd expresses great authority and responsibility. Nourishing the flock means that the shepherd must protect them from heresy, ever ready to defend the sheep from marauders. John tells us that Jesus himself proclaimed that he fulfilled Israel's hope for the coming of the good shepherd: "I am the good shepherd. The good shepherd lays down his life for the sheep" (John 10:11).

When Jesus withdraws with his disciples to a deserted place to rest, he attracts a great number of people to follow

228   *Words Made Flesh: Biblical Reflections for Year B*

them. Toward this people of the new exodus Jesus is moved with pity; he satisfies their spiritual hunger by teaching them many things, thus gradually showing himself the faithful shepherd of a new Israel.

When the Scriptures describe Jesus as having pity on his flock because they were "like sheep without a shepherd" in Mark 6:30-34, such an image is not original to Jesus in the Gospels. The image is drawn from Ezekiel 34, where God unleashes his anger at the shepherds of Israel who have fattened themselves on the weak and vulnerable, instead of caring for them (Ezekiel 34:10-12).

Sheep without a shepherd

Jesus' compassion is much more than a fleeting or temporary feeling of regret or sorrow. It is rather a deep anguish, a gut-wrenching type of anxiety and sorrow over the condition of people. Jesus was describing the spiritual lives of those who were living outside of the salvation so freely offered by God. Jesus felt gut-wrenching anguish over the souls of these people, who were facing spiritual starvation without someone to feed them, teach them, and lead them to true spiritual nourishment. They were in danger without a shepherd to protect them from false teaching. Like sheep without the good shepherd, they were alone and vulnerable to the attacks of the evil one, who roams around like a roaring lion, seeking someone to devour.

"Like sheep without a shepherd" is an accurate description of the spiritual lives of many 21st-century Christians in the world today. The expression describes many of our contemporaries who are directionless, helpless, and very vulnerable to the seductions and attacks of the evil one. "Sheep without a shepherd" are more than just a little lost. They are more than just a little vulnerable. They are facing danger and destruction.

Jesus' compassion

Jesus saw the sick and his compassion healed them. He saw those possessed by demons and his compassion freed them. He told the story of a king who was owed a huge debt by his servant. When the servant could not pay, the king ordered him thrown into slavery, along with his family. When the servant pleaded for mercy the king had compassion on him and forgave the huge debt (Matthew 18:21-35).

Jesus spoke about a man going down from Jerusalem to Jericho. That poor fellow fell among thieves who beat him, robbed him and left him to die. Two high-ranking religious officials passed by him, but a Samaritan stopped and had compassion on him. He bandaged the man's wounds and carried him to an inn where he nursed him through the night. The next day he paid the bill and gave the innkeeper his credit line, saying, "I will repay you whatever more you spend" (Luke 10:25-37).

Who can forget the thought-provoking story of the younger son who took his inheritance and squandered it in loose living? One day he "came to himself" and returned to his father's house, not hoping to be restored as a son, but wanting only to be hired as a servant. His father saw him coming and "was filled with compassion." Before the son could even utter his speech of repentance, the father placed on him a ring and robe and shoes and called for a royal feast (Luke 15:1-32).

The compassion of Jesus heals and feeds, forgives huge debts, nurses hurt bodies back to health and welcomes home sinners, restoring them to a place of honour. Jesus will not let his compassion stay with God or in heaven. He commands us: "Be merciful just as your Father is merciful" (Luke 6:36).

Jesus did a lot more than just feel compassion for those in today's Gospel story from Mark 6. His strong emotion moved him to act, far beyond what any shepherd would be expected to do for his sheep. The authentic shepherd, who models his or her life on Jesus, must love the people entrusted to him and imitate Jesus.

Where will we find such compassion for ourselves?

From time to time, despite our best intentions, we find ourselves among those in need, those who are like sheep without a shepherd. At times we ask ourselves: "Where on earth can we find this compassion to share with others?" I have learned that only in solitude before God, faced only with ourselves, can we learn the compassion of God. Perhaps it is not by accident that in the thick of his ministry and burdened by the unrelenting needs and demands of the crowd, Jesus called his disciples to join him in the desert: "Come away to a deserted place all by yourselves and rest a while" (Mark 6:31).

Could it not be the same for us, that away from the hustle and bustle of the everyday demands, we retreat in order to wrestle with our own hearts before God? And there we learn mercy and become in our day bearers of the compassion of Christ.

Leading people out

One of the most powerful and moving reflections on the theme of compassionate shepherding is found in Benedict XVI's inaugural homily of his Petrine Ministry on April 24, 2005:

"The pastor must be inspired by Christ's holy zeal: for him it is not a matter of indifference that so many people are living in the desert. And there are so many kinds of desert. There is the desert of poverty, the desert of hunger and thirst, the desert of abandonment, of loneliness, of destroyed love.

"There is the desert of God's darkness, the emptiness of souls no longer aware of their dignity or the goal of human life. The external deserts in the world are growing, because the internal deserts have become so vast. Therefore the earth's treasures no longer serve to build God's garden for all to live in, but they have been made to serve the powers of exploitation and destruction.

"The Church as a whole and all her Pastors, like Christ, must set out to lead people out of the desert, towards the place of life, towards friendship with the Son of God, towards the One who gives us life, and life in abundance."

This week may our prayer be for awareness, compassion and courage. Let us beg the Lord to make us more aware of the vast and growing deserts in which our contemporaries and perhaps even we are living today. Let us ask the Lord to give us his compassion for those who truly are sheep without shepherds. And let us pray for courage to help lead our friends out of their deserts and into the places of life and friendship with Christ, the Good Shepherd.

It Is Never Enough, Until We Give It Away

2 Kings 4:42-44;
Ephesians 4:1-6;
John 6:1-15

Today's Old Testament reading from 2 Kings 4:42-44 is a fitting prelude to John's version of the multiplication of the loaves and fishes (6:1-21). The author of Kings tells us about one of Elisha's servants who doubts that 20 loaves of barley is enough to feed 100 people. Elisha, however, trusts the promise of the Lord and overrules his servant. The miracle vindicates Elisha's trust. The numbers fed are modest in comparison with the feeding of the 5,000 in John's Gospel!

Bread is a symbol of the person and work of Jesus in John's great Eucharistic teaching in Chapter 6, and this Eucharistic theme continues over the next four weeks of Scripture readings. Today's Gospel is John's marvelous story of the multiplication of the loaves and fishes. The various accounts of the multiplication of loaves and fishes, two each in Mark and in Matthew and one each in Luke and in John, indicate the wide interest of the early Church in their Eucharistic gatherings (e.g., Mark 6:41; 8:6; 14:22); and recall also the sign of bread in Exodus 16; Deuteronomy 8:3-16; Psalm 78:24-25; 105:40; Wisdom 16:20-21. The miraculous event, recounted by the four evangelists, points forward to the idea of life in God's kingdom as a banquet at which the Messiah will preside.

Unique perspectives

Mark's readers saw this incident as an anticipation of the Last Supper (14:22) and the messianic banquet, both of which were celebrated in the community's Eucharists.

Matthew's addition of the number of people present and fed is significant, because the total figure could well have come to 20,000 or 30,000 people and the miracle is repeated again in 15:38. The sheer numbers of those fed give the feeding stories a distinct social character.

Luke links his feeding account with Jesus' prediction of his passion and his instructions about bearing one's cross daily (9:18-27). To celebrate the Eucharist in memory of Jesus (22:19) is to share not only his mission (9:1-6) but also his dedication and destiny, symbolized by the cross (9:18-27). The Eucharist is part of a journey in Luke's Gospel, nourishing and strengthening us for continuing faithfully in our way of life.

Johannine details

John's multiplication story is a central part of Jesus' important teaching on the Bread of Life (6:1-15). This story is immediately followed by Jesus' walking on water. John's multiplication story has been expanded in the introduction by the addition of 1) the vague chronological marker "after this"; 2) the specification of the place, Lake of Tiberias. This is also the place of the appearance of the risen Lord in John 21:1; 3) the motivation for the crowd – they have seen Jesus' healings (signs); and 4) the reference to the impending "Passover of the Jews."

As in other Johannine miracle stories, the initiative for this miracle clearly lies with Jesus. Philip does not perceive that Jesus' question is an appeal to his faith and simply refers to the amount of money required. Jesus teases Philip to have bigger dreams and better hopes rather than to reduce them down to reality. In verses 14-15, the crowds respond correctly that Jesus is the messianic prophet, but misunderstand what they are really saying. The true nature of Jesus' kingship, which is not that of a national liberator, will only be revealed at his trial (18:33-37; 19:12-15).

One unique Johannine touch is the role of the young boy in this miracle story. What human reason did not dare to hope became a reality with Jesus thanks to a young boy's generous heart.

Living bread

The multiplication of the loaves is an enduring image of the Eucharist. Jesus wanted to use this humble gift of a few loaves and fishes to feed a multitude, and more (12 baskets were left!). Logic and human reason often say to us, "We have no more than five loaves and two fish." But Jesus asks that even such meagre provisions as these, together with the trust and generosity of disciples of every age, be stretched to their limits. "Let's see. It will never be enough until we start to give it away."

For the believer, Jesus is much more than a miracle worker; he himself is heavenly food. The believer will never again experience hunger or thirst. As bread sustains life, Jesus will sustain all who approach him in faith. To acknowledge

Jesus as the living bread is the ultimate expression of God's love in Christ's death and glorification.

Prolonging the miracle

Whenever I read the miracle stories of the multiplication of the loaves and fishes, I recall these stirring words from Blessed Pope John Paul II's 1998 Apostolic Letter *Dies Domini* – On Keeping the Lord's Day (No. 71). These words illustrate what lies at the heart of today's miracle of the loaves and fishes and challenge each of us about our duties to truly put the Eucharist into practice in daily life: "The teachings of the Apostles struck a sympathetic chord from the earliest centuries, and evoked strong echoes in the preaching of the Fathers of the Church.

"St. Ambrose addressed words of fire to the rich who presumed to fulfill their religious obligations by attending church without sharing their goods with the poor, and who perhaps even exploited them: 'You who are rich, do you hear what the Lord God says? Yet you come into church not to give to the poor but to take instead.'

"St. John Chrysostom is no less demanding: 'Do you wish to honor the body of Christ? Do not ignore him when he is naked. Do not pay him homage in the temple clad in silk only then to neglect him outside where he suffers cold and nakedness. He who said: 'This is my body' is the same One who said: 'You saw me hungry and you gave me no food,' and 'Whatever you did to the least of my brothers you did also to me' … What good is it if the Eucharistic table is overloaded with golden chalices, when he is dying of hunger? Start by satisfying his hunger, and then with what is left you may adorn the altar as well.'

"These words effectively remind the Christian community of the duty to make the Eucharist the place where fraternity becomes practical solidarity, where the last are the first in the minds and attentions of the brethren, where Christ himself – through the generous gifts from the rich to the very poor – may somehow prolong in time the miracle of the multiplication of the loaves."

Questions for reflection

What does Jesus' Eucharistic presence mean for us? Does our participation in the weekly and daily celebrations of the Lord's meal transform us into people of gratitude, loving kindness, justice and charity? In what ways does the Eucharist symbolize the life we are living, and our life symbolize the Eucharist? How do we express gratitude? Is the Eucharist giving direction to our life?

Do we not often wonder where we shall get the means to accomplish what seems good and necessary? Today's miracle reveals the extraordinary resources of life within each of us. In order to sustain our hopes, we must believe in miracles. We must feast on the Body and Blood of the Lord for our real energy and life.

Give Us This Bread Always!

EIGHTEENTH SUNDAY IN ORDINARY TIME

Exodus 16:2-4, 12-15, 31a;
Ephesians 4:17, 20-24;
John 6:24-35

We can certainly understand God's frustration with his people in today's first reading from Exodus (16:2-4, 12-15).

The God of Israel has just delivered his people from slavery and has set them on the way to their promised land. Yet after crossing the Red Sea and celebrating their victory, the first recorded action in the Sinai proves to be grumbling and dissatisfaction, first over the bitter water at Mara (Exodus 15:22-27), and then more complaining and nostalgic longing for the fleshpots in the land of Egypt, where they were able to eat their fill!

Into this setting of ingratitude and lamentation, God rains down bread from heaven (manna) and quail for their food. The Exodus passage (16:2-4, 12-15) contrasts the nonbeliever (who grumbles that the manna and quail are meagre nourishment) with the believer (who sees these as God's generous gifts to the hungry).

A different kind of food

In today's Gospel text (John 6:24-35) that follows the miraculous multiplication of the loaves, Jesus says to the crowds who were seeking him: "Very truly I tell you, you are looking for me, not because you saw signs, but because you ate your fill of the loaves. Do not work for the food that perishes, but for the food that endures for eternal life, which the Son of Man will give you" (John 6:26-27).

Jesus' hearers continue the conversation and ask him, "What must we do to perform the works of God?" (John 6:28). Jesus answers: "This is the work of God, that you believe in him whom he has sent" (John 6:29). It is an exhortation to have faith in the Son of Man, in the giver of the food that does not perish. Without faith in him whom the Father has sent, it is not possible to recognize and accept this gift which does not pass away.

The miraculous multiplication of the loaves had not evoked the expected response of faith in those who had been eyewitnesses of that event. They wanted a new sign: "What sign are you going to give us then, so that we may see it and believe you? What work are you performing? Our ancestors ate the manna in the wilderness; as it is written, 'He gave them bread from heaven to eat'" (John 6:30-31). The disciples gathered around Jesus expecting a sign like the manna, which their ancestors had eaten in the desert. But Jesus exhorts them to expect something more than a mere repetition of the miracle of the manna, to expect a different kind of food. He says: "It was not Moses who gave you the bread from heaven, but it is my Father who gives you the true bread from heaven. For the bread of God is that which comes down from heaven and gives life to the world" (John 6:32-33).

Along with physical hunger there is within each of us another hunger, a more basic hunger, which cannot be satisfied by ordinary food. It is a hunger for life, a hunger for eternity, nostalgia for God. The sign of the manna was the proclamation of the coming of Christ who was to satisfy our hunger for eternity by himself becoming the "living bread" that "gives life to the world."

What is so startling about Jesus' remarks in this discourse is that he is not claiming to be another Moses, or one more messenger in a long line of human prophets. In giving us the bread of life, Jesus does not offer temporary nourishment; he gives us the eternal bread of his word. It will not pass away. It will nourish and give life forever. Jesus is this bread, and in offering to share it with us he calls us to faith in him.

Jesus invites us to "come to him," "believe in him," "look upon him," "be drawn to him," "hear him," and to "learn of him." All of these verbs invite the active response of our faith (cf. John 6:35, 37, 40, 44, 45). His word is nourishment for our faith.

Those who heard Jesus ask him to fulfill what had been proclaimed by the sign of the manna, perhaps without being conscious of how far their request would go: "Sir, give us this bread always" (John 6:34). How eloquent is this request! How generous and how amazing is its fulfillment! "I am the bread of life. Whoever comes to me will never be hungry, and whoever believes in me will never be thirsty."

Grumblings and ideologies

How difficult it was for Jesus' hearers to make this passage from the sign to the mystery indicated by that sign, from daily bread to the bread "which endures to eternal life"! Nor is it easy for us, the people of the 21st century to make such passages in our own life, from sign to mystery.

At times our grumblings and murmurings about the Eucharist and the Church often rise to fever pitch, not much different than the grumbling and murmuring of Israel in the desert. Excessive tensions arising from Church politics, gender issues, liturgical practices, language – all of these influence today's Eucharist – and can lead us to a feeling of God's absence.

Our Eucharistic celebrations are not taking place at Massah and Meribah – places of murmuring in the desert. We are often stuck in endless arguments between devotion and liturgy, or in a constant dispute between charity and justice: when devotion is treated as the enemy of liturgy and charity as the betrayer of justice, or when liturgy is reduced to private devotion and justice not recognized as constitutive to the Gospel.

Adoration rediscovered

Here is one concrete example to illustrate the above point about liturgy and devotion. Many of my generation have responded very negatively to the younger generation's rediscovery of Eucharistic adoration and devotion.

Benedict XVI has put a great emphasis on Eucharistic adoration and devotion in Catholic life. Many of us have failed to see that our public worship is intimately related to adoration, so much so that they could be considered as one. Piety and devotion can be springboards to mature faith. Each time we gather together to celebrate the Eucharist as the

Christian community, we profess, together with the whole Church, our faith in Christ the Eucharist, in Christ – the living bread and the bread of life.

At the 49th International Eucharistic Congress in Quebec City in 2008, Filipino Bishop Louis Antonio Tagle delivered a remarkable catechesis that concluded with a profound explanation of the meaning of authentic Adoration of the Eucharist (http://www.zenit.org/article-22964?l=english).

Bishop Tagle said: "In the Eucharist, the Church joins Jesus in adoring the God of life. But the practice of Eucharistic adoration enlivens some features of worship. We believe that the presence of Christ in the Eucharist continues beyond the liturgy. Adoration of the Blessed Sacrament connotes being present, resting, and beholding. In adoration, we are present to Jesus whose sacrifice is ever present to us. Abiding in him, we are assimilated more deeply into his self-giving. Beholding Jesus, we receive and are transformed by the mystery we adore. Eucharistic adoration is similar to standing at the foot of the Cross of Jesus, being a witness to his sacrifice of life and being renewed by it. The sacrifice or spiritual worship of Jesus on the cross is his supreme act of adoration."

This week let us ask ourselves: What does Jesus' Eucharistic presence mean for us? Does our participation in the weekly (and for some, daily) celebration of the Lord's meal transform us into people of gratitude, loving kindness and justice? Let us consider what Jesus requires of us who partake of the Eucharistic banquet. In what ways does the Eucharist symbolize the life we are living and our life symbolize the Eucharist?

How do we express gratitude? Is the Eucharist the spiritual exercise giving direction to our life?

May our Eucharistic celebrations continue to transform our parish communities and the society around us into a civilization of love! May they nourish in us a hunger and thirst for justice. May our longing for the Eucharist make us ever more patient and kind with one another. Let us pray that we may truly become what we receive in the Eucharistic meal.

Elijah's Power Food, and Ours

Nineteenth Sunday in Ordinary Time

1 Kings 19:4-8;
Ephesians 4:30–5:2;
John 6:41-51

I have always loved reading the Elijah cycle in the Book of Kings. The first book, Chapter 18, portrays Elijah as an invincible prophet who fearlessly stands up to king and prophets, but he remains extremely so human in the process! Today's first reading from 1 Kings 19 presents us with the great prophet who is vulnerable and subject to discouragement and fear.

Let us situate today's story in 1 Kings. In Chapter 19 we have the aftermath of Elijah's brilliant victory in the contest with Jezebel and the priests of Baal atop Mount Carmel. Just when Elijah should have been triumphant, he receives a message telling him of Jezebel's murderous intentions, and he is "afraid" (v 3). Elijah is persecuted for his faithfulness and for demanding total obedience to one God because such loyalty threatens the powers that be who have their own ideas about whom or what people should worship.

Israel's fiery prophet immediately flees south into the wilderness of the Negev Desert. His mood is one of defeat and desolation. After all he had done for the God of Israel, his victory now seems vitiated. He has not been given the divine protection he was promised and he only wants to die: "It is enough; now, O Lord, take away my life, for I am no

---

better than my ancestors." There, in the barren desert, Elijah lies down under a solitary broom tree and asks God to take his life, claiming that he is no better than his fathers. Elijah bemoans his discouragement at his lack of success in encouraging the Israelites to be faithful.

Energy from above

Suddenly, a messenger (angel) of the Lord awakens him and tells him to eat and drink. Whereas the wicked Jezebel sends a messenger of death to Elijah, the Lord God of Israel sends him a messenger of life, who serves Elijah food and water, two essentials for survival in the harsh wilderness.

Elijah eats, drinks, but then falls asleep again, indicating that he has not yet recovered from his lethargy or depression. The messenger wakes Elijah again and urges him to eat and drink, this time providing a reason, "otherwise the journey will be too much for you" (19:7).

What can we learn from Elijah in the desert wilderness? Here is a man who has given his life totally in faithfulness to the God of Israel. He has been totally "zealous for the Lord." His desperate cry, "I am no better than my ancestors" reveals a man who no longer believes in himself. He had believed himself to be a spectacularly exemplary servant of God. No one could outdo him in his zealousness. Now he believes it has been all in vain!

Dark night of the soul

Yet the God of Israel does not give up on Elijah. God's teaching moment begins when Elijah's famed resourcefulness runs out. Angels from God are needed to feed him in his weakness. Then God leads him through a time of reflection in the wilderness.

His journeying through Negev wilderness lasts for the significant time of forty days and forty nights. As the Hebrews wandered earlier in the wilderness in search of God, this most zealous prophet and servant of the Lord is led on a similar journey. Eventually Elijah comes to the sacred mountain of Horeb, where he spends the night in a dark cave. The dark cave and the dark night are reflective of his "dark night of the soul."

Mount Horeb is in some Old Testament traditions the name for Mount Sinai, the mountain associated with God's appearance. Forty days and nights in connection with Mount Sinai recalls the two sojourns of Moses on Sinai for forty days and nights (Exodus 24:18; 34:28).

The point of this moving story is not just that Elijah makes a physical trip to Mount Horeb or Mount Sinai, but rather something much more significant. In an act of sheer grace God intervenes, provides the prophet with life-giving food and water, and suggests a pilgrimage to the mountain that is the place forever associated with the source and essence of Israelite faith.

The Elijah story speaks powerfully to those who are worn-out, fearful, or in need of renewal and recommitment to their original call. The story suggests a way forward – eat and drink of God's life-giving sustenance, return to the core of faith, listen for God's still small voice. That may be the way to find new energy, new vision, and a new sense of purpose. Elijah must learn that God is not encountered in the sound and fury of loud and spectacular events. God will not be conjured up by the zealous or boisterous activity of the prophet who now stands quiet and broken atop the Lord's mountain.

Elijah discovers that God is encountered when the activity ceases and the words stop, when the heart is sad and the stomach is filled with pangs of hunger. When Elijah's mind and heart are finally empty of ambition and self-promotion, God is ultimately heard.

Bread of Life

For Elijah, for Jesus, and for us, bread is fundamental to life. Bread stands at the centre of life. Bread is life. And in today's Gospel (Jn. 6:41-51) we hear about Jesus who is the Bread of Life. Christ is life: He is the bread of life. To eat Jesus' body and to drink his blood means more than just to believe in him. The image of Jesus as the "bread of life" is at the heart of what renewal in the mystery of Christ is about.

When Jesus says that he is "the bread of life" his emphasis is not on the bread as such, but on himself as the "I" who declares it. Jesus is saying that what we long for to nourish our hungers is found in himself, the "I" who identifies his life with the bread he gives (cf. in 6:51). Jesus is more than mere bread for our bodily hunger. He is more than love to satisfy our emotional needs. He is the word that will satisfy our hunger for truth. He is bread for life itself; the total satisfaction for all our human hungers.

For all baptized believers the Eucharist is the primary way of celebrating and sustaining contact with the risen Lord. Let us consider for a moment the highly symbolic actions of Jesus as he gives us the living bread from heaven. Jesus took the bread. He has taken the bread of our lives and joined it with his own. Jesus blessed the bread. He has blessed us with his life. Baptism was the first moment of that blessing. Every other moment of contact with Jesus Christ is a deepening of that blessing.

Jesus broke the bread. Like Jesus, there are moments in our lives when we feel hurt, broken, lost, discouraged, disillusioned, empty, rejected and without energy and hope. We are like Elijah under the broom tree, waiting for our life to end. Yet even in these fractured moments, the Lord Jesus is present to us.

Jesus gave the bread. He gave of his time and his touch. He gave encouragement, but also his challenge. He gave both word and bread to feed and nourish. He gave most fully in giving himself. He gave till there was no more to give, declaring his life and work complete with the words, "It is finished" (John 19:30). Then bowing his head, he handed over his spirit, the same spirit he gave us when he appeared risen from the dead (cf. in 20:23).

In life, death, and resurrection, Jesus has given us a profound example, and challenges us to do the same. "Go and do likewise" is both a challenge and a commission. It is the commission to live the mystery of being bread blessed and broken for others. When life seems to be breaking apart, we should not forget the lesson of the bread broken for us. It cannot be broken without being firmly held in both hands. When it comes to the breaking of bread, or of our lives, both hold the challenge of the mystery of faith.

Let us pray that our sharing in the Eucharistic bread and wine may transform us more and more into what we eat and drink, and that we might truly become living bread, broken and shared with all people.

Health Food for the Soul

Proverbs 9:1-6;
Ephesians 5:15-20;
John 6:51-58

In chapter six of John's Gospel (v. 41-51), Jesus speaks of himself as "the living bread that came down from heaven" and invites his hearers to eat of this bread – that is, to believe in him.

He promises that those who do so will have eternal life. Jesus compares himself to the manna that came down from heaven to sustain the people of Israel in the wilderness. It is a vivid image that certainly evokes important memories for the people of Israel.

Then in John 6:51, Jesus says, "The bread that I will give for the life of the world is my flesh." Then his hearers ask: "How can this man give us his flesh to eat?" Did they respond in this way to give Jesus a chance to explain himself? Surely, they may have imagined, Jesus meant to say something else. After all, to eat someone's flesh appears in the Bible as a metaphor for great hostility (Psalms 27:2; Zechariah 11:9). The drinking of blood was looked upon as an abomination forbidden by God's law (Genesis 9:4, Leviticus 3:17; Deuteronomy 12:23).

Yet Jesus responds to the question by further explaining his initial declaration with explicit terms: "Unless you eat the flesh of the Son of Man and drink his blood, you have no life in you. Whoever eats my flesh and drinks my blood has eternal life, and I will raise them up on the last day; for my flesh is true food and my blood is true drink. Whoever eats my flesh and drinks my blood abides in me, and I in them."

No observant Jew would consider eating human flesh. We may ask ourselves: "Why couldn't Jesus continue using such pleasant terms as "abiding," "dwelling," "living in me" terminology? Was he advocating pure cannibalism with such vivid imagery and language?

Flesh and blood

Jesus makes his sacrifice on behalf of the world – not just Israel (see also John 3:16-17). The Hebrew expression "flesh and blood" means the whole person. To receive the whole Jesus entails receiving his flesh and blood. To encounter Jesus means, in part, to encounter the flesh and blood of him.

For those who receive Jesus, the whole Jesus, his life clings to their bones and courses through their veins. He can no more be taken from a believer's life than last Saturday's dinner can be extricated from one's body.

True reception of Jesus

In our cerebral approach to religion we often assume that what really matters is believing some important religious dogmas or truths. Receiving Jesus can be reduced to a matter of intellectual assent. There are times, however, when we can be particularly grateful that the presence of Christ is not something that can be recognized cerebrally, but can be received by other means as well.

The bread that Jesus used to feed the 5,000 on the mountaintop was something less than true bread, because it satisfied the people's hunger only momentarily. By way of contrast, Jesus' flesh and blood are true food because "whoever eats of this bread will live forever" (v 51) – and "has eternal life" (v 54).

"I am the living bread that came down from heaven" (v 51a). This "living bread" parallels the "living water" that Jesus offered the Samaritan woman (4:10). To eat of this bread, in this context, means the once-and-for-all action of accepting or believing in Christ.

Historical background

It is important to be aware of two things that were happening at the time of the writing of this Gospel that might have influenced John the Evangelist to emphasize the eating of Jesus' flesh and the drinking of his blood.

The first was the influence of Docetic and Gnostic heresies, both of which considered flesh to be evil and denied that Christ could have a physical body. The second was Jewish discrimination against Christian believers. Christians who observed the Lord's Supper were likely to be banned from synagogues.

The Eucharist fulfils the meaning hidden in the gift of manna. Jesus thus presents himself as the true and perfect fulfillment of what was symbolically foretold in the Old Covenant. Another of Moses' acts has a prophetic value: To quench the thirst of the people in the desert, he makes water flow from the rock. On the "feast of Tabernacles," Jesus promises to quench humanity's spiritual thirst: "Let anyone who is thirsty come to me and drink. As the Scripture has said, 'Out of the heart of the one who believes in me shall flow rivers of living water'" (John 7:37-38).

The ways we eat

Our eating style reflects and affects who and what we are. It identifies our approach to life. If we examine various societies and cultures, we see that each has its traditional foods and food rituals. "I am of Italian descent. I often eat spaghetti, lasagna, tortellini alla panna or pizza," or "I am a real American. I eat hamburgers, hot dogs, steak, coke, and French fries."

"I am Québecois. I feast on poutine and drink maple syrup." The French eat crepes, Belgians eat waffles, Chinese eat rice, Palestinians and Israelis eat falafel, the Swiss eat chocolate, and Inuit eat whale blubber. In short, the "way we eat" reveals how we identify ourselves. It reflects and often determines our worldview, our values, and our entire approach to life.

Foods are much more than just a collection of nutrients; they are a wealth of influences and connotations. Rare foods and spices are treasured as special culinary delights. Some foods are worshiped in various cultures as having an unusual holiness or are avoided altogether. The type of food we choose can affect our moods. Hot, spicy, or stimulating foods may influence many of us toward hot-temperedness or nervousness. Cooling foods can relax us and give us peace of mind. Foods can help us celebrate and can comfort us when we mourn. They are a sign of love and are a means of uniting people on many occasions.

The "ways we eat" are an important part of our heritage. The soul is not nourished by physical bread, as the body is. The food we eat is actually a combination of both a physical and a spiritual entity. The body is nourished by the physical aspects, or nutrients, contained in the foods we eat; the soul is nourished by the spiritual power which enlivens the physical substance of all matter, including food.

For all who seek the presence of Christ, Jesus' teaching in John's Gospel is good news indeed: "We are what we eat." We become what receive in the Eucharist. This week, let us examine our spiritual diets and look at the things that truly give us life, and those things that are junk foods that don't lead us to eternal life.

Do You Also Wish to Go Away?

Joshua 24:1-2a, 15-17, 18b;
Ephesians 4:32–5:2, 21-32;
John 6:53, 60-69

In today's Gospel (John 6:60-69), we hear of the mixed reactions of Jesus' disciples to the Bread of Life discourse that we have heard over the past weeks. Jesus provided bread, but his bread is not like the manna that God provided in the wilderness; this bread is himself, his very life; and those who eat it "will live forever" (verse 58).

As is often the case in John's Gospel, small, ordinary words such as bread and life are loaded with theological meaning. Centuries of Eucharistic theology and reflection give us a way to understand these words, but at the time they were first spoken, they were more than puzzling – they probably were offensive to some people. Rightly reading the mood of his audience, Jesus says, "Does this offend you?"

Jesus' challenge sets up a critical turning point in the Gospel. Not only are we told that one of Jesus' followers would betray him; we also learn that some of those who had been following Jesus "turned back and no longer went about with him" (v 66).

The group gets smaller as the stakes get higher. Whatever explanation Jesus gives, some choose to walk away, thus revoking their loyalty. John uses the word "disciples" for those who turn back. These were not casual or seasonal listeners:

They were disciples who knew him and were most likely known by him.

You too?

Then Jesus called the Twelve together and put the question to them straightforward: "Do you also wish to go away?"

Peter plays the role of spokesperson, just as he does in the other Gospels: "Lord, to whom can we go? You have the words of eternal life." While the words are different, this exchange is much the same as Peter's confession at Caesarea Philippi. There, Jesus asks, "Who do people say that I am?" – to which Peter responds, "You are the Christ" (Mark 8:27-30). In both cases, the miracle of the feeding is the backdrop for the crucial question: who is Jesus really?

Paul's marriage challenge

If we want to find out how the relationship between a man and woman in marriage should be according to the Bible, we must look at the relationship between Christ and the Church. In today's second reading from the letter to the community at Ephesus, Paul exhorts married Christians to a strong mutual love.

At the origin and centre of every Christian marriage, there must be love: "Husbands, love your wives, just as Christ loved the Church and gave himself up for her." Paul's teaching on Christian marriage was difficult then as it is today.

Holding with Genesis 2:24 that marriage is a divine institution (Ephesians 5:31), Paul sees Christian marriage as taking on a new meaning symbolic of the intimate relationship of love between Christ and the Church. The wife should serve her husband in the same spirit as that of the Church's service to Christ (Ephesians 5:22, 24), and the husband should care for his wife with the devotion of Christ to the Church (Ephesians 5:25-30).

Paul gives to the Genesis passage its highest meaning in the light of the union of Christ and the Church, of which Christ-like loyalty and devotion in Christian marriage are a clear reflection (Ephesians 5:31-33).

Parts of today's Ephesians reading can be problematic, especially when one takes the line, "wives, be subject to your husbands," out of context. Some have justified abuse of their spouse by taking this line (Ephesians 5:22) completely out of context. They have justified their bad behaviour, but the passage (v 21-33) refers to the mutual submission of husband and wife out of love for Christ: "Husbands should love their wives as they do their own bodies ... just as Christ loves the Church."

The Scriptures cannot be used to justify violence toward, or abuse of, any other human being. The Gospel calls all of us to show mutual care and respect to one another. This must be present in any healthy marriage or other committed relationship.

This mutual love and respect must also extend to relationships between nations and other groups of people. It must be reflected in the structures and rules of our society. Mutuality and loving, selfless service are the keys to an authentic, loving marriage, and of just relationships.

Foundations of society

In his encyclical, *Caritas in Veritate*, Benedict XVI writes: "It is thus becoming a social and even economic necessity once more to hold up to future generations the beauty of marriage and the family, and the fact that these institutions correspond to the deepest needs and dignity of the person.

"In view of this, states are called to enact policies promoting the centrality and the integrity of the family founded on marriage between a man and a woman, the primary vital cell of society, and to assume responsibility for its economic and fiscal needs, while respecting its essentially relational character" (44).

Though *Caritas in Veritate* is touted as a response to the current economic crisis, it is much more than that. A defence of family, the sanctity of life, a caution to not undermine the importance of human dignity: The Holy Father prudently explores each area, dissecting each topic on its own, as well as relating it to economics.

Regardless of any economic aspect, the wisdom shared concerning these areas stands on its own. It serves us well to take note of this as we strive for authentic human development. This is not some antiquated teaching or remnant of the past. It is the living foundation for the present and the future of humanity. And like many of Jesus' words, some will take offence at this and "walk away."

Without married people, we cannot build the future of society and the Church. I am convinced beyond any doubt that from solid families will come forth vocations to serve the

Church. The "vocation crisis" in many parts of the world is due in great part to the break up and dissolution of the family.

A scandalous teaching

The depth and significance of Christ's message, and the teaching of the Church, scandalizes, in the sense that it is often a stumbling block for the disbeliever and it is a test for the believer.

The theme of scandal in the New Testament is connected with faith, as free acceptance of the mystery of Christ. Before the Gospel we cannot remain indifferent, lukewarm or evasive: The Lord calls each of us personally asking us to declare ourselves for him (cf. Matthew 10:32-33).

When we are faced with the difficult teachings of Jesus and the Church, do we also wish to go away? Is it not true that many times, because of the complexity of the issues, and the pressures of the society around us, we may wish to "go away?"

Peter's response to Jesus' question – "Do you also wish to go away?" – in today's Gospel is striking. He doesn't say, "yes, of course," but he doesn't quite say "no" either.

Instead, in good Gospel-style, he answers back with another question: "To whom can we go?" It is not the most flattering answer in the world, but it is honest. Peter and the others stay with Jesus precisely because he has been a source of life for them. Jesus liberated them and has given them a new life.

Following Jesus and the teaching of the Church may not always be easy, or pleasant, or even totally comprehensible, but when it comes to the eternal-life business, there's not much out there in the way of alternatives.

This week let us not forget the words of Jesus: "Whoever eats me will live because of me." Let us give witness to our Catholic faith and to God's plan that marriage be the sacred union of one man and one woman, to family life as the foundation of our society.

Blessed are we if we do not take offence, but are led by these words to abundant life.

Caught Up in the Externals

Deuteronomy 4:1-2, 6-8;
James 1:17-18, 21-22, 27;
Mark 7:1-8, 14-15, 21-23

How many times have we heard, or perhaps even said ourselves: "So-and-so is a Pharisee." "That person is so Pharisaical."
"They are caught up in Pharisaism."

Today's Gospel (Mark 7:1-8, 14-15, 21-23) offers us a
good opportunity to understand the role of the Pharisees in
Judaism, and why Jesus and others had such strong feelings
against their behaviour. Who were the Pharisees of Jesus' time,
and who are their modern-day contemporaries?

Let me try to simplify a very complex topic to help us
understand today's Gospel. The Pharisees sought to make the
Law come alive in every Jew, by interpreting its commandments in such a way as to adapt them to the various spheres
of life.

The doctrine of the Pharisees is not opposed to that of
Christianity. At the time of Jesus, the Pharisees were the "con-
servative party" within Judaism. They adhered strictly to the
Torah and the Talmud and were outwardly very moral people.
They were the leaders of the majority of the Jews and were
revered by their followers for their religious zeal and dedication. Their main opposition was the party of the Sadducees,
who were the "liberal party" within Judaism. The Sadducees
were popular among the high-class minority.

Pharisees are mentioned when John the Baptist condemns them and the Sadducees in Matthew 3:7-10: "But when he saw many Pharisees and Sadducees coming for baptism, John said to them, 'You brood of vipers! Who warned you to flee from the wrath to come?'" Why would John the Baptizer say that the Pharisees, who were outwardly moral, zealous, and religious, were the offspring of vipers?

Jesus reserved his harshest words for the Pharisees as well. In Matthew 16:6, Jesus warned the disciples, "Watch out and beware of the yeast of the Pharisees and Sadducees." What were the disciples to beware of? Were they to beware of the immorality of the Pharisees and Sadducees?

Adherence to the law

The Pharisees in Jesus' time promoted adherence to the law with a genuine interior response and advocated ordinary day-to-day spirituality. There were some Pharisees who were caught up only in external prescriptions, but they would have been criticized by other Pharisees even as the prophet Isaiah criticized hypocrisy in the past. Similarly, Jesus reprimanded aberrant Pharisees occasionally and had some clashes with them over his reinterpretation of the law. Jesus did not condemn Pharisaism as such or all Pharisees.

The Pharisees "trusted in themselves that they were righteous"(Luke 18:9). They believed that their own works – their doing what God commands and their abstaining from what God forbids – were what gained and maintained God's favour and recommended them to God. The Pharisees self-righteously and hypocritically despised all others who did not meet the same standard of law keeping that they met.

They would not eat with the tax collectors and other sinners, because they were self-righteously aloof. They spent their time murmuring about who was eating and drinking with Jesus. Jesus said to them, "Those who are well have no need for a physician, but those who are sick; I have come to call not the righteous but sinners to repentance" (Luke 5:31-32).

No etiquette lesson!

In today's Gospel passage (Mark 7:1-8, 14-15, 21-23), the Pharisees and scribes come from Jerusalem to investigate Jesus. Jesus abolishes the practice of ritual purity and the distinction between clean and unclean foods. The watchdogs of religious tradition cite Jesus for running a rather lax operation! Some of his disciples were eating with unwashed hands (Mark 7:2). Pharisees and scribes seize this infraction of the law and challenge Jesus, "Why do your disciples not live according to the tradition of the elders, but eat with defiled hands?" (v 5).

Jesus doesn't respond with an etiquette lesson or an explanation of personal hygiene. Instead, he calls the Pharisees and scribes what they are: "you hypocrites" (v 6). Quoting Isaiah, Jesus exposes the condition of the legalists' hearts. They cling to human precepts and put their trust in the traditions of their elders over the commandment of God (v 8).

Against the Pharisees' narrow, legalistic, and external practices of piety in matters of purification (Mark 7:2-5), external worship (7:6-7), and observance of commandments, Jesus

---

sets in opposition the true moral intent of the divine law (7:8-13).

But he goes beyond contrasting the law and Pharisaic interpretation of it. Mark 7:14-15 in effect sets aside the law itself in respect to clean and unclean food. Jesus' point is well taken – and most Pharisees would have agreed – that internal attitude is more important than the externals of the law.

Pharisaical notion of sin

Jesus rejects the Pharisees' and the scribes' notion of sin. For Jesus, sin is the human spirit gone wrong, not a failure to distinguish between types of food. Jesus' attitude toward sin is consistent with his views regarding the Sabbath. The letter of the law without compassion is dehumanizing.

We can see how Jesus wants his message to be made known to the Pharisees and scribes (v 1-8), the crowd ("Listen to me, all of you, and understand" v 14-15) and his disciples (v 21-23, see also v 17). It is good news to all that God doesn't desire legalism. Instead, because of what God has done in Jesus Christ, the Father offers a new kind of life. One doesn't have to worry about how well one is obeying the rules and keeping oneself clean.

Having been made clean, we are now free to use our hands to serve others. We might even get them dirty in the process. God gives freedom from the law. God offers his grace. That is the same good news we get to share as we serve the legal-minded, the crowds, and even the disciples of Jesus who are around us.

Contemporary Pharisees

Who are the modern-day Pharisees and their followers? The blind modern-day Pharisees and their blind followers are very religious, moral, zealous people. They strive to keep God's law, and they are zealous in their religious duties. They diligently attend Church every Sunday. They are hardworking, outwardly upright citizens. They keep themselves from and preach against moral evil.

In addition to being moral and religious and zealous, modern-day Pharisees and their followers do not believe that salvation is conditioned on the work of Christ alone; instead, they believe that salvation is ultimately up to human efforts and what the sinner adds to Christ's work!

In contrast to the modern-day Pharisees and their followers, true Christians are those who boast in Christ crucified and no other, meaning that they believe that Christ's work ensured the salvation of all whom He represented and is the only thing that makes the difference between salvation and condemnation. They know that their own efforts form absolutely no part of their acceptance before God. They rest in Christ alone as their only hope, knowing that it is the work of Christ by the grace of God that guarantees salvation.

Jesus showed that only those who were sinners in need of a healer, who do not have righteousness in themselves, who are devoid of divine entitlement, who do not deserve to be in fellowship with God, are the ones He came to call to repentance.

The medicine of mercy

Whenever I hear Jesus' words about legalism in today's Gospel, I cannot help but recall with gratitude and emotion Blessed Pope John XXIII. In his historic, opening address on October 11, 1962, at the beginning of the momentous Second Vatican Council, Blessed John XXIII made it clear that he did not call Vatican II to refute errors or to clarify points of doctrine. The Church today, he insisted, must employ the "medicine of mercy rather than that of severity."

The "Good Pope" as he was called, rejected the opinions of those around him who were "always forecasting disaster." He referred to them as "prophets of gloom" who lacked a sense of history, which is "the teacher of life." Divine Providence, he declared, was leading the world into a new and better order of human relations. "And everything, even human differences, leads to the greater good of the Church."

"Papa Roncalli" was a human being, more concerned with his faithfulness than his image, more concerned with those around him than with his own desires. With an infectious warmth and vision, he stressed the relevance of the Church in a rapidly changing society and made the Church's deepest truths stand out in the modern world. He knew that the letter of the law without compassion is dehumanizing.

"Papa Giovanni" was beatified by his successor, John Paul II (who has also been beatified) in 2000. May he soften the hearts of the modern-day Pharisees and Sadducees who are alive and well in the Church and world today!

Quality Communication

Isaiah 35:4-7;
James 2:1-5;
Mark 7:31-37

In the magnificent piece of biblical poetry in Isaiah 35:4-7 (today's first reading) the prophet Isaiah announces the end of the Babylonian captivity.

The Exodus of God's people from bondage in Egypt became a model for thinking about salvation and a symbol of the great pilgrimage of the human family towards God. The prophet Isaiah encountered a dispirited community of exiles. Isaiah responded by recalling the joyous memories of the Exodus from Egypt.

A second exodus is in store, symbolized by the healing granted to the blind, the lame, and the mute, and new life to the dead. Delivered and saved by God, all peoples shall return to their own land by way of the desert, in a new exodus. Isaiah prophecies that there shall be one, pure road, and it will be called the way of holiness upon which the redeemed shall walk.

In the midst of the desert, streams will break forth. God's saving power also embraces afflicted humans, healing every ill that comes upon people. Isaiah addressed specific afflictions that God would heal: "Then the eyes of the blind shall be opened, and the ears of the deaf unstopped; then the lame shall leap like a deer, and the tongue of the mute sing for joy."

Isaiah's prediction of this abundant, new life underlies Mark's understanding of Jesus' cure of "a deaf man who had an impediment in his speech" (Mark 7:31-37). Mark's story of the healing of this hearing and speech impaired man invites us to consider some important points about sickness and suffering in the New Testament.

Sick people in the Bible are those who have fallen from an appropriate human state or condition of human integrity or wholeness. Jesus heals people by restoring them to a proper state: Those who are leprous are made clean, blind people see, mute persons speak, etc.

We have little information about how Jesus' healings episodes were accomplished. Jesus did not perform miracles as someone waving a magic wand or clicking his fingers. The man cured by Jesus was deaf and dumb; he could not communicate with others, hear his voice and express his feelings and needs. The sigh uttered by Jesus at the moment of touching the ears of the deaf man tells us that he identified with people's suffering; he participated deeply in their misfortune and made it his own burden.

"Ephphatha, Be opened!"

The early Church was so impressed by the healing miracle of the deaf man that it attached deep significance to it, incorporating the Lord's action into the Baptismal Rite of new Christians. To this day, the minister of baptism puts his fingers into our ears and touches the tip of our tongue, repeating Jesus' word: "Ephphatha, Be opened!" He has made both the deaf hear and the dumb speak.

We learn by hearing and listening

Sight deals with things, while hearing deals with human beings. Sight has to do with science, with observation, with objectivity. Hearing has to do with personal relationships, with subjectivity. When I use my eyes to look at people or things, I am in complete control of the information that comes to me, for I can shut my eyes when I wish. When I am reading the words of scripture by myself, I can close my eyes and stop reading. But the ear is unlike the eye. I cannot shut my ear. The only way I can stop the sound is to leave the room!

We learn about other people by hearing and listening to what they have to say. Language reveals the inside of another person, something sight can never do. If we want to learn about God, we must listen to his Word with all our heart, all our soul and all our mind.

When we read the Bible, do we "hear" what it says? The Bible does not tell us to read the Word of God but to hear it, to listen to it. That is the great Jewish prayer: "Shema, Israel," "Hear, O Israel." Someone else must read the Word so that I may hear it and truly understand it.

Biblical faith cannot be individualistic but must be communal. Speaking and hearing involve mutual submission. Mutual respect and submission is the essence of community, and the only way I can get away from hearing is to leave the room, to leave the community and go off by myself. Sadly this is the case for many who have left the Church community and claim to have found freedom, autonomy, and truth in solitude, away from the community of faith!

What they have found is not solitude, but loneliness, selfishness and rugged individualism. Authentic hearing and listening involve submission to authority and membership in community.

Physical and spiritual deafness

The healing stories reflect Jesus' intimate, powerful relationship with God and his great compassion. He healed with words, touch and physical means. Physical deafness and spiritual deafness are alike; Jesus confronted one type in the man born deaf, the other type in the Pharisees and others who were unreceptive of his message. Jesus was concerned not only with physical infirmity but also spiritual impairment and moral deafness.

Our contemporary world has grown deaf to the words of Jesus, but it is not a physical deafness, it is a spiritual deafness caused by sin. We have become so used to sin that we take it as normal and we have become deafened and blinded to Jesus and his daily call to us.

If deafness and dumbness consist in the inability to communicate plainly with one's neighbour or to have good relationships, then we must acknowledge that each of us is in some way impaired in our hearing and speech. What decides the quality of our communication, hearing and speech is not simply to speak or not to speak or hear, but to do so or not to do so out of love.

We are blind and deaf when we show favouritism or discrimination because of the status and wealth of other people (see James 2:1-5). We fail to recall that divine favour consists in God's election and promises (James 2:5).

We are deaf when we do not hear the cry for help raised to us and we prefer to put indifference between our neighbour and ourselves. In doing so we oppress the poor and blaspheme the name of Christ (James 2:6-7).

Parents are deaf when they do not understand that certain dysfunctional behaviours of their children betray deep-seated cries for attention and love.

We are deaf when we turn inward and close ourselves to the world because of selfishness, pride, resentment, anger, jealousy and our inability to forgive others.

We are deaf when we refuse to recognize those who suffer in the world around us, and do not acknowledge glaring situations of inequality, injustice, poverty and the devastation of war.

We are deaf when we refuse to hear the cry of the unborn, of those whose lives are in danger because they are elderly, handicapped, and chronically ill, while others wish to end their lives out of misguided mercy.

Beethoven's deafness

The German composer and virtuoso pianist Ludwig van Beethoven (1770-1827) was one of the most loved composers of all time. What I never knew until recently was that Beethoven started losing his hearing at the age of 28. The deafness gave Beethoven insights into that which existed beyond that which could be seen and heard.

Beethoven was aware of the oneness of music with God from a very early age. And he was conscious of this while composing his music. "Ever since my childhood my heart and soul have been imbued with the tender feeling of goodwill. And I have always been inclined to accomplish great things." In many of his letters Beethoven expresses his desire to serve God and humanity with his music. "Almighty God, you see into my heart … and you know it's filled with love for humanity and a desire to do good."

Beethoven's life is a paradox. On one hand, his solitary life was burdened by his deafness and on the other his spiritual insights flashed through his music. Many a times his deafness drove him to the edge and he cursed it. Yet, he also accepted it. It may have been out of frustration, but there was an acceptance of the divine will.

Today may the words Jesus spoke over the deaf man be addressed once again to each of us: "Ephphatha, Be opened!" May our ears, eyes and hearts be opened to the Gospel!

Affirmation, Identity and Purpose
of Jesus' Mission

TWENTY-FOURTH SUNDAY IN ORDINARY TIME

Isaiah 50:5-9;
James 2:14-18;
Mark 8:27-35

Today's Gospel story (Mark 8:27-35) is about affirmation, identity and purpose of Jesus' mission. Mark makes this episode the centrepiece of his Gospel. It comes immediately after Jesus' healing of the blind man of Bethsaida.

This restoration of sight must surely set the scene for Peter's confession of faith and the glorious moment of the Transfiguration. Jesus' nature is now gradually revealed to the disciples. Their blindness is cured but they still do not understand the full meaning of what they see. From this point on, everything in Mark's Gospel moves toward the crucifixion.

If there was ever a "turning point" in Mark's account of Jesus' public ministry, it is today's story. During my graduate studies in Israel in the 1990s, I had the privilege of working closely with the Israeli archeological team on the excavations in Caesarea Philippi, now known as "Banias" referring back to "Paneas" or the Greek god Pan. Sexual excess and violence ran rampant in this centre for the worship of the Greek god Pan.

At the time of Jesus, a fertility cult was thriving in this pagan temple on the border of northern Israel and Syria at the foot of majestic Mount Hermon. Jesus and his disciples entered the area of Caesarea Philippi as part of a long journey from their familiar surroundings.

Caesarea Philippi had been built by Philip, another generation of the Herodian family, and it was a garrison town for the Roman army. Here in this centre of pagan worship to the Greek god Pan, Jesus asks about their understanding of his identity. Jesus asks what people are saying about him. How do they see his work? Who is he in their minds? Probably taken aback by the question, the disciples dredge their memories for overheard remarks, past conversations, opinions and gossip circulating in the fishing towns of the lake area. Jesus himself is aware of some of what is being said and knows only too well the hurtful attitudes of his own townsfolk of Nazareth.

In response to Jesus' question, the disciples list a whole series of labels that people have applied to Jesus. These names reveal the different expectations held about him. Some thought of him as an Elijah, working toward a real confrontation with the powers that be. Some saw him more like Jeremiah, no less vehement but concentrating more on the inner journey, the private side of life.

Jesus pursues the question further – "Who do you say that I am?" and Peter responds, "You are the Christ" of the one true God. Jesus acknowledges this identification but forbids them from making his messianic role known to avoid confusing it with ambiguous contemporary ideas associated with that title. Then Jesus goes on to say, somewhat enigmatically, that the Son of Man must suffer, be rejected, die, and rise again.

The concept of Messiah in Judaism

There was no single concept of "Messiah" in Judaism. The idea of Messiah "anointed one" as an ideal king descended from David is the earliest known to us, but in the Maccabaean period (163-63 B.C.) the Greek Testaments of the Twelve Patriarchs give evidence of belief in a Messiah from the tribe of Levi, to which the Maccabaean family belonged. The Dead Sea Scrolls contain various ideas: a priestly Messiah and the (lay) Messiah of Israel; a prophet like Moses (Deuteronomy 18:18-19) who is also the star coming out of Jacob (Numbers 23:15-17); but also the Davidic Messiah. Melchizedek is a deliverer also, but is not called Messiah.

To proclaim Jesus as the Messiah was a loaded and dangerous statement. It was all that Jesus' enemies needed to use against him, and already there were many who were ready to enlist under the banner of a royal pretender. But, far more than this, such a role was not Jesus' destiny. He would not and could not be that kind of militaristic or political Messiah.

Identifying Jesus' role today

The struggle to identify Jesus and his role as Messiah continues today. Some say individual Christians and the whole Church should be Elijah figures, publicly confronting systems, institutions and national policies. That was the way Elijah saw his task. Read the First Book of Kings (Chapters 17 to 21) to see what Elijah endured. Those filled with violence don't usually bring about peace and justice in situations that are terribly unjust and wrong. Some say, like Jeremiah, that the reign of

Christ, through his Church, is the personal and private side of life. And there are indeed many who would like to reduce religion and faith to a private affair in our world today.

Jesus probes beyond both approaches and asks, "You, who do you say I am." In Peter's answer, "You are Christ," blurted out with his typical impetuosity, we are given a concept that involves both of the above ideas and goes beyond them. The Messiah came into society, and into individual lives, in a total way, reconciling the distinction between public and private. The quality of our response to this question is the best gauge of the quality of our discipleship. Everyone at some stage must come to Caesarea Philippi and answer the question, "You, who do you say I am?"

Some facts about Jesus

As we continue to give answer to the question: "Who is Jesus for us?" let us recall certain facts about Jesus' background, identity and mission that have prepared the mission of the Church in the world today:

1) Jesus was born of political tribe of Judah – not the priestly tribe of Levi nor the priestly family of Zaddok. Jesus was not a politician.

2) Jesus did, however, have a keen sense of politics. World mission cannot be undertaken independently without serious interaction with politics.

3) Jesus established himself at Capernaum rather than at Qumran in the desert or in some remote village or place away from the thick of things. In Capernaum, on the northwest shore of the Sea of Galilee, there was a main

road, tax collectors, and dealings with the Roman centurion. Jesus was very much at home in Capernaum, not in Jerusalem.

4) Jesus bonded himself with the unclean, the sick and dying, with sinners, and those living on the fringes of society. Through his life, Jesus puts biblical justice into practice in proclaiming the Beatitudes. Authentic justice is a bonding of one's self with the sick, the disabled, the poor and the hungry. But he did not neglect others as well. He dined with the rich and the mighty as well as with the poor and downtrodden. He befriended sinners and the wretched of his times – never condoning their behavior, but inviting them to an alternative lifestyle. He teaches us that by "being with people" he also teaches and heals. His human solidarity with the unclean, the unjust and sinners also saves.

5) Jesus did not preach the political kingdom of David but the Kingdom of God. He had a great ability to appeal to everything and incorporate everything into his vision of kingdom. During his lifetime, he only tried to fulfill the hopes of Israel. The Good News he preached was ultimately about love. Contrary to some popular opinions still around today, Jesus was not a social revolutionary. He did not denounce injustice, but confronted it with love. It is striking how many of his parables assume situations of injustice, not to condemn the injustice but to show the zeal, ingenuity and perseverance of the unjust as a model for those who would live by love. Still, those who lived by injustice made no mistake when they recognized in Jesus

and in those who followed him a fundamental challenge to their way of life.

Following Jesus today

Jesus' words at the end of today's Gospel "Whoever wants to become my follower, let him deny himself and take up his cross and follow me. For whoever wants to save their life will lose it, but whoever loses their life for my sake, and for the sake of the Gospel, will save it." (v 34-35) challenge all believers to authentic discipleship and total commitment to himself through self-renunciation and acceptance of the cross of suffering, even to the sacrifice of life itself. The Way of the Cross was not for Jesus alone but also for everyone who professed to follow him. There might be victory and glory ahead, but it was only for those who could take up the Cross. If Peter or anyone else should reject this demand it meant to be on the side of Satan. Life seen as mere self-centred earthly existence and lived in denial of Christ ends in destruction, but when lived in loyalty to Christ, despite earthly death, it arrives at fullness of life.

The Meaning of Christian Wisdom

TWENTY-FIFTH SUNDAY IN ORDINARY TIME

Wisdom 2:12, 17-20;
James 3:16-4:3;
Mark 9:30-37

The picture of the righteous one in today's first reading from the Book of Wisdom is based on the fourth Servant Song (Isaiah 52:13-53:12), as well as on Isaiah 42:1 and Psalm 22:8. Though the Book of Wisdom was not accepted into the canon by the rabbis of Palestine, nonetheless it seems to have influenced the writers of the New Testament, especially in their portrait of Jesus, the righteous one who was unjustly condemned.

The haunting description of the wicked who lie in wait for the righteous in today's first reading (Wisdom 2:12 and 17-20) leaves the hearers shocked. The thoughts and actions of the wicked are cold and calculated: "Let us see if his words are true, and let us test what will happen at the end of his life; for if the righteous one is God's son, God will help him, and will deliver him from the hand of his adversaries. Let us test him with insult and torture, so that we may find out how gentle he is, and make trial of his forbearance. Let us condemn him to a shameful death, for, according to what he says, he will be protected" (2:17-20).

The righteous one is attacked because his lifestyle is a condemnation of the wicked: "Who reproaches us for sins against the law" (2:12). The righteous one's fidelity is vindicated. He

---

does not die because he shares community with God. The righteous person is characterized by gentleness and patience, is tested, persecuted and even killed by the self-confident wicked. They resolve to persecute the righteous one because his life and words are a reproach to them (2:12-16), and they determine to test the claims of the righteous one (17-20). The wicked invite death by their evil deeds.

Who is wise among you?

The question introduced beginning at James 3:13 frames the entire discussion: "Who is wise and understanding among you?" In other words, how is wisdom perceived? James (3:13-4:3) addresses the symptoms of wisdom, both godly wisdom and another kind of wisdom, which is "earthly, unspiritual, devilish" (3:15). With 4:4, James spells out a sharp dichotomy between the wise and the unwise, characterizing the wise person as one who is an enemy of the world and the unwise as one who is "an enemy of God" (4:4). "Wisdom from above is first pure, then peaceable, gentle, willing to yield, full of mercy and good fruits, without a trace of partiality or hypocrisy" (3:17).

True Christian wisdom is dedicated to others; jealousy and strife are self-centred. This passage makes it clear that we should imitate wisdom rather than fame and wealth.

Ingredients

Today's Gospel passage (Mark 9:30-37) is the second of the Passion predictions of Jesus in Mark's Gospel. Jesus' announcement of his passion and death leaves the disciples without words. In the meantime, they argue who was the most important among them. We find the same pattern as in last week's Gospel – the prediction, misunderstanding, and instruction on the nature of discipleship.

For Mark, these scenes contain all the ingredients of Christian wisdom. Like the other predictions, today's passage is followed by a series of sayings on discipleship (9:30-37). In this brief discussion with Jesus, three features of the disciples are revealed.

First, even after failure, the disciples are singled out for special instruction. The immediate preceding incident details the inability of the disciples to help the father and his son who was troubled with an unclean spirit (9:14-29). Jesus scolds them harshly, since their failure has led to another confrontation with the scribes: "How much longer must I be among you?" (9:19). Yet the weakness of the disciples has not diminished his zeal to prepare them for life in the Kingdom of God.

Second, the disciples find Jesus' message baffling. This is the second time that Jesus predicts his destiny in Jerusalem, yet the disciples fail to understand and are so intimidated that they will not even ask any questions (9:32). When Jesus asks them what they are arguing about on the road, they were so embarrassed that they had nothing to say. They may not have understood much but they knew enough that their argument was completely out of order. They are baffled and humiliated. But Jesus has not given up on them yet.

The third thing that happens to the disciples is that they learn a profound lesson about what it means to be servant. When Mark uses the word "servant" in today's Gospel, he is using the Greek word which also means deacon. This word is first used of the waiters who serve the water-made-wine at the wedding feast at Cana (John 2:5, 9). Matthew uses it for the king's servants in the parable of the marriage feast (Matthew 22:13). St. Paul describes himself as a servant of the Gospel (Colossians 1:23; Ephesians 3:7), servant of the Church (Colossians 1:25), servant of the new covenant in the Spirit (2 Corinthians 6:4). John uses it of Jesus' adherents in general; they are his "deacons," his servants (John 12:26).

Greatness redefined

The whole notion of greatness is redefined for the disciples. New categories are established for determining success and failure, winning and losing, achievement and unfulfillment. At this point Jesus introduces the child into their midst. It is not the child's naïveté or innocence, trustfulness or playfulness that is highlighted here, but the child's lowly status, as one always under the authority of another and without rights. Jesus forges a new system of relationships: welcome the little child in my name and you welcome me; welcome me and you are welcoming no less than God himself. A communion of hospitality is established between the little child, Jesus, and God.

The child is an apt symbol for powerlessness and total reliance on others. Mark teaches us to welcome the powerless and the disenfranchised. Through this gesture, Jesus illustrates the qualities of the little child within each of us. Jesus possessed the child within in himself and he expects nothing less than these childlike qualities from his disciples.

The disciples become mirrors in which we see ourselves all too clearly. Their failures, their inability to understand typify the patterns of future generations of disciples like us who are also slow to understand the radical message of Jesus.

Wisdom and virtue

One of the profound, universal lessons about acquiring true wisdom was taught by the Blessed Pope John Paul II during his historic address to the General Assembly of the United Nations in New York City on October 5, 1995. Those words still ring in my heart and mind today. Addressing the leaders of the nations of the world, the Holy Father said:

"We must overcome our fear of the future. But we will not be able to overcome it completely unless we do so together. The 'answer' to that fear is neither coercion nor repression, nor the imposition of one social 'model' on the entire world. The answer to the fear which darkens human existence at the end of the 20th century is the common effort to build the civilization of love, founded on the universal values of peace, solidarity, justice, and liberty. And the 'soul' of the civilization of love is the culture of freedom: the freedom of individuals and the freedom of nations, lived in self-giving solidarity and responsibility.

"We must not be afraid of the future. We must not be afraid of man. It is no accident that we are here. Each and every human person has been created in the 'image and likeness' of the One who is the origin of all that is. We have within us the capacities for wisdom and virtue. With these gifts, and with the help of God's grace, we can build in the next century and the next millennium a civilization worthy of the human person, a true culture of freedom. We can and must do so! And

---

in doing so, we shall see that the tears of this century have pre-pared the ground for a new springtime of the human spirit."

Let us pray that the Lord will bring to harvest the seeds of righteousness, wisdom and virtue sown in human hearts. Without these gifts, the civilization of love and the culture of freedom for which we all long will not be possible.

The Importance of Self-Criticism and Humility

Twenty-Sixth Sunday in Ordinary Time

Numbers 11:25-29;
James 5:1-6;
Mark 9:38-43, 45, 47-48

The biblical prophet is one who has received a divine call to be a messenger and interpreter of the Word of God. The word that comes to the prophet compels him to speak.

Amos asks: "The Lord God has spoken; who can but prophesy?" (Amos 3:8). Jeremiah, despondent because of his unrelieved message of woe to the people he loved would stifle the word: "If I say, 'I will not mention him, or speak any more in his name,' then within me there is something like a burning fire shut up in my bones; and I am weary with holding it in, and I cannot" (Jeremiah 20:9). Whatever the form of the message, the true Israelite prophet's vision of God has permeated the manner of his thoughts so that he sees things from God's point of view and is convinced that he so sees them. Fundamental to the mission of the prophet is obedience to God's Word.

Would that all the Lord's people were prophets!

In today's first reading from Numbers (11:25-29), God sent the spirit of prophecy upon others who took Moses by surprise. Moses had earlier complained to God that he could not provide for Israel in the desert all by himself. To alleviate the situation, God promised to confer Moses' prophetic spirit on 70 elders. Even though Eldad and Medad were not present in

---

the camp when God conferred Moses' spirit, they still received the gift and began to prophesy.

When Moses' aide, Joshua, wished to squelch the so-called rebellion against authority, Moses replies: "Are you jealous for my sake? Would that all the Lord's people were Prophets, and that the Lord would put his spirit on them!" (Numbers 11:29). Moses is pleased that the spirit of prophecy is shared with those not immediately present in the first commissioning of the elders. Joshua is upbraided for his jealousy. Spiritual authority can lead to serious abuses. It must be handled carefully, humbly and justly. The lesson is that God's ability to share the spirit is not restricted. God is the measure.

The present worthlessness of wealth

The severe denunciation of the unjust rich in today's second reading from the Letter of James (5:1-6) is reminiscent of the Old Testament prophets (e.g., Amos 8:4-8). It is not intended to influence the rich to whom it is rhetorically addressed, but is rather a salutary warning to the faithful of the terrible fate of those who abuse riches and perhaps also a consolation to those now oppressed by the rich (James 2:5-7). The identical mode of introduction in 5:1-6 and 4:13-17 and the use of direct address throughout indicate the parallelism of the two sections. However, the present passage is harsher in tone and does not seem to allow the chance for repentance. In 5:2-3, the perfect tense of the verbs used (rotted, moth-eaten, rusted) probably indicate the present worthlessness of wealth.

Furthermore, although silver and gold do not actually rust (verse 3), the expression used for them indicates their basic worthlessness.

This reading from James does not parallel the other two readings, especially in the matter of spiritual gifts manifesting themselves outside the immediate circle of Jesus' disciples. Nevertheless it offers hard words against the wealthy who abused their workers and withheld wages as well as insight into abuse of power. James is speaking explicitly of the secular realm of employment, salaries and just recompense for work. The author of James maintains that the rich have mistreated their employees. Since they withheld the wages that were due, their silver and gold will corrode and their garments will fall prey to ravaging moths. The wealthy have not realized that God is the God of the poor, and intercedes on their behalf.

Problems in Mark's church community

Today's Gospel passage (Mark 9:38-43, 45, 47-48) is rather loosely put together and seems to reflect the problems of Mark's church community. First there is the exchange between John and Jesus about the foreign exorcist (9:38), followed by Jesus' rejection of the elitism of the disciples (v 39-40). In the second part (v 41), anyone who gives the disciple a drink will belong to Christ; in the third part (v 42), Jesus holds up the little ones as totally dependent on God, whom no one may lead astray.

There is a certain irony about Jesus' explanation of the disciples' action in trying to stop the foreign exorcist. In 9:14-29, the disciples, themselves, fail to exorcise an unclean spirit from a young boy and are sharply rebuked by Jesus. Now they want to restrain a successful exorcist simply because he is not part of their own group. The issue is clearly not whether the exorcist is acting in the name and power of Jesus, but whether he is part of their own chosen establishment. The exclusivist attitudes of the disciples are exposed for all to see. The success of the foreign exorcist is a threat to the status of the "official" disciples! Jesus answers with an inclusive word, and yet one that realistically recognizes the problem of unauthorized ministries (9:39). The disciples need to nurture the gifts of generosity and graciousness.

The need for self-criticism

In the second half of the passage, we find a miscellaneous collection of sayings that call for a stance of self-criticism. The disciples are directed to reflect on their own style of life and ministry. Do any of their words or actions serve as stumbling blocks for the children of the Church? Mark uses words of Jesus against scandal and the misuse of one's hands, eyes and feet. Jesus does not mandate mutilation. He has a typically Semitic way of speaking – graphic, vivid, even exaggerated. Nothing, no one comes before Christ. Jesus' command to "cut it off" is not mutilation, but rather an invitation to liberation. It liberates us to love without reservation, not trapped in the self-love where everything and perhaps everyone, even God, himself, must revolve around me. The fascinating paradox of this story is this: The more we focus on the God who lives in us, on the people God cherishes in a special way because they are more needy, and on the earth that God saw as being "very good" (Genesis 1:31), the richer will be our delight in ourselves. Human life is a matter of relationships: with God, with people, with earth.

Despite its disjointedness, today's Gospel passage provides a strong antidote to the ever-present temptation to overestimate one's own position as the chosen of God. Human nature tends to be judgmental. Sometimes our inclination to judge results in elitism, concluding that others are not worthy of our company. We make difficulties, not thinking of others but blindly plunging ahead with feet, hands and eyes. We ignore God's consecration of our hands to work, of our eyes to perceive, and of our feet to walk God's special ways. We reject others as outsiders, foreign to our own ranks and status in life. Instead of questioning the validity of other active and perhaps successful groups, we are reminded in graphic fashion of the importance of self-criticism and humility.

A final thought on humility

Jesus said, "learn from me, for I am gentle, and humble in heart, and you will find rest for your souls" (Matthew 11:29). Most of the saints prayed for and manifested humility in their lives. Many of us live in societies and cultures that value self-promotion of worth, assertiveness, competitiveness, communicating our accomplishments if we wish to get anywhere and make a difference.

The virtue of humility is a quality by which a person considering his or her own defects has a lowly opinion of himself and willingly submits himself or herself to God and to others for God's sake. How can we strike a balance between being humble and meek, and assertive enough to succeed in the world today? Or do we need to sacrifice one for the other? In living just and upright lives, we can do a good job as a humble leader, but that is different from been able to succeed and being placed in greater positions of responsibility.

Mother Cabrini's humility

When I was growing up in an Italian-American household, we often heard stories of the saints and blesseds from my grandparents and parents. Two Italians, of course, were at the top of the list: Mother Cabrini and Padre Pio. St. Frances Xavier Cabrini (1850 - 1917) was the first American citizen to be canonized by the Church. As a child, Mother Cabrini's prayer for humility was given to us and I have kept it ever since in my Bible. The life of Mother Cabrini and the words of this prayer embody many of the thoughts found in today's Scripture readings.

"Lord Jesus Christ, I pray that you may fortify me with the grace of your Holy Spirit, and give your peace to my soul, that I may be free from all needless anxiety and worry. Help me to desire always that which is pleasing and acceptable to you, so that your will may be my will.

"Grant that I may be free from unholy desires, and that, for your love, I may remain obscure and unknown in this world, to be known only to you.

"Do not permit me to attribute to myself the good that you perform in me and through me, but rather, referring all honor to you, may I admit only to my infirmities, so that renouncing sincerely all vainglory which comes from the world, I may aspire to that true and lasting glory that comes from you. Amen."

Marriage and the Family: Humanity's Future

TWENTY-SEVENTH SUNDAY IN ORDINARY TIME

Genesis 2:7ab, 15, 18-24;
Hebrews 2:9-11;
Mark 10:2-16

Rather than commenting in detail on each of the readings for the 27th Sunday in Ordinary Time (Year B), I would like to offer some general reflections on marriage and family life that flow from today's readings. In today's Gospel (Mark 10:2-16) the Pharisees once again confront Jesus with the divisive issue of divorce and its legitimacy: "Is it lawful for a man to divorce his wife?"

"What did Moses command you?" Jesus asked. They replied that Moses permitted a husband to write a bill of divorce and dismiss the wife. Jesus declares that the Law of Moses permitted divorce (Deuteronomy 24:1) only because of the hardness of hearts (Mark 10:4-5). In citing Genesis 1:27 and 2:24, Jesus proclaims permanence to be the divine intent from the beginning concerning human marriage (Mark 10:6-8). He reaffirms this with the declaration that what God has joined together, no human being must separate (v 9).

Jesus wisely and prudently responds to the loaded question by appealing to God's plan of complete unity and equality in drawing men and women together in marriage. He affirms that husband and wife are united so intimately that they actually become one and indivisible. In answering a direct question that was deliberately designed to entrap him,

Jesus was speaking of the nature of marriage and of that only. His emphasis is on its holiness and covenant fidelity and not on the illegitimacy of divorce. The goal of marriage is not divorce and annulment!

Divorce, annulment and remarriage

Jesus did not condemn people who did their best and ended up divorced. He was not judging such people, throwing them out of the community of the Church, or assigning them places in hell. He was only affirming the outlook taken by couples themselves when they stand before the Church's minister and pronounce their wedding vows.

Today Catholic annulments look to many like a simple Catholic divorce. Divorce says that the reality of marriage was there in the beginning and that now the reality is broken. Annulment is a declaration that the reality was never there. The Church declares many marriages invalid because of some impediment present at the time of the marriage.

Over the years of my pastoral ministry, I have met many divorced people who feel very alienated from the Church. For many, divorce was the last thing they ever dreamed of or wanted. In many instances, it hit them unexpectedly, forcefully and tragically. No one I met ever told me that they looked forward to a divorce. They simply didn't see any other alternative.

Some divorced men and women have erroneously been told by well-meaning people that they are excommunicated from the Catholic Church, which is certainly not true. Their pain is often enormous; their need for understanding and acceptance is great. They need unambiguous Catholic teaching to enlighten them and lead them to Christ. They need friends, people to pray for and with them, and they need God in their lives in the midst of rupture and brokenness. They deserve our understanding and our prayerful care.

A positive teaching on annulments should be offered in every parish community. Though it may be a tedious and painful process for some people, an annulment can be an instrument of grace, healing, closure, and peace of mind and heart.

The future of humanity
passes through marriage and the family

In the papal encyclicals from *Humanae Vitae* (1968) to *Evangelium Vitae* (1995) and especially the apostolic exhortation *Familiaris Consortio* (1981) and the magnificent *Letter to Families* (1994), Popes Paul VI and Blessed John Paul II have dedicated much attention to marriage and the family in today's culture. From the first year of his pontificate, Blessed John Paul II constantly emphasized: "the family is the way of the Church." The family is a school of communion, based on the values of the Gospel.

On the occasion of the 40th anniversary of the encyclical *Humanae Vitae*, in 2008, the bishops of Canada released a very important document in which they wrote (#19): "In short, Pope Paul VI's encyclical *Humanae Vitae* and the subsequent 'theology of the body' developed by Blessed John Paul II issue an immense challenge to a world that is too often occupied with protecting itself against the extraordinary life potential of sexuality. In the wake of these two prophetic

Popes, the Church, 'expert in humanity,' issues an unexpected message: Sexuality is a friend, a gift of God. It is revealed to us by the Trinitarian God who asks us to reveal it in turn in all its grandeur and dignity to our contemporaries at this start of the third millennium. The theology of the body has been compared to a revolution that would have positive effects throughout the 21st century of Christianity. We invite the faithful to be the first to experience its liberating potential."

Signs of hope for marriage, family life and vocations

To accept Jesus' teaching on marriage requires the openness of children and a sense of dependence on God's strength matching the child's sense of dependence on parents. When love is authentic, strong, sincere and firm, it is accompanied by vision, joy and creativity, new life and a desire for holiness. When married couples allow Christ to be at the centre of their project, they experience deeply the peace outpoured by God – a peace that flows forth to their children and grandchildren.

The crisis of vocations in the Western world requires that we rethink not only our manner of promoting vocations, but the terrain where seeds of vocations are sown. This fertile soil for vocations is the family, the domestic church. This reality is brought about by the presence of Christ in the home, from the graces of the sacraments, especially the Eucharist, and from fidelity to the Gospel and the teachings of the Church.

There are some voices in our society and Church that don't have much hope for the sacrament of marriage and for family life. I beg to differ with such voices of doom and despair. Each of us is responsible for fostering a true culture of marriage and family life as well as a culture of vocations to the priesthood and religious or consecrated life.

Over the past year in particular, I have witnessed some very hopeful signs for marriage and family life among young adults in various parts of the world. I had the privilege of leading two retreats for university students – one for the John Paul II Catholic Chaplaincy of Sheffield's Hallam University in England and the other for the Catholic Students' Association of Victoria University in British Colombia in Canada.

The wise, ecclesial leadership of university chaplains – Sister Anne Lee, NDS in Hallam and Father Dean Henderson in Victoria – gathered together some remarkable young adults from many countries of the world. They are the young men and women of the generations of Blessed John Paul II and Benedict XVI, freed from the ideological strangleholds and liberated from the barren, spiritual wastelands of my generation. Their eyes are fixed on Christ and they love the Church with all of her shadows and light.

I never had more open conversations about marriage and family life than I did with those students in Hallam and Victoria over those months. Many spoke openly about their parents who were divorced and alienated or simply absent from the Church. The students said that they learned from the mistakes and losses of their parents, and wanted to pursue the path of a holy marriage and family life. They desire to have Christ, the sacramental life, and the teachings of the Church at the centre of their lives.

I have also been very moved and edified by the young men and women who form the staff of the Salt and Light Television Network in Canada. Their simple and clear faith, deep joy, sterling commitment, visible love of Christ and the Church and ardent desire for evangelization is inspiring. Over the past six years, I have been privileged to witness the religious professions and ordinations of several Salt and Light colleagues, and to celebrate seven marriages of my staff – several who worked with me in preparing World Youth Day 2002. And now we are into the season of baptisms! It is from this generation of children that will come forth vocations for the Church. How could there not be vocations when the terrain was so fertile and the parents so open to the Gospel and to the Church?

For reflection, discussion and prayer

We must never forget that other bonds of love and inter-dependency, of commitment and mutual responsibility exist in society. They may be good; they may even be recognized in law. They are clearly not the same as marriage; they are something else. No extension of terminology for legal purposes will change the observable reality that only the committed union of a man and a woman carries, not only the bond of interdependency between the two adults, but the capacity to bring forth children.

This week, let us recommit ourselves to building up the human family, to strengthening marriage, to blessing and nurturing children, and to making our homes, families and parish communities holy, welcoming places for women and men of every race, language, orientation and way of life.

In our pastoral strategies, programs and preaching, how do we welcome the sanctifying role of Jesus Christ in the marriage of a man and woman? Are we ready to offer Jesus' teaching on marriage with the openness to children? What are some of the weaknesses and painful situations that afflict marriages today? Can these marriages be saved and the brokenness in the husband-wife relationships be healed? What is the role of faith in all of this?

Let us pray today for married people, that they may grow in this awareness of the sacramentality of marriage and its capacity to reflect the love of God to our world. Let us continue to help one another to bear the blessings, burdens and crosses that the Lord has given to us. And let us never forget those who have loved and lost, and those who have suffered the pain of separation, divorce and alienation. May they find healing in the community of the Church, and welcome from those whose marriages have borne much fruit.

How to Inherit Eternal Life

Wisdom 7:7-11;
Hebrews 4:12-13;
Mark 10:17-30 **or** *10:17-27*

Mark's Gospel story of Jesus' encounter with the man seeking eternal life is essentially a vocation story (Mark 10:17-30). It is the only story in Mark in which the individual called responds not by following, but by going away.

The story is narrated in all three Synoptic Gospel accounts. Matthew (19:16-22) tells us that the man was young; only Luke (18:18-23) tells us he was a ruler. The three evangelists agree that the man was rich, and in Mark, this is the only description given. The rich man's concern is to "inherit eternal life."

Let us consider several aspects of Mark's account of the Gospel episode. First of all, Jesus repudiates the term "good" for himself and directs it to God, the source of all goodness, who alone can grant the gift of eternal life.

Is Jesus' directive to this man with many possessions a requirement for all who wish to inherit eternal life? Is it true that Jesus did not ask other disciples to sell their possessions (1 Timothy 6:17-19)? Wasn't Peter able to keep his house and boat for a short period of time (Mark 1:29; John 21:3)? Didn't the women of Galilee continue to have access to their personal, material resources (Mark 15:41), just as Joseph of Arimathea did (15:43)?

It seems that in the case of this man with many possessions in Mark's story, Jesus issued a very personal invitation
for very specific reasons. Why does this young man find the
teaching of Jesus so difficult to accept? In the Old Testament,
wealth and material goods are considered a sign of God's
favour (Job 1:10; Psalm 128:1-2; Isaiah 3:10).

Religious Jews believed that wealth was a sign of God's
blessing. Rich people were regarded as those God had blessed,
and poor people were regarded as those God had cursed.

Power of possessions

The words of Jesus in Mark 10:23-25 provoke astonishment
among the disciples because of their apparent contradiction with the Old Testament concept (Mark 10:24.26). Since
wealth, power, and merit generate false security, Jesus rejects
them utterly as a claim to enter the kingdom. The negative
outcome of the man's choice to walk away strikes a note of
realism.

It also attests the special power of possessions to hinder
Christian discipleship. Jesus uses the rich man's departure as
a teaching moment to instruct his disciples about the dangerous snare that earthly possessions, success and prosperity can
have. Total detachment from one's possessions is required
of every authentic disciple. Jesus saw the danger of material
possessions. They can fix our heart to the world and make us
think of everything in terms of price rather than value.

Jesus was trying to completely overturn what the apostles
and all other good Jews had been taught. But his teaching
on wealth and richness was incomprehensible to the listeners. When Jesus said, "how hard it will be for those who

have wealth to enter the Kingdom of God!" the Gospel says, "They (the disciples) were greatly astonished and said to one another, 'Then who can be saved?'" (v 23, 26).

Anyone of us would naturally ask the same question! Jesus reminded them that salvation is purely a gift from God. Grace is God's gift and only those whose arms and hands are empty of self can stretch out to receive the gift of grace. The achievement of salvation is beyond human capability and depends solely on the goodness of God who offers it as a gift (Mark 10:27).

A Christian contradiction

In many societies, wealth is a sign of God's approval, and poverty and hardship are the signs of God's disapproval. Every Christian is challenged by the teaching of Jesus and the values of the society, which upholds the principle that worth really does come from material wealth; for example from the number of cars we own, the size of our homes, the amount in our investment portfolios.

When capitalist systems are solely market-driven, heartless, and materialistic, they contradict the Gospel teachings of Jesus. The Gospel of Jesus challenges the "prosperity gospel mentality." Jesus is not speaking against material wealth, but condemns being enslaved to and enchained by wealth. It becomes a blessing when it is shared with others, and it becomes an obstacle and a prison for those who do not have the wisdom to share it with others.

As Jesus looked at the rich young man, he looks at each one of us with love. He is reminding us to do "one thing more." We have to allow his loving gaze to penetrate us to the core, and unlike the young man we must open ourselves to transform our lives, upset our values and rearrange our priorities.

When, considering his language too demanding, many of his disciples left him, Jesus asked the few who had remained: "Will you also go away?"

Peter answered him: "Lord, to whom shall we go? You have the words of eternal life" (John 6:67-68).

And they chose to remain with him. They stayed because the Master had "the words of eternal life," words that promised eternity and also gave full meaning to life here and now.

Wisdom and happiness

King Solomon, as seen in the first reading (Wisdom 7:7-11), realized that only true wisdom could bring happiness. He prayed for it and it alone, rather than power, riches, health or good looks. God gave him everything.

For us, wisdom has become a person and his name is Jesus. Wisdom was born in a manger and died on a cross, and in between said that our only shot at ever being filled up is if we follow him in the life of self-emptying love.

Looking at Jesus, we see what it means to be poor in spirit, gentle and merciful, to mourn, to care for what is right, to be pure in heart, to make peace, to be persecuted. This is why he has the right to say to each of us, "Come, follow me!"

He does not say simply, "Do what I say." He says, "Come, follow me!"

In the end, Jesus looks intently and lovingly at each one of us and reminds us that life is to be had in its fullness not by accumulating things, honours, privileges, reputations, and prestige, but by letting go of things.

Initially, his invitation might surprise, upset, shock, and grieve us. With God's grace, may we realize Jesus' word is living and effective, sharper than any two-edged sword, penetrating even between soul and spirit, joints and marrow, and able to discern reflections and thoughts of the heart (Hebrews 4:12-13). Hopefully, we will not go away sad.

Ordinary life

Following today's Gospel, I encourage you to consider three important teachings of our Catholic tradition, from the *Catechism of the Catholic Church* and Benedict XVI's encyclical, *Caritas in Veritate*.

1) The *Catechism of the Catholic Church* teaches (2404-2405) that our material goods are entrusted to us by God not for our own personal advantage but for the privilege of using them for the good of others. "The ownership of any property makes its holder a steward of Providence, with the task of making it fruitful and communicating its benefits to others, first of all his family. Goods of production – material or immaterial – such as land, factories, practical or artistic skills, oblige their possessors to employ them in ways that will benefit the greatest number. Those who hold goods for use and consumption should use them with moderation, reserving the better part for guests, for the sick and the poor."

2) "The second truth is that … authentic human development concerns the whole of the person in every single
dimension. Without the perspective of eternal life, human
progress in this world is denied breathing space. Enclosed
within history, it runs the risk of being reduced to the
mere accumulation of wealth; humanity thus loses the
courage to be at the service of higher goods, at the service
of the great and disinterested initiatives called forth by
universal charity.

"Man does not develop through his own powers, nor can
development simply be handed to him. In the course
of history, it was often maintained that the creation of
institutions was sufficient to guarantee the fulfillment
of humanity's right to development" (No. 11 *Caritas in
Veritate*).

3) "While the poor of the world continue knocking on the
doors of the rich, the world of affluence runs the risk of
no longer hearing those knocks, on account of a conscience that can no longer distinguish what is human.
God reveals man to himself; reason and faith work hand
in hand to demonstrate to us what is good, provided we
want to see it; the natural law, in which creative Reason
shines forth, reveals our greatness, but also our wretchedness insofar as we fail to recognize the call to moral truth"
(No. 75 *Caritas in Veritate*).

Christ and the Priesthood

Isaiah 53:10-11;
Hebrews 4:14-16;
Mark 10:35-45 **or** *10:42-45*

The readings for the 29th Sunday in Ordinary Time of Cycle B invite us to prayerfully consider the priesthood and priestly ministry. The first reading is the passage of Isaiah's mysterious suffering servant who takes upon himself the people's iniquity (Isaiah 53:2-11).

The second reading speaks of Christ the high priest, tried in every way like us but sin, and the Gospel passage speaks of the Son of Man who has come to give his life in ransom for many (Mark 10:35-45). These three passages bring to light a fundamental aspect of the heart of priestly ministry and one that we celebrate together as God's people in the Eucharistic mystery.

Recognizing that many priests around the world read these reflections each week, I offer these thoughts that are particularly inspired by the second readings from this Sunday and next Sunday (Hebrews 4:14-16 and 5:1-6).

Isaiah's mysterious servant

First, allow me to offer a brief thought on today's reading from the prophet Isaiah (53:10-11). Isaiah's mysterious figure of the "suffering servant" is not only a sign of God's love for us, but he also represents all human beings before God.

Only God appreciated his servant's true greatness. Because he suffered, he was regarded as a sinner and therefore as one to be spurned. Because the servant fulfilled the divine will by suffering for the sins of others, the servant will be rewarded by the Lord.

Jesus, our great High Priest

In the letter to the Hebrews 4:14-16, the author calls Jesus a great high priest (v 14). Jesus has been tested in every way, yet without sin (v 15); this indicates an acquaintance with the tradition of Jesus' temptations, not only at the beginning (as in 1:13) but throughout his public life (cf. Luke 22:28). The similarity of Hebrews 4:16 to Hebrews 10:19-22 indicates that the author is thinking of our confident access to God, made possible by the priestly work of Jesus. Jesus' entire life is steeped in the Scriptures of Israel and he lived and acted out of God's Word.

Our "great high priest" is Jesus, the Child of Bethlehem who becomes the *Ecce Homo* of Jerusalem, not one distant from us and our condition, but he is the one who sympathizes with us, for he has experienced our weakness and pain, even our temptations (Hebrews 4:14-15). We must ask ourselves: Are we priestly people like he was? Do we live for others? Is the world any less violent, any less hostile, any more merciful, patient, kind and just, because of us?

In his very memorable and ever valid 1975 apostolic exhortation *Evangelii Nuntiandi* (On Evangelization in the Modern World), Pope Paul VI rightly noted: "Modern man listens more willingly to witnesses than to teachers, and if he does listen to teachers, it is because they are witnesses."

Lest we experience emptiness, and the effectiveness of our ministry be compromised, we need to constantly ask ourselves: Are we truly inhabited by the Word of God? Is that Word truly the nourishment we live by, even more than bread and the things of this world? Do we really know that Word? Do we love it? Do we act upon it? Are we deeply engaged with this Word to the point that it really leaves a mark on our lives, shapes our thinking, and motivates and inspires others to act?

Old and New

The Old Testament never dreamed of requiring the high priest to make himself like his brothers and sisters, but was preoccupied on the contrary with separating him from them. No text ever required that the high priest should be free from all sin. In the Old Testament, an attitude of compassion toward sinners appeared to be incompatible with the priesthood.

Unlike the Levitical priests, the death of Jesus was essential for his priesthood. He is a priest of compassion. His authority attracts us – because of his compassion. Ultimately, Jesus exists for others: he exists to serve. He has been tested in all respects like us – he knows all of our difficulties; he is a tried man; he knows our condition from the inside and from the outside – only by this did he acquire a profound capacity for compassion.

The opposite of a priestly person is a consumer: one who buys, amasses, collects things. The priest is one who spends and consumes himself for others. Is it any wonder that vocations to the priesthood face immense challenges in cultures of wealth, abundance, consumption, and excess?

Are you able to drink this cup?

In today's Gospel, Jesus asks the enigmatic question: "Are you able to drink the cup that I drink, or be baptized with the baptism I am baptized with?" (Mark 10:38-40): the metaphor of drinking the cup is used in the Old Testament to refer to acceptance of the destiny assigned by God.

In Jesus' case, this involves divine judgment on sin that Jesus, the innocent one, is to expiate on behalf of the guilty (Mark 14:24; Isaiah 53:5). His baptism is to be his crucifixion and death for the salvation of the human race. The request of James and John for a share in the glory (Mark 10:35-37) must of necessity involve a share in Jesus' sufferings, the endurance of tribulation and suffering for the Gospel (Mark 10:39). The authority of assigning places of honour in the kingdom is reserved to God (Mark 10:40).

Whatever authority is to be exercised by the disciples must, like that of Jesus, be transformed into service to others (Mark 10:45) rather than for personal aggrandizement (Mark 10:42-44). The service of Jesus is his passion and death for the sins of the human race (Mark 10:45).

Today's Gospel passage concludes with one of the most important Gospel sayings that indicates Jesus' messianic mission: "For the Son of Man came not to be served but to serve, and to give his life as a ransom for many."

Jesus did not come into the world seeking personal gain, privilege or prestige. Rather, he came for service, and this entailed giving his life up as a ransom.

The Old Testament never explained how God could "pay a price" for his people. Only in the passion, suffering and death of his only Son does the price become clear. We become capable of salvation only by offering our flesh and blood.

All of the sinfulness and evil in the world around us must be borne on our shoulders and in our own flesh. In this way, we share the pain in our own flesh and bones, making it part of our very selves just as Jesus did. For as St. Paul tells us in his second letter to the Corinthian community: "God made Christ to be sin who knew no sin, so that in Christ we might become the righteousness of God" (2 Corinthians 5:21).

Difficult times

As priestly shepherds, we are given a share in arduous and awesome duties in difficult and trying times. We are ordained to gather God's people, to boldly proclaim the Word of the Lord, to baptize, to celebrate the breaking of the Bread, and to constantly give thanks to God for so many gifts.

We are also commissioned to assist those in need and to rouse generosity to the poor. Our ordained ministry demands that we lead by wholehearted example.

Nevertheless we remain unworthy servants, yet sent to do the work of Christ. Who of us can ever be worthy of such a great calling? As human beings, we priests can err, but the priestly gestures we carry out at the altar or in the confessional, are not invalid or ineffective because of our weakness and sinfulness.

God's people and ours are not deprived of divine grace because of our own unworthiness. After all it is Christ who baptizes, celebrates, reconciles and forgives; the priest is only the instrument.

Only if we are servant shepherds who suffer will people be stung by Jesus' call to tend one another, and to wash the feet of the world. Only if we allow our own hearts to be broken over and over again, in joyful service of God's people, will we be effective priests and good shepherds to the Lord's people.

It is this broken, wounded heart that lies at the heart of authentic ministry and shepherding today in the Church. Not a heart broken in a state of despair, but one opened in loving embrace to the world, a broken heart that leads to ultimate joy because we have given it all to God and made place for the entire world in our own hearts.

Jesus is the perfect priest who burns, spends and consumes himself gladly for his brothers and sisters; one who lays down his life for others. The suffering servant of the Lord lives in union, communion and sympathy with the entire human family. Just as the Son of Man did not come to be served but to serve and to give his life as a ransom for many, so must it be for us.

Above and beyond eloquent words in homilies and written texts, we must know Christ and love him. Our friendship with him will be contagious to our contemporaries, and others might recognize the Lord's nobility, beauty and greatness though our faces, our smiles, our hands, our feet, our heart and our weaknesses. We cannot forget that people will fall in love with the Lord in spite of us, and hopefully because of us.

Master, I Want to See!

Jeremiah 31:7-9;
Hebrews 5:1-6;
Mark 10:46-52

Mark's healing stories of the blind man of Bethsaida (8:22-26) and the healing of Bartimaeus, the blind man on the road to Jericho (10:46-52) were undoubtedly popular stories in the early Church and they remain very significant stories for the contemporary Church.

These miracles have always fascinated me because I grew up with my father who was an eye doctor. How frequently we spoke about sight impairments, eye diseases, astigmatisms, cataracts and 20/20 vision! My father was also a member of a charitable society that assisted the blind, and I vividly remember volunteering as a child with my father and his doctor colleagues who hosted memorable Christmas parties for blind people.

Road to Jericho

Mark tells the story of Jesus' encounter with Bartimaeus, a blind man and a beggar (10:46-52) in the Gospel for the 30th Sunday in Ordinary Time (Year B). Jesus had made the long, arduous journey down the desert valley from Galilee in the north. He was on his way to Jerusalem, a daunting climb from an oasis on the desert floor to the hills of Judea.

As Jesus passed through Jericho, Bartimaeus heard the din of the crowd and knew that the chance of a lifetime was within his grasp. Bartimaeus was not about to miss this opportunity! From the roadside, he began to cry out, "Jesus, Son of David, have mercy on me!" Some people in Jesus' entourage were embarrassed to have this dirty, rude beggar bother the master and they attempted to silence him.

What were they embarrassed about? Bartimaeus was simply trying to engage the culture around him and let the people know that he, too, had a right to see Jesus. If individuals in the crowd had heard the rumours about Jesus' healing powers, wouldn't they be kind to this poor beggar and bring him to Jesus for healing?

Bartimaeus would not be denied – and neither would Jesus. As the shouts of the beggar reached his ears, Jesus brushed aside the restraints of his disciples and called to the blind man. Bartimaeus threw off his cloak and drew near to that welcoming voice, which responded to his pleas, "What do you want me to do for you?"

"My teacher, let me see again." And Bartimaeus did see, not just with his eyes but more importantly, with his heart. Though Bartimaeus was blind to many things, he clearly saw who Jesus is. Seeing "who Jesus is" is the goal of faith, and it leads to discipleship. At the end of the story, Bartimaeus regained his sight and followed Jesus on the way. Given that the very next verse in Mark narrates the entry into Jerusalem, we can be certain that Bartimaeus followed Jesus on the way to the cross.

Blindness metaphor

Compassion for the outcast was a hallmark of Jesus' ministry and healing stories in the Gospels never seem to be simply a reversal of physical misfortune. In the stories of those who "once were blind, but now they see," the connections between seeing and believing are so strong that these miracles worked by Jesus are more about growing in faith than letting the scales of blindness fall away.

Disciples of Jesus have vision problems. How often do we use the metaphor of blindness to describe our inability to grasp the meaning of the suffering we endure? We sometimes describe our blindness as an inability to see the forest for the trees, but that is a rather simplistic analysis. More worrisome is the inherited blindness which so often assumes that there are no lessons left to learn. Arrogance is very often the root of our blindness. We need the miracle of restored sight each day.

What corners of the Church, of society and of our culture need serious healing, restoration and reformation in our time? Where are our blind spots? Where are the big problems with near-sightedness and far-sightedness? How often do we prefer monologue to dialogue, refusing to believe that we might learn from those who oppose us and disagree with us; refusing to engage the culture around us and preferring a narrow, obstinate and angry way of existing? How often do we say that there are no other ways to look at an issue than our way ... or the highway!

How often do we behave like those who tried to prevent Bartimaeus from seeing and meeting the Lord? Against the cries of the scoffers and cynics in our midst, do we dare to bring our friends, colleagues and loved ones into the very presence of the Lord? How can we not, when we know the result of a lifetime without Christ?

Healing, restoration and sight

Abortion is the most serious wound inflicted not only on individuals and their families who should provide the sanctuary for life, but inflicted as well on society and its culture, by the very people who ought to be society's promoters and defenders. It is important to recall Benedict XVI's words and pro-life vision at the opening ceremony of World Youth Day 2008 in Sydney, on July 17, 2008:

"And so we are led to reflect on what place the poor and the elderly, immigrants and the voiceless, have in our societies. How can it be that domestic violence torments so many mothers and children? How can it be that the most wondrous and sacred human space – the womb – has become a place of unutterable violence?"

The Roman Catholic Church offers a teaching on the inviolability, the sacredness and the dignity of the human person: a 20/20 vision for which we must strive each day if we claim to be pro-life.

Opposition to abortion and euthanasia does not excuse indifference to those who suffer from poverty, violence and injustice. We must strive to see the whole picture, not with tunnel vision.

To say that we are pro-life means that we are against whatever is opposed to life itself, such as any type of murder, genocide, abortion, euthanasia or wilful self-destruction.

We stand firmly against whatever violates the dignity of the human person such as mutilation, torments inflicted on body or mind, attempts to coerce the will itself, whatever insults human dignity such as subhuman living conditions, arbitrary imprisonment, deportation, slavery, prostitution, the selling of women and children, and disgraceful working conditions where people are treated as instruments of gain rather than as free and responsible persons. All of these things and more destroy human life and poison human society.

Capuchin Cardinal Sean O'Malley, archbishop of Boston, recently wrote: "Our ability to change people's hearts and help them to grasp the dignity of each and every life, from the first moment of conception to the last moment of natural death, is directly related to our ability to increase love and unity in the Church, for our proclamation of the Truth is hindered when we are divided and fighting with each other."

Being pro-life is one of the deepest expressions of our baptism: We stand up as sons and daughters of the light, clothed in humility and charity, filled with conviction, speaking the truth to power with firmness, conviction and determination, and never losing joy and hope.

Being pro-life is not an activity for a political party or a particular side of the spectrum. It is an obligation for everyone: left, right and centre! If we are pro-life, we must engage the culture around us, and not curse it. We must see others as Jesus does, and we must love them to life, even those who are opposed to us.

As we recognize the things that blind us from the Lord and paralyze us from effective action, let us never cease begging the Lord to heal us! "Lord, that I may see!" And when our vision is restored, let us get up to follow him joyfully along the way to the Kingdom.

A Prayer for Sight
Origen (185-253)

May the Lord Jesus touch our eyes,
As he did those of the blind.
Then we shall begin to see in visible things
Those which are invisible.
May he open our eyes to gaze not on present realities,
But on the blessings to come.
May he open the eyes of our heart
 to contemplate God in Spirit,
Through Jesus Christ the Lord,
To whom belong power and glory
 through all eternity. Amen.

The Beatitudes:
Blueprint for Holiness

SOLEMNITY OF ALL SAINTS

Revelation 7:2-4, 9-14;
1 John 3:1-3;
Matthew 5:1-12a

The words of Salesian Cardinal Angelo Amato, prefect of the Congregation for Saints' Causes, spoken during the 2008 Synod of Bishops on the Word of God, still resound in my mind and heart today on the Solemnity of All Saints:

"Jesus says: 'Learn from me, for I am gentle and humble in heart, and you will find rest for your souls' (Matthew 11:29). For more than 2,000 years, men and women, old and young, wise and ignorant, in the East as in the West, applied themselves to the school of the Lord Jesus, which caused this sublime commandment to echo in their hearts and minds: 'You must therefore be perfect, just as your heavenly Father is perfect' (Matthew 5:48).

"Their library was largely composed of the life and the words of Jesus: blessed are the poor, blessed are those who mourn, blessed are the gentle, blessed are those who hunger and thirst for uprightness, blessed are the merciful, blessed are the pure in heart, blessed are the peacemakers, blessed are those who are persecuted. The saints, understanding that the beatitudes are the essence of the Gospel and the portrait of Christ himself, became their imitators."

A new recipe

The beatitudes in Christ's Sermon on the Mount (Matthew 5:1-12) are a recipe for extreme holiness. As has been pointed out by many others in the past, though the Mount of the Beatitudes is a few dozen feet above sea level, it is the really the highest peak on earth!

On this holy mountain in Galilee, Jesus proclaimed the new law that was the expression of Christ's holiness.

They are not an abstract code of behaviour. Jesus is the poor in spirit, the meek, the persecuted, and the peacemaker. He is the new "code of holiness" that must be imprinted on hearts, and that must be contemplated through the action of the Holy Spirit. His Passion and Death are the crowning of his holiness.

Holiness is a way of life that involves commitment and activity. It is not a passive endeavour, but rather a continuous choice to deepen one's relationship with God and to then allow this relationship to guide all of one's actions in the world. Holiness requires a radical change in mindset and attitude. The acceptance of the call to holiness places God as our final goal in every aspect of our lives.

Looking at Jesus, we see what it means to be poor in spirit, gentle and merciful, to mourn, to care for what is right, to be pure in heart, to make peace, to be persecuted. This is why he has the right to say to each of us, "Come, follow me!"

Jesus does not say simply, "Do what I say." He says, "Come, follow me!"

Taking stock

The saints and blesseds are travel companions along our journey, in joy and suffering. They are men and women who wrote a new page in their lives and in the lives of so many people. This was the core of Blessed Pope John Paul II's message to humanity: Holiness is not a gift reserved for a few.

We can all aspire to it, because it is a goal within our capacity – a great lesson reaffirmed by the Second Vatican Council and its call to universal holiness (*Lumen Gentium*).

Today's solemnity of All Saints is a wonderful opportunity for the whole Church to take stock once again of the way that the Blessed John Paul II, changed our way of viewing the saints and blessed. In nearly 27 years of his pontificate, John Paul II, who is now also numbered among the blessed, gave the Church 1,338 blessed and 482 saints.

The Polish Pontiff reminded us that the heroes and heroines the world offers to young people today are terribly flawed. They leave us so empty. The real "stars" of his pontificate are the saints and blessed who did not try to be regarded as heroes, or to shock or provoke.

To believe greatness is attainable, we need successful role models to emulate. There is a desperate need for real heroes and heroines, models and witnesses of faith and virtue that the world of sports, cinema, science and music cannot provide.

Standing at the radical centre

Many think that sainthood is a privilege reserved only for the chosen few. Actually, to become a saint is the task of every Christian, and what's more, we could even say it's the task of everyone! How many times have we thought that the saints are merely "eccentrics" that the Church exalts for our imitation; people who were so unrepresentative of and out of touch with the human scene?

It is certainly true of all those men and women who were "eccentric" in its literal sense: they deviated from the centre, from usual practice, the ordinary ways of doing things, the established methods. Another way of looking at the saints is that they stood at the "radical centre."

Saints of the new millennium

Blessed John Paul II spoke much to young people about the call to holiness and the vocation to be saints. In his message for World Youth Day 2000 in Rome, he wrote to his "dear young friends" throughout the world unforgettable words that became the rallying cry for the Jubilee's greatest celebration:

"Young people of every continent, do not be afraid to be the saints of the new millennium! Be contemplative, love prayer; be coherent with your faith and generous in the service of your brothers and sisters, be active members of the Church and builders of peace.

"To succeed in this demanding project of life, continue to listen to his word, draw strength from the sacraments, especially the Eucharist and penance. The Lord wants you to be intrepid apostles of his Gospel and builders of a new humanity."

Two years later for our World Youth Day 2002 in Canada, Blessed John Paul II took up once again the theme of holiness and saints in his message to us:

"Just as salt gives flavor to food and light illumines the darkness, so too holiness gives full meaning to life and makes it reflect God's glory.

"How many saints, especially young saints, can we count in the Church's history! In their love for God their heroic virtues shone before the world, and so they became models of life which the Church has held up for imitation by all. (…)

"Through the intercession of this great host of witnesses, may God make you too, dear young people, the saints of the third millennium!"

At the concluding World Youth Day Mass at Downsview Park in Toronto on July 28, 2002, Blessed John Paul II issued a stirring challenge:

"And if, in the depths of your hearts, you feel the same call to the priesthood or consecrated life, do not be afraid to follow Christ on the royal road of the Cross!

"At difficult moments in the Church's life, the pursuit of holiness becomes even more urgent. And holiness is not a question of age; it is a matter of living in the Holy Spirit, just as Kateri Tekakwitha did here in America and so many other young people have done."

True reformers

Benedict XVI continued the momentum of Blessed John Paul II's invitations and exhortations to holiness at World Youth Day 2005 in Cologne, Germany. At the opening ceremony on August 18, 2005, Benedict XVI addressed the throng of young people from the entire world:

"Dear young people, the Church needs genuine witnesses for the new evangelization: men and women whose lives have been transformed by meeting with Jesus, men and women who are capable of communicating this experience to others. The Church needs saints.

"All are called to holiness, and holy people alone can renew humanity. Many have gone before us along this path of Gospel heroism, and I urge you to turn often to them to pray for their intercession."

Benedict XVI continued this theme at the great vigil on Saturday evening August 20, 2005 at Marienfeld:

"It is the great multitude of the saints – both known and unknown – in whose lives the Lord has opened up the Gospel before us and turned over the pages; he has done this throughout history and he still does so today.

"In their lives, as if in a great picture book, the riches of the Gospel are revealed. They are the shining path which God himself has traced throughout history and is still tracing today."

Then Benedict XVI cried out in that great assembly of over one million young people gathered in prayer at Marienfeld in Cologne: "The saints (...) are the true reformers. Now I want to express this in an even more radical way: Only from the saints, only from God does true revolution come, the definitive way to change the world."

At the core

Every crisis that the Church faces, every crisis that the world faces, is a crisis of holiness and a crisis of saints. Holiness is crucial because it is the real face of the Church.

The core of the proclamation of the saints and blessed was always hope, even in the midst of the darkest moments of history. It's almost as if in those times of darkness the light of Christ shines ever more brightly. We are living through one of those times, and the Lord is still taking applications for his extreme form of holiness and sanctity.

Believers in Jesus and his message must allow themselves to be enticed and enchanted by his life and message contained in the beatitudes.

Today we must hold up the beatitudes as a mirror in which we examine our own lives and consciences. "Am I poor in spirit? Am I humble and merciful? Am I pure of heart? Do I bring peace? Am I 'blessed,' in other words, happy?"

Jesus not only gives us what he has, but also what he is. He is holy and makes us holy.

Love of God and
Loving-Kindness Towards One's Neighbor

Deuteronomy 6:2-6
Hebrews 7:23-28
Mark 12:28-34

Today's first reading from the Book of Deuteronomy 6:2-6 and the section from Mark's Gospel (12:28-34) contain the fundamental prayer of the *Shema*, the Hebrew profession of faith: "Hear, O Israel, the Lord our God is one Lord" (Deuteronomy 6:4). Just as we profess our faith with the Creed in Christian worship, the Jewish people profess their faith with the *Shema* in their synagogue services. The *Shema* is a summary of true religion: "Hear, O Israel: the Lord is our God, the Lord alone. You shall love the Lord your God with all your heart, and with all your soul, and with all your might."

Central to the Hebrew profession of faith is this truth: there is only one God, the Creator of heaven and earth, who is thus the God of all. All other gods are not God, and the universe in which we live has its source in God and was created by him. This notion of creation is found elsewhere, yet only here does it become absolutely clear that it is not one god among many, but the one true God himself who is the source of all that exists. The entire whole world comes into existence by the power of his creative Word.

The priesthood of Jesus Christ

In today's second reading from Hebrews 7:23-28, we read of the former priests of the Old Covenant who though were many, were prevented by death from remaining in office. We also hear of the priesthood of Jesus Christ who, because he remains forever, has a priesthood that does not pass away. Jesus, the new high priest, guarantees the permanence of the New Covenant. Therefore, he is always able to save those who approach God through him, since he lives forever to make intercession for them. Jesus was not a priest after the Jewish tradition. He did not belong to the line of Aaron but to that of Judah, and thus the path of priesthood was legally closed to Him. The person and activity of Jesus of Nazareth did not follow in the line of the ancient priests, but in that of the tradition of the prophets of ancient Israel.

As Pope Benedict pointed out in his homily for the Solemnity of the Most Holy Body and Blood of Christ (Corpus Christi) in Rome on June 3, 2010: "Jesus distanced Himself from a ritualistic conception of religion, criticizing the approach that attributed value to human precepts associated with ritual purity rather than to the observance of God's commandments; that is, to love for God and for neighbor, which 'is much more important than all whole burnt offerings and sacrifices'. ... Even His death, which we Christians rightly call 'sacrifice', was completely unlike the ancient sacrifices, it was quite the opposite: the execution of a death sentence of the most humiliating kind: crucifixion outside the walls of Jerusalem." The priesthood of Christ involves suffering. Without this fundamental principle and vision, any of our efforts to form the Church of Jesus Christ are in vain.

An important teaching moment for Jesus

Jesus was a threat to the scribes and they often depicted as being hostile to him. Yet today's Gospel story from Mark 12:28-34 presents us with a rather friendly conversation rather than the usual controversial discussion between Jesus and the scribes.

In order to fully grasp today's Gospel passage, it is important to understand the role of the scribe in Judaism. The scribe was not a member of any Jewish sect or political party such as a Pharisee, Sadducee, Essene or Zealot, even though many of the scribes were indeed Pharisees who abided by a strict interpretation of the Law. Scribes were the scholars and intellectuals of Judaism. Their scholarship was the knowledge of the Law, which they regarded as the sum of wisdom and the only true learning. The position of scribe in the Jewish community was a respected place of leadership.

In today's text, the scribe appears to be impressed with Jesus' previous responses (24-27) to the question regarding whose wife and seven husbands in the resurrection. The scribe approaches Jesus and wants to know more.

Today's key question "Which is the first of all the commandments?" offers Jesus an important teaching moment. The teachers of the Torah (scribes and rabbis) had always argued about the relative importance of the commandments in the Old Testament. In response, Jesus quotes Deuteronomy 6:4-5 (today's first reading), and indicates the opening verses of the *Shema*, recited daily by the Jews. Even though Jesus is asked for one commandment, he provides two in his response. The second is this: You shall love your neighbor as yourself, from Leviticus 19:18, which was also not among the 613 commandments. What is remarkable is that the scribe expresses agreement with Jesus by paraphrasing him without any hint of hostility or irony.

In referring to heart, soul, and mind, and strength, (30) they do not refer to the various components of the person but are a way of stressing that the whole person should love God with everything the person has and is. The Deuteronomy text only lists heart, soul, and strength while today's Gospel cites heart, soul, mind and strength (as does Matthew's Gospel text 22:37). Jesus probably equated the mind (knowledge) with strength.

Today's Gospel immediately calls to mind the story of the rich man who is close to the kingdom of heaven. The scribe's correct understanding and humble openness to learn from Jesus is unique (Mark 10:13-16). The difference between the story of the rich man and the scribe is that unlike the rich man, Jesus doesn't add that there is one more thing (Mark 10:21); because the scribe has understood, nothing impedes him from entering the kingdom.

Moses teaches in the *Shema* (cf. Deuteronomy 6:5; Leviticus 19:34) – and Jesus reaffirms in the Gospel (cf. Mark 12:19-31), that all of the Commandments are summed up in the love of God and loving-kindness towards one's neighbor. Every time that Jews recite the *"Shema Israel"* and that that Christians recall the first and second great commandments, we are, by God's grace, brought closer to each other. Whenever we make the sign of the cross, we are tracing the *Shema* upon our bodies as we touch our head (soul), heart, and shoulders (strength) and pledge them to God's service.

Lectio Divina: listening to the Word of God

Today's readings invite us to a special kind of listening to God's Word. This listening requires prolonged silence so that the Holy Spirit can reveal the intent and understanding of the Word of God and unite himself silently to our own spirit (cf. Romans 8:26-27). In this light I would like to make a few comments about the ancient art of *Lectio Divina*. *Verbum Domini*, the Apostolic Exhortation from the Synod on the Word of God in the Life and Mission of the Church offers *Lectio Divina* as a method of approaching, understanding, praying and loving the Word of God.

Verbum Domini states: "The Synod frequently insisted on the need for a prayerful approach to the sacred text as a fundamental element in the spiritual life of every believer, in the various ministries and states in life, with particular reference to *Lectio Divina*. The Word of God is at the basis of all authentic Christian spirituality." (#86)

In *Verbum Domini*, Pope Benedict describes in detail the method of *Lectio Divina* (#87): "I would like here to review the basic steps of this procedure. It opens with the reading (*lectio*) of a text, which leads to a desire to understand its true content: what does the biblical text say in itself? Without this, there is always a risk that the text will become a pretext for never moving beyond our own ideas.

"Next comes meditation (*meditatio*), which asks: what does the biblical text say to us? Here, each person, individually but also as a member of the community, must let himself or herself be moved and challenged.

"Following this comes prayer (*oratio*), which asks the question: what do we say to the Lord in response to his word? Prayer, as petition, intercession, thanksgiving and praise, is the primary way by which the word transforms us.

"Finally, *Lectio Divina* concludes with contemplation (*contemplatio*), during which we take up, as a gift from God, his own way of seeing and judging reality, and ask ourselves what conversion of mind, heart and life is the Lord asking of us? In the Letter to the Romans, Saint Paul tells us: 'Do not be conformed to this world, but be transformed by the renewal of your mind, that you may prove what is the will of God, what is good and acceptable and perfect' (12:2).

"Contemplation aims at creating within us a truly wise and discerning vision of reality, as God sees it, and at forming within us 'the mind of Christ' (1 Corinthians 2:16). The word of God appears here as a criterion for discernment: it is "living and active, sharper than any two-edged sword, piercing to the division of soul and spirit, of joints and marrow, and discerning the thoughts and intentions of the heart' (Hebrews 4:12). We do well also to remember that the process of *Lectio Divina* is not concluded until it arrives at action (*actio*), which moves the believer to make his or her life a gift for others in charity."

Thanks to this simple adherence to and humble respect for the whole biblical text, *Lectio Divina* is an exercise in total and unconditional obedience to God who is speaking to human beings who are listening attentively to the Word.

Two Mighty and Courageous Widows

Thirty-Second Sunday in Ordinary Time

1 Kings 17:10-16;
Hebrews 9:24-28;
Mark 12:38-44 **or** *12:41-44*

Today's Old Testament reading from 1 Kings 17:10-16 and the Gospel story from Mark 12:38-44 present us with two remarkable widows who challenge us by their conviction, generosity and faith.

They force us to reexamine our understanding of the poor and poverty, and look at our own ways of being generous with others.

I would like to offer some reflections on the stories of these two biblical figures and then apply their example to our own lives, through the lenses of Pope Benedict XVI's encyclical letter *Caritas in Veritate.*

Elijah's faith

Whenever I read stories from the Elijah and Elisha cycle in the first and second books of Kings, I always say a prayer of thanksgiving for one of my professors from the Pontifical Biblical Institute in Rome, Jesuit Father Stephen Pisano, who taught the best course I had in the Old Testament: "The Man of God in the Books of Kings." God knows how many times I have gone back to those notes and appreciated anew the stories of Elijah and his disciple Elisha, and their efforts to make God's Word known and loved in the land of Israel!

In I Kings 17:8-16, God continues to test the Prophet Elijah. While today's lectionary reading begins with Verse 10, it is important to go back to Verse 8 to understand the full meaning of the text. In Verse 8 we read: "Then the word of the Lord came to him, saying... ."

Elijah did not set out until he received the message from God. It is essential for us to be in communication with God through listening to God's Word before setting out on mission.

Elijah is then told to go to Zarephath (v 9), which is part of Sidon. Verse 9 contains three commands: "arise," "go," and "stay." The prophet will be tested with each of these commands through faith, trust, obedience, availability and commitment. When Elijah is told to "arise," it is not only a physical movement but a spiritual one. For Elijah, following the Lord obediently is the result of his own spiritual reawakening.

The second command – "go to Zarephath" – carries with it the idea of a journey, including risks, hardships and dangers. Elijah is sent to a specific place, Zarephath, which means "a smelting place, a place of testing." Furthermore, Zarephath was in the land of Sidon, which belonged to the wicked Jezebel. Elijah is hardly being sent to a vacation destination for rest and relaxation!

The third command – "stay there" – was a great challenge to his commitment, trust and vision as a man of God who was simply seeking to serve the Lord. Elijah's provision would come from a poor, destitute, depressed widow facing starvation in the pagan nation of the Sidonians who represented the forces clearly in opposition to the God of Israel.

Elijah encounters his benefactress, not living in a large house and sharing her excess with itinerant prophets, but rather at the gate of the city, collecting a few sticks since she had no fuel at home to cook even a meagre meal.

The God who commanded the ravens and who provided for Elijah in the desert (I Kings 17:1-7), was the same God who had commanded the widow and would provide for the prophet through her. At Zarephath, the poor woman listened to Elijah's instruction and it was just as he had promised according to the Word of the Lord. She saw the power of God: The widow, her son, and Elijah were all sustained.

What lessons can we learn from this passage?

Because of a poor woman's generosity and goodness, and Elijah's faithfulness, God strengthened the prophet's faith, renewed his capacity for ministry, using him to comfort the widow and her son at the same time. The Lord God will provide for us, beyond outward appearances of weakness, failure and fear. God always does far more than we can ever ask for or imagine.

Just a mite

In today's well-known Gospel story (Mark 12:38-44), Jesus praises the poor widow's offering, and makes it clear that the standard measurement for assessing gifts is not how much we give to the works of God or how much we put in the collection

---

basket, but how much we have left for ourselves. Those who give out of their abundance still have abundance left.

Is Jesus exalting this woman because she emptied her bank account for the temple? Is Jesus romanticizing and idealizing the poor? I have yet to meet people who dream of growing up destitute, poor, hungry and homeless. I don't know anyone who delights in living from one government social assistance check to the next, nor people who enjoy rummaging through garbage bins and are proud that they cannot afford to pay for electric and water bills for their inadequate and even danger-ous housing situations during cold Canadian winters.

The woman in today's provocative Gospel story was poor because she was a widow. She was completely dependent on her male relatives for her livelihood. To be widowed meant not only losing a spouse, but more tragically, losing the one on whom you were totally dependent. Widows were forced to live off of the generosity of other male relatives and anyone in the community who might provide for one's needs.

The two coins in the woman's hand were most likely all she had. When one has so little, a penny or two isn't going to move that person from complete social assistance to employ-ment. With the coins or without them, the widow was still a dependent person. She had no status in life. She was totally dependent on the grace of God, yet she was indeed rich in God's mercy.

Jesus never condemns the rich but simply says that they will find it difficult to enter the kingdom. What matters is not how much money is stored in bank accounts or kept in stocks and bonds, but rather for what that money is destined.

Will the money be used to assist others, to make the world a better place? Will be it used to feed the hungry, clothe the naked, provide for the homeless and destitute poor? Will it be used to build a culture of life? Do our lives revolve around the money or are we dependant on God who truly makes us rich? Do we behave as owners or live as stewards?

The widow tossed her only signs of independence into the collection basket, but she maintained her complete dependence on God and neighbour. Her example of faith is grounded in the love of God: her love for God and God's love for her. She was a steward and not an owner of her meagre possessions. This poor widow teaches us that dependence, far from being oppressive and depressive, can really lead to a life lived in deep joy and profound gratitude.

Charity in truth

Four brief sections from Benedict XVI's encyclical letter *Caritas in Veritate* merit our careful reflection and meditation this week.

1. "The search for love and truth is purified and liberated by Jesus Christ from the impoverishment that our humanity brings to it, and he reveals to us in all its fullness the initiative of love and the plan for true life that God has prepared for us. In Christ, charity in truth becomes the Face of his Person, a vocation for us to love our brothers and sisters in the truth of his plan. Indeed, he himself is the Truth (cf. John 14:6)."

23. "The mere fact of emerging from economic backward-ness, though positive in itself, does not resolve the complex issues of human advancement, neither for the countries that are spearheading such progress, nor for those that are already economically developed, nor even for those that are still poor, which can suffer not just through old forms of exploitation, but also from the negative consequences of a growth that is marked by irregularities and imbalances."

42. "For a long time it was thought that poor peoples should remain at a fixed stage of development, and should be content to receive assistance from the philanthropy of developed peoples. Paul VI strongly opposed this mentality in *Populorum Progressio*.

"Today the material resources available for rescuing these peoples from poverty are potentially greater than before, but they have ended up largely in the hands of people from developed countries, who have benefited more from the liberalization that has occurred in the mobility of capital and labor. The world-wide diffusion of forms of prosperity should not therefore be held up by projects that are self-centred, protectionist or at the service of private interests."

75. "While the poor of the world continue knocking on the doors of the rich, the world of affluence runs the risk of no longer hearing those knocks, on account of a conscience that can no longer distinguish what is human. God reveals man to himself; reason and faith work hand

in hand to demonstrate to us what is good, provided we want to see it; the natural law, in which creative Reason shines forth, reveals our greatness, but also our wretchedness insofar as we fail to recognize the call to moral truth."

Know That He Is Near, at the Gates

THIRTY-THIRD SUNDAY IN ORDINARY TIME

Daniel 12:1-3;
Hebrews 10:11-14, 18;
Mark 13:24-32

Today's Gospel story is taken from the most difficult chapter of Mark's Gospel (13:24-32) and is often interpreted as announcing the end of the world.

Mark 13 is often called the "little apocalypse." Like Daniel 7-12 and the Book of Revelation, it focuses on a world of persecution. When we take the chapter as a whole, we will be able to see that we are dealing with the theme of meaning rather than chronology.

Jesus' prediction of the destruction of the temple (Mark 13:2) provoked questions that the four disciples put to him in private regarding the time and the sign when all these things are about to come to an end (Mark 13:3-4). The response to their questions was Jesus' eschatological discourse prior to his imminent death. It contained instruction and consolation exhorting the disciples and the Church to faith and obedience through the trials that would confront them (Mark 13:5-13).

The sign is the presence of the desolating abomination (Mark 13:14; see Daniel 9:27), i.e., of the Roman power profaning the temple. Flight from Jerusalem is urged rather than defence of the city through misguided messianic hope (Mark 13:14-23). Intervention will occur only after destruction

(Mark 13:24-27), which will happen before the end of the first Christian generation (Mark 13:28-31).

No one but the Father knows the precise time, or that of the parousia (Mark 13:32); hence the necessity of constant vigilance (Mark 13:33-37). Luke sets the parousia at a later date, after "the time of the Gentiles" (Luke 21:24). See also the notes on Matthew 24:1-25, 46.

Son of Man

Jesus' words in today's Gospel deal with two realities: Jesus himself will fulfill the Old Testament Scripture texts about the end and the disciples are not to worry about the precise time of Jesus' second coming. When we read v. 26, we know that Jesus is the heavenly being who will come in power and glory.

Like Daniel's Son of Man, Mark's Jesus will return and gather his elect "from the four winds, from the end of the earth to the end of heaven" (Mark 13:27). When Jesus spoke, he didn't paint a glistening future for his disciples. He addressed the very era in which Mark's first readers lived and, indeed, in which we ourselves live. Jesus foretold wars, earthquakes and famines, and identifies these as "the beginning of the birth pangs:" the prophesied events signal the painful advent of the new age, which comes about even as the powers of the old age struggle to prevent it.

Jesus described to the people of his day all the things that would arouse fear in people today: wars, persecution, catastrophes, scandals, and people in misery. Jesus used these predictions of distress as a basis for hope. We are invited to fix our gaze on him! I take great consolation in the words of

Jesus in today's Gospel (v 29-31): "When you see these things taking place, you know that he is near, at the very gates. Truly I tell you, this generation will not pass away until all these things have taken place. Heaven and earth will pass away, but my words will not pass away."

Eschatological testing

Eschatological testing will take a variety of forms. First, there will be betrayals. Just as Jesus was "betrayed" or "handed over" to the hands of sinners for testing, so Mark's readers will be "betrayed" or "given over" to councils, beaten in synagogues, and called to give testimony before governors and kings. They will be "betrayed" or "given over" to death not only by their enemies, but even by their fathers and children, their own kin!

Second, false Christs and false prophets will appear, to "lead many astray." These deceivers will promise deliverance and perform signs and wonders so as to trick people into abandoning their faith in Jesus.

Third, there will be trials or temptations even for those who enjoy relative peace and stability. Jesus speaks about this last sort of trial in his concluding parable in chapter 13, about a man who goes on a journey, having put his servants in charge and commanded his doorkeeper to "watch" or to "keep awake." The parable suggests that Mark's readers are in danger of failing to "watch," of falling asleep. They are threatened by "the cares of the world and the lure of wealth," (Matthew 13:22) and the desire for other things which Jesus elsewhere warns may choke out the seed before it matures.

Mark's Gospel teaches us that all who follow Jesus will be put to the test. They will be tested by great affliction or by powerful seducers who do signs and wonders to lead them astray. They will be tested by the ordinary routines of daily existence and by fleshly desires. Whatever the form of the tests we face, Mark tells us that we must remain vigilant and pray, for if we have divided minds and hearts, we will fail the tests and so be unprepared to greet the master and be vindicated before him when he comes.

We shall be put to the test, but we need not fear, for Jesus has changed forever the context in which testing occurs. Because of his endurance of his own testing, Jesus offered himself as the perfect sacrifice to God, thereby rendering the cult in the Jerusalem temple obsolete. From now on, the appropriate "offerings" of the righteous will be prayers made in the gathered community of believers, rather than sacrifices made in the temple. God accepted Jesus' self-offering as sufficient to atone for human sin; those who follow Jesus have therefore been "ransomed" from wrathful punishment by the just God. They can be confident that they are destined for salvation.

The community of those who pray

Mark indicates that in the wake of the temple's destruction, the community of those who pray will be the "house of prayer for all nations," the new temple to be raised up by Jesus. Single-minded prayer is the hallmark of this new community, the temple built of living stones. But how might Mark and his readers have understood this notion of "single-minded prayer"? How did one go about praying in such a manner, and what were the consequences of such prayer for daily life? Jesus promised that faithful prayer will be answered, but his promise is qualified: Those who pray must not doubt in their hearts.

In the darkness and anguish of Gethsemane, Jesus earnestly requests that God save him from the agony that lies ahead, and he is fully convinced that God can do so. But at the same time, Jesus submits himself to the will of God his Father. Jesus' endurance, his single-mindedness, his deliberate laying aside of his own vision for himself in favour of God's vision for him is what triumphs in the garden at the foot of the Mount of Olives. For Mark, this prayer in Gethsemane is a model of how "disciples on trial" ought to pray.

Put to the test

What are the great cataclysmic events that shake us in our world today? How are we being put to the test daily? Are experiences of rejection, or suffering, death or loss, deprivation and emptiness leading us to give up the Word of life that we once received with joy? Are our concerns about money, success at work or in school, health, release from addiction, job security, status and recognition, family or relationships choking out the word of God which has been planted in our hearts? Are we gripped by passions such as anger, grief or lust, which block us from following Jesus? Is there any joy left in our life?

The Good News of Mark's Gospel is that we do not have to replicate Jesus' faithfulness in time of trial by the sheer force of our own will. We do not have to face satanic tests devoid of divine power. Jesus of Nazareth has changed our situation forever. Mark phrases the Good News in terms of the empowering of believers that takes place in prayer. The Christian community is empowered to engage in single-minded prayer that cannot be derailed by fear, grief, persecution, or deceptive powers at work in the world. Jesus has atoned for human sin and undermined the very powers that seek to separate humans from God. Therefore all things are possible when we come to God in prayer.

Bigger picture

Let us never lose sight of the bigger picture of salvation history as we face the setbacks, losses and tragedies of daily life. As Christians, we are invited each day to respond to the dialectics of hope and gloom, which often have gripped our age. Collective anxiety can easily become mass hysteria in the mist of any crisis.

That is why it is so important to be firmly established in the Word of God, to draw life from that Word and live in that Word. It is then that we realize the Prophet Daniel's words (12:1-3) in our daily life: "The wise shall shine like the brightness of the sky, and those who lead many to righteousness like the stars forever and ever."

The King Who Did Not Bow Down

SOLEMNITY OF OUR LORD JESUS CHRIST,
KING OF THE UNIVERSE

Daniel 7:13-14;
Revelation 1:5-8;
John 18:33b-37

The liturgical year ends with the Solemnity of Our Lord Jesus Christ, King of the Universe. In John's poignant trial scene of Pilate and Jesus (18:33-37), we see a great contrast between power and powerlessness.

In coming to the Romans to ensure that Jesus would be crucified, the Jewish authorities fulfilled his prophecy that he would be exalted (John 3:14; 12:32-33). Pilate asks Jesus: "Are you the King of the Jews?" (v 33). The accused prepares his answer with a previous question, which provokes the Roman official: "Do you ask this on your own, or did others tell you about me?" (v 34).

Pilate's arrogance does not intimidate Jesus, who then gives his own answer in the well-known words: "My kingdom is not from this world" (v 36). At once, Jesus gives the reason: 'My kingdom does not use coercion, it is not imposed.' Jesus reiterates his point: "My kingdom is not from this world."

Pilate is very astute. He does not see in Jesus' answer a denial of his kingship. In fact, Pilate infers and insists: "So you are a king" (v 37). Jesus accepts his claim without hesitation: "You say that I am a king ... For this I came into the world."

For what? To inaugurate a world of peace and fellowship, of justice and respect for other people's rights, of love for God and for one another. This is the kingdom that penetrates our human history, illuminating it and leading it beyond itself, a kingdom that will have no end. When we pray the Our Father, we pray for this kingdom to come in its fullness.

In this Gospel scene, Pilate reveals himself as a deeply perplexed leader as he encounters one who is Truth. What is there of Pilate inside of each of us? What prevents us from being free? What are our fears? What are our labels? What costumes and masks are we wearing in public and really don't care to jeopardize? What is our capacity for neglecting and trampling on others for the sake of keeping up appearances, maintaining the façade, or the important job, or people's good opinion with regard to our respectability, our reputation or good name?

The Kingdom of Jesus

In the Fourth Gospel, the focus is on the kingship of Christ. The core of Jesus' message is the kingdom of God, and the God of Jesus Christ is the God of the kingdom, the one who has a word and an involvement in human history from which the image of the kingdom is taken. In the kingdom of Jesus, there is no distance between what is religious and temporal, but rather between domination and service.

Jesus' kingdom is unlike the one that Pilate knows and is willingly or unwillingly part of. Pilate's kingdom, and for that matter the Roman kingdom, was one of arbitrariness, privileges, domination and occupation. Jesus' kingdom is built on love, justice and peace.

Jesus proclaims the kingdom of God, the kingdom of holiness and grace, of justice, love and peace. This kingdom is God's final aim and purpose in everything he has done from the beginning. It is his final act of liberation and salvation. Jesus speaks of this kingdom as a future reality, but a reality that is mysteriously already present in his being, his actions and words and in his personal destiny.

If today's solemnity of Christ's kingship upsets some of us, is it not due to our own disillusionment of earthly kings and leaders, rather than the kingship of Jesus? The kingship and leadership of God's Son refuses rank and privilege, and any attempt to be master of the world. In him there is no lust, greed and ambition for power. He, the innocent king who executes no one, is himself executed. His reign completely overturns our notions of earthly kingship. His is a kingship of ultimate service, even to the point of laying down his life for others.

In John's Gospel, Jesus goes to his death as a king. The crucifixion is Jesus' enthronement, the ultimate expression of royal service. Because of Christ, the coronation of suffering is no longer death, but rather eternal life. Very few can measure up to Jesus' kingly stature, remaining powerless in the face of the powerful. Many of us resist with power, even though we resort to very refined forms of pressure and manipulation. Jesus never responded to violence with more violence.

Two crowns

The Solemnity of Our Lord Jesus Christ, King of the Universe has had particular significance for me since I lived at Ecce Homo Convent, the Sisters of Sion Center on the Via Dolorosa in Jerusalem's Old City during the years of my graduate studies in Scripture. The whole complex is built over what is believed to be Pontius Pilate's judgment hall, the setting for today's striking Gospel scene between Jesus and Pontius Pilate.

The holy sites in Jerusalem, which commemorate events in the life, passion and death of Jesus, often have two feasts throughout the year, feasts that remember the joyful and sorrowful aspects of Jesus' life. Ecce Homo Convent's "patronal" feasts are the joyful solemnity of Christ the King at the end of the liturgical year, and the sorrowful feast of Jesus crowned with thorns on the first Friday of Lent.

Two feasts, two crowns, two images of Jesus the Lord set before the Christian community to ponder and imitate.

The feast of Christ the King presents us with the image of Christ crowned – first with thorns, then with the victor's laurel hat, the evergreen crown of glory. On the day of our baptism, the crown of our head was smeared with the holy oil of chrism, that royal oil that makes us another *Christos*, another Anointed One. We have the power to live faithfully and love fiercely as Jesus did. The crown of glory – Christ's very own – is promised to each of us. Which crown is found at the centre of our faith and our proclamation?

Who, if not the condemned Saviour?

Jesus answered the Roman governor's questions by declaring that he was a king, but not of this world (cf. John 18: 36). He did not come to rule over peoples and territories, but to set people free from the slavery of sin and to reconcile them with God. He states: "For this I was born, and for this I have come into the world, to testify to the truth. Everyone who belongs to the truth listens to my voice" (John 18: 37).

What is this "truth" that Christ came into the world to witness to? The whole of his life reveals that God is love: So this is the truth to which he witnessed to the full with the sacrifice of his own life on Calvary. Jesus established the kingdom of God once and for all from the cross. The way to reach this goal is long and admits of no short cuts: Indeed, every person must freely accept the truth of God's love.

God is Love and Truth, and neither Love nor Truth is ever imposed. They stand gently knocking at the doors of our minds and hearts, waiting for us to open the door and welcome them. Yet so often we are afraid to usher in such guests into our lives and earthly kingdoms because of the serious implications associated with such gifts. Many of us resist the Truth with power, while others will resort to very refined forms of pressure and manipulation to keep the Truth at bay.

As we contemplate Christ crucified, we understand something of why Christ has remained a king even up to modern times: He didn't bow down. He who was Truth incarnate never imposed himself on others. He stood, waited and knocked. He never responded to violence with more violence.

At the conclusion of the Stations of the Cross at Rome's Coliseum on Good Friday night in the Jubilee Year 2000, Blessed Pope John Paul II spoke these moving words: "Who, if not the condemned Saviour, can fully understand the pain of those unjustly condemned?

"Who, if not the King scorned and humiliated, can meet the expectations of the countless men and women who live without hope or dignity?

"Who, if not the crucified Son of God, can know the sorrow and loneliness of so many lives shattered and without a future?"

Jesus took his wounds to heaven, and there is a place in heaven for our wounds because our king bears his in glory.

On this last Sunday of the liturgical year, our Crucified King hangs in our midst, arms outstretched in loving mercy and welcome. May we have the courage to ask him to remember us in his kingdom, the grace to imitate him in our own earthly kingdoms, and the wisdom to welcome him when he stands knocking at the doors of our lives and hearts.